Migrant Workers in Russia

Russia has a very large pool of economic migrants, up to 25 per cent of the workforce according to some estimates. Although many migrants, many from former Soviet countries which are now independent, entered Russia legally, they frequently face bureaucratic obstacles to legal employment and Russian citizenship, factors which have led to a very large 'shadow economy'. This book presents a comprehensive examination of migrant labour in Russia. It describes the nature of migrant labour, explores the shadow economy and its unfortunate consequences, and discusses the rise of popular sentiment against migrants and its likely impact. The book also sets the Russian experiences of migrant labour in context, comparing the situation in Russia with that in other countries with significant migrant labour workforces.

Anna-Liisa Heusala is a senior researcher in the Aleksanteri Institute, University of Helsinki, Finland.

Kaarina Aitamurto is a researcher in the Aleksanteri Institute, University of Helsinki, Finland.

Routledge Contemporary Russia and Eastern Europe Series

Migrant Workers in Russia

Global challenges of the shadow economy
in societal transformation

Edited by
Anna-Liisa Heusala and Kaarina Aitamurto

Routledge
Taylor & Francis Group
LONDON AND NEW YORK

First published 2017 by Routledge

2 Park Square, Milton Park, Abingdon, Oxfordshire OX14 4RN

711 Third Avenue, New York, NY 10017

Routledge is an imprint of the Taylor & Francis Group, an informa business

First issued in paperback 2018

British Library Cataloguing in Publication Data
A catalogue record for this book is available from the British Library

Library of Congress Cataloging in Publication Data
Names: Heusala, Anna-Liisa, editor. | Aitamurto, Kaarina, editor.
Title: Migrant workers in Russia : global challenges of the shadow economy
   in societal transformation / edited by Anna-Liisa Heusala and Kaarina
   Aitamurto.
Description: Abingdon, Oxon ; New York, NY : Routledge, 2017. | Series:
   Routledge contemporary Russia and Eastern Europe series ; 72 | Includes
   bibliographical references.
Identifiers: LCCN 2016017514| ISBN 9781138100831 (hardback) | ISBN
   9781315657424 (ebook)
Subjects: LCSH: Foreign workers–Russia (Federation) | Informal sector
   (Economics)–Russia (Federation) | Labor policy–Russia (Federation) |
   Russia (Federation)–Emigration and immigration–Economic aspects.
Classification: LCC HD8530.2 .M498 2017 | DDC 331.5/440947–dc23
LC record available at https://lccn.loc.gov/2016017514

ISBN: 978-1-138-10083-1 (hbk)
ISBN: 978-1-138-58818-9 (pbk)

DOI: 10.4324/9781315657424

Typeset in Times New Roman
by Taylor & Francis Books

Contents

List of figures

Contributors

Sergey N. Abashin is a professor at the European University at St Petersburg. He received his postgraduate degrees from Moscow State University. From 1990 to 2013 Dr Abashin worked at the Institute of Ethnology and Anthropology at the Russian Academy of Sciences, and has conducted fieldwork in Uzbekistan, Tajikistan, Kyrgyzstan and Kazakhstan. He is the author of *Natsionalizmy v Sredney Azii: V Poiskakh Identichnosti* ('Nationalisms in Central Asia: Searching for Identity') 2007; *Sovetskiy Kishlak: Mezhdu Kolonializmom i Modernizatsiey* ('Soviet Kishlak: Between Colonialism and Modernization') 2015.

Kaarina Aitamurto received her doctoral degree from the University of Helsinki. Her dissertation analysed Russian contemporary paganism and nationalism. Aitamurto holds a position of a postdoctoral researcher at the Aleksanteri Institute and is a member of the Finnish Centre of Excellence in Russian Studies – Choices of Russian Modernisation, funded by the Academy of Finland. In her postdoctoral studies, Aitamurto focuses on Muslim minorities in ethnically Russian areas. She is the editor of the book *Modern Pagan and Native Faiths in Central and Eastern Europe* and author of *Paganism, Traditionalism, Nationalism. Narratives of Russian Rodnoverie.*

Linda J. Cook received her Ph.D. from Columbia University in 1985. She is Professor of Political Science and Slavic Studies at Brown University and Associate of the Davis Center for Russian and Eurasian Studies at Harvard University. Cook authored *The Soviet Social Contract and Why It Failed: Welfare Policy and Workers' Politics from Brezhnev to Yeltsin* (1993); *Postcommunist Welfare States: Reform Politics in Russia and Eastern Europe* (2007/2013). Her work has been published in *Post-Soviet Affairs, Comparative Politics, Communist and Post-Communist Studies, Studies in Comparative International Development,* and *Voprosy gosudarstvennogo i Munitsiplann'nogo Upravlenie,* as well as other journals and collected volumes.

Anna-Liisa Heusala received her doctoral degree in political science from the University of Helsinki in 2005. She is a senior researcher in the Aleksanteri Institute at the University of Helsinki and a fellow in the Finnish Centre of Excellence in Russian Studies – Choices of Russian Modernisation, funded by the Academy of Finland (2012–2017). Her research interests include comparative studies on Russian public administration, comprehensive security and Russian security policy. Her recent works include articles in *International Review of Administrative Sciences* and *Review of Central and East European Law.*

Markku Kangaspuro is a professor and the Research Director of the Aleksanteri Institute at the University of Helsinki. His background is contemporary history (Ph.D.) and his expertise covers political history of the Soviet Union, Russia's political development after the fall of the Soviet Union, identity politics and nationalism. His latest publications are: *The Dilemma of Perception on Russian Strong State and Demand of Modernization: Authoritarian Modernization in Russia: Ideas, Institutions, and Policies* (ed. V. Gel'man, 2016); *History Politics and the Changing meaning of Victory Day in contemporary Russia: The Long Aftermath. Cultural Legacies of Europe at War, 1936–2016* (ed. M. Bragança and P. Tame, 2015); *Naming the War and Framing the Nation in Russian Public Discussion – Canadian Slavonic Papers 54/2012.*

Jussi Lassila works as a postdoctoral researcher at the Aleksanteri Institute, Finnish Centre for Russian and Eastern European Studies, of the University of Helsinki. His book *The Quest for an Ideal Youth in Putin's Russia II: The Search for Distinctive Conformism in the Political Communication of Nashi, 2005–2009* was published in late 2012. The second and revised edition of the book was published in 2014. His core areas of expertise are discourse analysis, political communication, post-Soviet identity politics, nationalism and populism. His papers have been published in the journals *Europe–Asia Studies, Demokratizatsiya, Canadian Slavonic Papers, Forum noveishei vostochnoevropeiskoi istorii i kul'tury, Finnish Review of East European Studies,* as well as in numerous collected volumes.

Rustamjon Urinboyev is a postdoctoral research fellow at the Department of Sociology of Law at Lund University, Sweden. He has a Ph.D. in sociology of law (2013) from Lund University; his research focuses on state–society relations, pre-Soviet (Islamic) traditional governance structures, corruption and legal pluralism, legal ethnography with regional focus on Central Asia, and migration governance in Russia. His current research focuses on the everyday life and socio-legal integration of Central Asian migrant workers in Moscow, Russia, specifically investigating how migrants negotiate and manoeuvre around Russian legal system (e.g. police, immigration officials, border guards) and informal structures (e.g. racketeers, middlemen).

Yuliya Zabyelina is an assistant professor in the Political Science Department at John Jay College of Criminal Justice, City University of New York (CUNY). She came to John Jay from a Newton postdoctoral fellowship at the University of Edinburgh's law school funded by the Royal Society and British Academy. At John Jay, Dr Zabyelina teaches in the BA and MA programmes in international criminal justice. Her research is focused on the emergence and functioning of illegal markets, various manifestations of organized (transnational) crime and corruption, and the nexus between crime and state failure. She has published broadly in edited books, peer-reviewed academic journals, and specialized policy magazines and has been recognized with numerous awards, including the Academy of Criminal Justice SAGE Junior Faculty Teaching Award (2015), The Aleksanteri Institute Visiting Scholars Fellowship (2015), and the Donald EJ MacNamara Junior Faculty Award (2016).

1 Introduction

Russian societal transformation and migrant workers in the shadow economy

Anna-Liisa Heusala

In the post-Soviet period, Russian societal transformation has been shaped by globalised phenomena and interactions, and this interconnectedness has cut across traditional spheres of interests and influenced the reconstruction of new ones. Globalisation has contributed to the development of various new mechanisms to follow the movement of people, goods and communication across borders. One important unintended consequence of globalisation in Russia has been the persistence of a large-scale shadow economy. The human security dimensions (Kaldor *et al.* 2007; Laszlo 1999) of the shadow economy have become inextricably linked to many key processes of Russian societal transformation at both the domestic and international levels. The shadow economy connects questions of globalised economic competitiveness involving huge interests inside the Russian market with internal security and foreign policy goals of a regional security complex (Buzan 1991) in Central Asia.

Various definitions for the shadow economy exist (Gerxhani 2004), underlining different sides of the phenomenon. Here, the shadow economy is the segment of the economy where transactions generally leave no formal trace (Nardo 2011: 50), where an activity may be spontaneous but often has become a more or less institutionalised custom. The shadow economy includes all economic activities that contribute to the officially calculated GDP but are unregistered (Schneider and Enste 2000) to avoid legal obligations in the production process. Commonly used explanations for the growth of the shadow economy in the developed, industrialised world include the rise and burden of taxes and social security contributions, increased regulation in the official labour markets, forced reductions of weekly working time, earlier retirement, unemployment, and the decline of civic virtue and loyalty towards public institutions combined with a declining tax morale. Individuals, groups and organisations may react against a state when control is experienced as arbitrary, unequal and corrupt (Schneider and Enste 2000: 77, 82). In addition to many of these reasons, the shadow economy in Russia is closely linked with the distribution of inequalities and economic growth opportunities among the former Soviet states.

The shadow economy leads to direct monetary losses and indirect societal consequences through unhealthy market competition, loss of entrepreneurial innovativeness and structural corruption. Shadow economic activities are not

DOI: 10.4324/9781315657424-1

protected legally, which increases entrepreneurial risks. Growth prospects can be compromised due to the lack of social infrastructure. Public finances can suffer as the tax base shrinks, thus weakening the government's capacity to generate revenue (Blackburn *et al.* 2012). For the state, the shadow economy makes policy planning and implementation difficult, as official indicators on unemployment, the labour force, income and consumption are unreliable (Schneider and Enste 2000: 78). The shadow economy, through these channels and mechanisms, reproduces unwanted economic, legal and social consequences.

Transitional countries have faced similar types of difficulties, which can be found in, for instance, African societies, where obstacles for doing business legally create a need for shadow economic activity. This type of situation is, then, different from the industrialised developed world scene of tax evasion (Schneider and Williams 2013). Nardo (2011: 50) underlines that the shadow economy is not necessarily the same as an illegal economy, although these often overlap, and the shadow economy provides a favourable environment for illegal economic activity. In fact, the division between 'clearly' illegal activities and 'shadow' activities depends on the legislation of states, although transnational categories exist, which are commonly part of the legislation of industrialised societies. Such illegal activities include corruption, extortion, fraud and illegal trafficking. The shadow activities would then include payment means and payment structures (inclusion in final price, separate service payment), sheltered tax locations, financial-banking instruments and channels, and privileged goods (Nardo 2011: 53).

The use of illegal migrant workforce is criminalised in the legislation of many countries as extortionate work discrimination (Aerschot and Daentzer 2014). Alvesalo *et al.* (2014: 121) define this type of an exploitation of migrant labour with the help of a criminological category of corporate crime, thus underlining the effect which exploitation has on the business culture in a society. Exploitation covers everything from human trafficking and forced labour to less aggravated coercion.

In many parts of the world, the shadow economy employment is the rule.[1] Unregistered work is created as a result of both barriers to official employment and individuals voluntarily staying out of official structures (Schneider and Williams 2013). There are various incentives for individuals to join the shadow economic workforce which include the availability of personal networks and ease of entry into shadow work ('friend-to-friend' systems); autonomy and flexibility in the market (small business strategy); and individual survival (the need of workers to just simply find any work, anywhere) (Gerxhani 2004). I will add a fourth reason, which I name the 'loyalty motive'; namely, the understanding that one should sustain family economies with the salary earned abroad. The latter, of course, is important for the understanding of the regional consequences of Russian labour conditions and the constraints of economic development in its neighbouring Southern societies.

Several perspectives or hypotheses on large-scale immigration and migrant workers have been at the core of public debates in many societies, particularly in the US. There, commentators on migrations have used several basic arguments against liberal migration policies and their perceived societal consequences, such as the economic threat hypothesis, the culture threat hypothesis, the core (national) values hypothesis, the cultural affinity hypothesis, the race affinity hypothesis and the group threat hypothesis (Buckler 2008). These hypotheses, although not specifically linked with the shadow economy, help to structure discussions concerning the migrant labour force. Arguments regarding the protection of the domestic labour force, the negative effects of growing multiculturalism and the threats posed by transnational crime spread by the migrant communities, are ongoing everywhere. The migrant agent is the focus of critical discussion. The shadow economy, which is based on structural arrangements and the legal provisions enabling them, as well as on practices and ways of thinking condoning these practices, appears less often in the focus of wide public dismay and subsequent effective political action.

The aim of this joint volume is to look at the wide array of consequences for societal transformation in Russia created by the use of a large-scale migrant workforce[2] under shadow economic and globalised conditions. We view societal transformation as a complex, non-linear process consisting of both abrupt changes and more incremental institutional change and adaptation, often dominated by both negative and positive unintended consequences. The scope of societal change ranges from individual behaviour to relations inside and between groups, and finally to the change of values in a society (Cotterrell 1992: 47). As Castles (2010: 1576) has previously pointed out, social transformation is mediated by local circumstances, which affect the acceptance and resistance of change from nationalistic political movements to family-level livelihood strategies. Migration studies have paid increasing attention to how migration itself and practices connected to it – such as management of migration or cultural practices of the migrants – affect societal transformation.[3] Our addition to this general perspective is to bring in the concept of the shadow economy in a detailed manner. We examine the dynamics in three transformational areas of Russian society – politics, law and institutions – at different hierarchical levels and geographical dimensions of the Russian state and society. Our attention focuses on the institutional settings and 'players' in the system as well as incentives and perspectives for accepting, using or opposing the current conditions (Nardo 2011: 56). Both individual strategies connected to the shadow economy and the economic, cultural, political and social context (e.g. Castles 2010; Collinson 2009) of migrant labour use are given attention in order to create a rich account of linkages between politics, law and social institutions in today's Russia.

Legal and institutional context of the Russian shadow economy

One of the starting points in this volume is the idea that perhaps the most significant element in Russian post-Soviet societal transformation has been the 'collision with' and 'adaptation to' economic globalisation (Legvold 2011). In the past twenty-plus years, researchers have concentrated on the abrupt shock created by the collapse of the Soviet Union and have marvelled at the complexities of institutional change in Russia with the help of path dependency and legacy explanations (Meyer-Sahling 2009). However, the collapse of the Soviet Union has also been interpreted as the end result of an attempt to integrate selected features of globalised public sector changes into the Soviet system (Sakwa 2013), a change which was implemented more effectively only after Vladimir Putin rose to power in 1998 (Collier 2011; Gel'man and Starodubtsev 2014).

As elsewhere, the past two decades plus of globalisation have further challenged the autonomy of the nation-state and made intervention in societal processes a complex undertaking for the Russian government. In Russia, deregulation of the economy through trade and commerce liberalisation, and shifts in the balance of power towards new actors (Mugarura 2014: 383, 385) radically influenced the planning and implementation of state policies in the 1990s. Russian economic and labour market changes have coincided with the general globalisation of the public sector everywhere – often referred to as the neo-liberal (neo-classical economic) development. Since the end of the 1990s, the state of Russia has decentralised, deregulated and delegated resource-using powers. The Russian state no longer provides all services, but instead directs attention to the regulation and control of actors in the Russian market society. The post-Soviet space has seen the movement of people and capital redefine the contours of national sovereignty by blurring the meaning of borders.

Studies on public administration in post-Socialist and non-democratic societies have shown that administrative and legal reforms have collided with old cultures and lack of well-functioning democratic administrations (Bouckart *et al.* 2011; Drechsler 2005; Liebert *et al.* 2013). This has led to continuous and unsystematic legal, economic and administrative reforms based on different modes of agency autonomy and control (Randma-Liiv *et al.* 2011). The radical restructuring of the economy through shock therapy in the 1990s made the strategic planning of Russian state reforms very difficult in such areas as the legal system and the civil service. All in all, the major overhaul of the state administration received specific attention rather late in the first post-Soviet decade. The effect on the creation of functioning labour markets with credible systems of government control, modernised tax laws and an overall sufficient level of institutional trust, particularly in the legal sector, has been immense. Still today, questions related to the level of institutional trust, with the subsequent willingness to pay taxes, develop and provide services, obey laws and cooperate with authorities who in turn provide adequate services dominate in the evolution of the Russian labour market.

Kar and Freitas (2013), who use an estimation of 43.8 per cent as the Russian average shadow economy between 1999 and 2007, find that illicit flows (transactions) fuel the growth of the shadow economy more than they add to the productive capacity of official GDP. The shadow economy, in turn, drives illicit flows. Their conclusion is that for Russia, this underscores the need for broad reforms to strengthen the business environment, curtail illicit flows and adopt specific policies to close the governance deficit. They point out the success story of the tax reform (Gel'man and Starodubtsev 2014) as a turning point in the fight against the shadow economy. The tax reform was aimed at broadening the tax net, simplifying the taxation and strengthening the tax and customs administrations. The implementation of a flat tax in 2001 has reduced the size of the shadow economy relative to official GDP. Citing a 2002 IMF report, they point out that revenue collections in 2001 were at the highest level since the break-up of the Soviet Union, the result of improvements in tax compliance. The improvement in tax compliance since 2001 is perhaps an important reason behind the shrinking of the underground economy relative to GDP.

Against this background, the legislative changes concerning the Federal Migration Service (FMS) and immigrant labour regulations, as well as developments in the provision of basic welfare services, deserve attention. The evolution of the FMS and the conflicting regulations for migrant workers, examined in this volume by Sergey Abashin, give us an account of a transitional institution in search of its institutional place and identity. The challenges of social services 'on the ground' analysed in the case study by Linda Cook give us another side of the story, from the experiences of persons needing those basic social security benefits normally attached to 'full', official employment. Forms of labour movement control and social security provision are among the key practical consequences of Russia's economic integration with its Southern neighbours. The considerable public resistance against migrants themselves, as stated in the chapters by Abashin, Kangaspuro and Heusala, and Lassila, creates formidable barriers to finding solutions for the future, when Russia's economy will need more foreign hands again.

Estimates of legal labour migrants in Russia have varied from approximately 8 to 25 per cent of the Russian labour market. In the 1990s, Russia received an influx of 4.5 million immigrants from former Soviet republics, followed by 1.5 million persons between 2000 and 2008 (Ioffe and Zayonchkovskaya 2010: 105). The decline in the birth rate and increase in the adult mortality rate in the 1990s (Kulmala *et al.* 2014) has had a long-lasting effect on Russian economic potential. In 2007, these processes coincided with a negative turn in the balance between the working age population, deaths and retirements (Ioffe and Zayonchkovskaya 2010: 105). Until the economic recession of 2014, the demand in the Russian economy for a migrant workforce and immigration more generally was a much-debated issue. Growing immigrant communities have not been accepted by either politicians or the Russian public, and – as Kaarina Aitamurto shows in her chapter – not even many of the Muslim communities which these migrants could in principle join.

Increasing legal migration – and creating the conditions for it – has been rejected as a policy which is contrary to the interpretation of Russian national interests. Negative public opinion towards illegal migration and demands for more effective control of migrants in general has remained in the focus of policy- and opinion-makers, and has also been actively fostered by its members, as examined in Jussi Lassila's chapter. In the 1990s, Russia was second on the list of countries receiving immigrants, after the US, with a total of 12.5 million persons. Illegal migrants in Russia have several origins. Most arrived in Russia based on bilateral visa-free agreements among CIS countries. Their undocumented or poor legal status has affected the whole Russian immigration system, which has concentrated on control enforcement and mechanisms of deportation (Ivakhniouk 2004: 41). As Madeleine Reeves' (2013) work and Rustamjon Urinboyev's chapter in this volume demonstrate, the financial and legal constraints on the legitimisation of migrant status continue to evolve alongside new laws and regulations.

Well before the establishment of the current Eurasian Economic Union, the labour market shared by Russia and its neighbours has de facto created an area of economic integration, which has affected social, political and security developments in these societies. In this context, societal transformation in Russia has included an important component of 'semi-legality'. At the macro level, a society's reliance of the economy on persons whose status is 'in between' (e.g. Kubal 2013) forces them to balance their domestic policies and the demands of international economic and political regimes. National political cultures and economic integration may clash.

As is shown in the chapters of this volume, at the micro level, migrant workers will often move between different statuses where their agency is changed (Kubal 2013). This is seen in the way in which local communities integrate migrant workers and provide them necessary services, a question approached in Linda Cook's chapter. Tyuryukanova and Kostyrya (2008) have previously pointed out that migrants coming to Russia from countries with large and established diasporas have been better off in terms of surviving in new economic and legal conditions. Therefore, immigrants from Armenia and Azerbaijan have benefited from well-developed ethnic resources in comparison to migrant workers coming from Central Asia. However, in the 2000s, traditional ethnic communities have been replaced by more flexible and unstable networks of new migrants. These migrant worker communities do not become members or part of the cultural and social fabric of the surrounding society, but live in a reality of informal and illegal systems and mutual assistance. The primary logic of migration is not to integrate, but instead to sustain family economies from abroad. Kaarina Aitamurto's account of cultural assimilation and fear of Islamic radicalisation among migrants brings out an important effect which these questions have in the Russian society.

In globalised conditions migration policies are affected by various official outsourcing and privatisation policies which states carry out as part of their economic reforms. In transitional conditions, where the institutional boundaries are not yet consolidated and practices are formulated in often legally obscure conditions, bureaucratic functions organised by a 'third party' often lead to corruption (Kubal 2013).[4] Ioffe and Zayonchkovskaya (2010) show how Russian open door polices in the 1990s led to an inaccurate recording of immigrants and their exploitation, including forced labour, human trafficking and fraudulent recruitment schemes. Increasing negative public opinion on 'too many foreigners' prompted the Russian government to introduce the 2002 Federal Law on the legal status of foreigners in the Russian Federation. A type of border control was instituted in the practice of employment authorisation, which was to be procured by the prospective employer, preceded by a residential approval stamp on the migrant's passport. Ioffe and Zayonchkovskaya point out that these rules offered a substantial outlet for corruption. Intermediary services (which could also be called privatised border and immigration officials) offered residential registration and employment authorisation for a significant fee.

Examination of law and institutions 'on the ground' is important, because changing practices and ways of thinking is a complex long-term challenge, often resulting in unintended consequences. Laws that cannot be enforced, or invoked by citizens, do not change ways of thinking or practices (Cotterrell 1992: 51). In 2006, a new law on the records of foreign citizens in Russian Federation stipulated that temporary migrants no longer had to apply for registration and receive a stamp on their passport, but must instead notify the Federal Migration Service of their arrival. According to the 2006 amendments, an employment authorisation card could be handed directly to the applicant by the local office of the Federal Migration Service. These changes did have some positive effects in terms of growing the number of registered migrant workers. Ioffe and Zayonchkovskaya (2010) report that in 2007, 8 million entries for temporary stay were recorded and 1.7 million job authorisations were granted to temporary migrants, up from 1.0 million in 2006. In addition, the tax base of the foreign labour force doubled (Zayonchkovskaya *et al.* 2009: 58). However, even as the rights and freedom of migrants were being strengthened, shadow employment in Russia continued. Still in 2007, around 40 per cent of registered migrants were being hired unofficially (Zayonchkovskaya *et al.* 2009: 58), which implies that persons who had a legal right to work in the Russian Federation were still being employed in the shadow economy.

Schneider and Enste (2000) have concluded that the impact, which the shadow economy has on official institutions, norms and rules, is even more important than the loss of state revenue. Shadow economies by nature foster conditions where different forms of adjunct crime can take place (Friman 2004; Tyuryukanova and Kostyrya 2008; Zabyelina 2012). Lavezzi's (2014: 7) study on the conditions for organised crime in Italy points out that where firms use workers illegally, criminal organisations emerge as intermediaries, often to keep workers' salary claims low. Yuliya Zabyelina's (2012) study on the illicit shuttle trade in Moscow shows that the success of informal trade often partly depends on a combination of illicit transactions, imperfections in customs regulations, and corruption. Thus, the destructive impact of the shadow economy can be felt both in the deformed structure of national economies and in the damaged fiscal and law enforcement capacities of state institutions. Schneider and Enste point out that shadow economic activities are an indicator of the social order and legitimacy of rules in the official economy, and that the illegality of shadow activities is in fact an important constraint on the Leviathan state (2000: 108). These features are aggravated by transitional conditions where both the legacies of the previous political system and the globalised changes in state–individual relations influence societal transformation, as is shown in the case studies of this volume.

Our case studies

The first three chapters address dominant transformations in Russian politics. As the chapters demonstrate, questions related to identity and politics of belonging (Amelina 2016: 6, Yuval-Davis 2011: 18–21) are among significant factors which influence both domestic and foreign policy goals and implementation of migrant labour policies. In Sergey Abashin's chapter, the author examines the formation of the current Russian policies on transnational labour mobility between 2000 and 2014, a time period characterised by continuous, significant growth in migration to Russia from the ex-Soviet states. He argues that there is not one, but several competing, even conflicting, migration policies, lobbied for by different actors with their own interests and views. The conclusion has been that the issue of migration has turned into an instrument of political manipulation as the 'migrant' has come to represent the main 'Other'.

Abashin addresses the negotiations over the Russian legislature and within state institutions which govern regulation concerning migration. The focus is on changes in the development as well as ways in which different arguments and aims have been grounded. The analysis demonstrates the contradictory and inconsistent nature of the policy; liberal actions and positive rhetoric concerning migration in governmental programmes have been followed by the restrictive measures and negative rhetoric of the implementing institutions. The second part focuses on the political and societal debates concerning migration in Russia. The analysis detects the different configurations and framings of the issue by political actors, and the main definitions and images concerning migrants that prevail in Russian societal discussions.

Markku Kangaspuro and Anna-Liisa Heusala look at the evolution of Russian foreign policy thinking as an attempt to merge identity political and economic interests in the Eurasian Economic Union. The chapter takes a brief look at the public dispute on the initiative of Russia's leadership in the Eurasian Economic Union and the anti-migration criticism related to the integration project. The main political goal of the ambitious plan is to strengthen Russian influence over the former Soviet area and to allow Russia more economic security in globalised competition. It is challenged by the overwhelming legal and administrative requirements connected to the common economic area and free movement of goods and people. The chapter examines the case of the construction field where questions related to working conditions, qualifications of workers and industrial standards, entrepreneurial integrity and state control over legality have gained momentum in recent times. The chapter analyses the various dimensions through which the shadow economy (*tenevaya ekonomika*) is approached by both the national organisation of developers and the Russia's biggest trade union, the Federation of Independent Trade Unions in the Russian Federation.

Jussi Lassila examines two political cases in Russia which are intertwined with the issue of migration: the Moscow mayoral elections in 2013 and the discussion on Ukrainian refugees as a result of the dramatic events in Ukraine since early 2014. The Moscow mayoral election illustrates how the challenger candidate, the opposition's new frontman, anti-corruption blogger Alexei Navalny, skilfully harnessed Muscovites' anti-immigration mood into his vision of a modern, European capital of Russia. In comparison, the views of Ukrainian refugees as a 'wanted' workforce in Russia show how official state patriotism struggles with the combination of national policies that are largely based on statist–imperial legacies and the exploitation of cheap workforce.

Lassila argues that Russia's demographic needs for immigrants, reactivated neo-imperial ideas of anti-Westernism and Eurasianism and anti-immigration mood towards 'non-European' newcomers create a complex source of political capital in Russia. The chapter also finds answers to the question of how the Russian shadow economy and its implications are understood and presented in these processes. In this respect, state policies and popular dissent around the issue of migration not only reflect general European trends of xenophobic populism and islamophobia but, perhaps more importantly, the growing tension in Russian identity politics between defensive nation-state nationalism and traditional statist nationalism based on imperial myths.

The following four chapters by Rustamjon Urinboyev, Yuliya Zabyelina, Kaarina Aitamurto and Linda Cook address transformations in Russian law and institutions. In Rustamjon Urinboyev's chapter, the author shows how globalisation, even as it necessitates the harmonisation of rules and practices, also produces new, 'ethnic' forms of adaptation within legal and administrative systems. Particularly in the shadow economy, migrant workers import and adapt 'traditional' practices to their new surroundings, which are outside regulated communication and decision-making. Thus, definitions of 'legality' and 'illegality' are affected by the legal cultures of their home states and local communities.

Urinboyev points out how a common feature of previous studies on informality in Russia is a focus on informal practices and their regulatory structures that take place within the boundaries of a single nation-state, thereby confining informality to particular places, fields or people. This chapter situates itself in these 'informality' debates by arguing that the nature of informal practices in Russia is changing, not only in terms of their content, form and magnitude, but, more importantly, in terms of geographical scope, due to the massive, unrelenting inflow of migrant workers from Central Asia and the Caucasus to Russia. Migrant workers remain part of the fabric of everyday life and social relations in their home state, while simultaneously becoming part of the socio-economic processes in their receiving state, leading to a daily flow of ideas, social practices and cultural symbols between the sending and receiving societies. These processes are especially visible in the construction sector in Moscow, where informal employment in the shadow economy is prevalent and carried out through so-called *po rukam* (informal, handshake-based) work contracts, which involve multiple actors with very different kinds and locations of power, such as migrant workers, construction firms, Russian immigration officials, police, *posredniks* (informal inter- mediaries), protection racketeers, imams (religious leaders), family members and village networks from the migrants' home states.

Yuliya Zabyelina addresses the marginalisation and exploitation of irre- gular migrants, as well as their coping mechanisms under the conditions of the shadow economy. She reviews the organisation of 'trafficking economies', and the culture of corruption connected with labour exploitation. The pre- dicament of the shadow economy is that it generates high and fast revenues that positively influence the development of national economies and provide jobs to local residents as well as migrant communities. Informal economic practices, however, are not limited to administrative fraud and low-scale tax evasion. The success of informal trade often depends partly on a combination of illicit transactions, imperfections in customs regulations and corruption. Moreover, the shadow economy is often connected to organised crime and various forms of trafficking. Within the twenty years of the post-Soviet eco- nomic reforms and market transformation, the Russian government has unfortunately been able to formalise its large informal trade. Zabyelina criti- cally evaluates the persistence of the shadow economy, and suggests some policy-relevant remedies that could help to legalise informal trade and inter- rupt criminal activities without upsetting economic growth and harming low-income groups.

Migrants themselves are the subjects of various types of cultural, legal and political regimes which are constantly overlapping. As Rustamjon Urinboyev and Kaarina Aitamurto show in this volume, 'regimes' exist in both official state functions and unofficial societal networks (Nonini 2002). Aitamurto analyses how in Western Europe, it has become increasingly common to talk about Islam as a religion in discussions concerning the integration of immi- grants. Given that a substantial portion of new immigrants in Russia are Muslims, similar debates have begun to emerge in Russia, even though Muslim communities have a long history in many areas of the country. Rus- sian scholars disagree on whether Islamic religiosity helps or hinders the integration of migrants into contemporary Russian society. While some point out the benefits of the religious community for newcomers, others claim that overt religiosity isolates migrants from the rest of society. In nationalist rhetoric, racist claims are increasingly translated into 'cultural criticism' of the clash of civilisations or religions. Moreover, the problems of inequality and the shadow economy are explained in 'cultural terms'. The popular isla-mophobia also influences authorities' reluctance to assimilate Islamic reli-giosity, which is manifested, for example, in the denial of permission to build new mosques or in the registration of Islamic organisations. Both of these enforce feelings of exclusion for Muslim migrants. In spite of the official rhetoric on the capacity of 'traditional religions' to guarantee morality in migrants, the scarcity of the resources the Russian government is allocating to Islamic organisations to carry out social work among migrants provides evi-dence of the suspicious attitudes towards Islam and also encourages informal practices in the domains of the integration of migrants.

The short-term profitability of the shadow economy for employers and the inconsistent and conflicting government responses to the matter ensure the continuation of societal fragmentation. Tension created by newcomers in institutionalised religious networks and the fragmentation of social services for these newcomers illustrate the negative impact for transitional government institutions which are 'swallowed' by new challenges before they come into being. In these circumstances, new insecurities and inequalities emerge, as Linda Cook's chapter shows. She analyses how a new structure of inequality has developed over the past two decades that has negative implications for societal well-being, public health in Russia and sending countries, and the breadth and integrity of the state's obligations to provide basic services to its population. The chapter addresses the demand for publicly funded social services for illegal migrants working in the shadow economy and examines how marginalised labour migrants contribute to the fragmentation of Russia's welfare state. The focus is on Tajik migrants' social rights in Russia, particu-larly their access to health and welfare services in Moscow. The Russian economy relies on their labour, while Tajikistan, one of the world's most remittance-dependent states, relies on their remittances for up to half of its annual GDP. Thus, migration now constitutes an institutionalised part of the political economies of both Russia's highly stratified 'global cities' and the Eurasian periphery.

Securitisation and migrant workers in the shadow economy

Finally, I wish to make some remarks about the connection between the shadow economy in the Russian labour market and the enormous growth in the securitisation of societal questions in the post-9/11 world. When societal and economic questions are defined in the context of security, their management, the norms connected with this management, and the self-understandings of persons involved take on new dimensions. Sergey Abashin demonstrates how the content of the Russian 'illegality discourse' (i.e. public discourse on illegal immigrants) is one of the main political consequences of the shadow economy and the socio-economic interdependencies between Russia and its neighbours in regional cooperation. The successes and failures of Russian migration policies have significance for European security, since Russia can prevent a mass influx of illegal migrants and forms of crime from penetrating into Western Europe.

As Abashin's account also testifies, in Russia's transition, this has meant a shift towards underlining the national security framework in state policy planning and implementation (Legvold 2011). In 2001, the Russian Security Council declared that the scale of illegal immigration had grown into a real threat to national security (Ivakhnouk 2004: 37). The contents of the newly minted current national security framework (31 December 2015) are defined in strategy and policy documents, security and administrative legislation and the yearly policy speeches of the president.[5] Migration policy, along with transnational crime prevention and border control, is high on the list of matters which the Russian government vows to take seriously.

The implementation of prioritised policies is coordinated by the Security Council, which is a structure that overlaps with the state administration. In the current national security framework, the main challenges of Russian national security are linked with the promotion of economic growth and the building of defence and state capacity. The predictability of the Russian state is built on the ability of its leadership to strengthen the Russian welfare system, prevent crime (particularly organised and narcotics crime, and terrorism) and reverse the demographic crisis of the 1990s. In its current foreign policy, Russian national security interests are connected to the creation of a multipolar world order where Russia is one of the key great powers. Increasing emphasis on various forms of identity politics, including the legal sphere (Antonov 2012), have emerged as a reflex in the face of this evolution, together with an attempt to create a regional security complex (Buzan 1991) in the ex-Soviet states.

Historically, the emphasis on security thinking and control inside the Russian state bureaucracy has happened as a result of institutional risks which have been serious enough to undermine reform goals. The Russian leadership has attempted to find ways to contain and solve these risks to reduce goal ambiguity and increase control through legalistic decision-making, hierarchical organisation and centralisation (Heusala 2013). In the area of migration polices, restrictions on immigrant labour have been enforced through a centralised assignment of quotas for foreign workers. The system itself has been more accessible to large firms than small businesses or individuals willing to hire persons legally. In 2009 the Federal Migration Service issued Directive No. 36, which attempted to protect domestic labour by way of limiting the authorised working period to one year, a rule which pressured employers and migrant workers to bypass the law and use corruption (Ioffe and Zayonchkovskaya 2010: 120–2).

As this example shows, attempts to control the shadow economy amid institutional consolidation have not been easy to execute. The economic and social costs of unofficial practices, and their toleration in the future – by migrants, Russian officials and the general public (Ackerman 2014; Buckler 2008) – come to the fore. Securitisation of migration is the chosen mode of action in the current European context, while Russia is again underlining the importance of anti-extremist and anti-terrorism action. Therefore, a more 'law and order' approach to immigration control and workforce registration remains along with the complex political and legal changes aiming at building regional economic cooperation and harmonisation of structures. In this delicate balance there are both new possibilities and new risks for the long-term development of practices and ways of thinking which would curtail the wider phenomenon of the shadow economy in the Russian society.

Notes

1 Schneider and Williams (2013) cite a 2009 study by the OECD which found that more than half of all jobs in the non-agricultural sectors of developing countries can be considered informal. The informal economy in the developing world consists of persons who are self-employed and work independently or who own and manage very small enterprises.
2 Definitions for undocumented migrants vary in literature. Commonly used definitions include illegal migrants and irregular migrants. Both of these terms are used also in this joint volume. We are aware of the Resolution 3449 of the UN General Assembly (9 December 1975), which recommends the use of the terms non-documented or irregular migrants to avoid incriminating migrants. In this volume, the term 'illegal migrant worker' is used for persons who work without a legal work permit and who are thus employed without a formal contract. 'Illegality' refers to their legal status and does not imply anything else with regard to their behaviour or personal characteristics.
3 A large body of literature exists on the evolution of migration and migration policy. Here we refer to examples such as Amelina *et al.* (2016: 1–6) and Castles (2010).
4 Kubal (2013: 556) shows how after 2004 and 2007, Eastern Europeans migrating to old EU member states held an ambiguous legal status for several years. Although EU citizens, they did not have full access to the labour markets. In 2007, this legal incoherence extended to over 102 million persons who were legal residents but illegal workers.
5 Ukaz Prezidenta Rossiiskoi Federatsii ot 31 dekabrya 2015 goda N. 683 'O Strategii natsional'noi bezopasnosti Rossiiskoi Federatsii'; federal'nye zakon ot 28 dekabrya 2010 g. N. 390-FZ 'O bezopasnosti'; federal'nye zakon ot 28 iyunya 2014 g. N. 172-FZ 'O strategicheskom planirovanii v Rossiiskoi Federatsii'.

References

Ackerman, E. 2014. 'What part of illegal don't you understand? Bureaucracy and civil society in the shaping of illegality', *Ethnic and Racial Studies*, 37(2): 181–203.
Alvesalo, A., N. Ollus and A. Jokinen. 2014. 'The exploitation of migrant labour and the problems of control in Finland'. In P. Van Aerschot and P. Daentzer (eds) *The Integration and Protection of Immigrants. Canadian and Scandinavian Critiques.* Ashgate: Farnham, pp. 121–138.

Amelina, A., K. Horvath and B. Meeus (eds) 2016. *An Anthology of Migration and Social Transformation. European Perspective.* Dordrecht: Springer.

Antonov, M. 2012. 'Theoretical issues of sovereignty in Russia and Russian law', *Review of Central and East European Law*, 37, 1–40.

Beck, U. 2007. 'Beyond class and nation: Reframing social inequalities in a globalizing world', *British Journal of Sociology* 58(4): 679–705.

Blackburn, K., N. Bose and S. Capasso. 2012. 'Tax evasion, the underground economy and financial development', *Journal of Economic Behavior & Organization*, 83: 243–253.

Bouckart, G. and C. Pollitt. 2011. *Public Management Reform. A Comparative Analysis. New Public Management, Governance and the Neo-Weberian State.* Oxford: Oxford University Press.

Buckler, K. 2008. 'Public opinion on illegal immigration: A test of seven core hypotheses', *Journal of Crime and Justice*, 31(1): 113–147.

Buzan, B. 1991. *People, States and Fear: An Agenda For International Security Studies in the Post-Cold War Era.* Hertfordshire: Harvester Wheatsheaf.

Castles, S. 2010. 'Understanding global migration: A social transformation perspective'. *Journal of Ethnic and Migration Studies*, 36(10): 1565–1586.

Chandler, A. 2001. 'Globalization, social welfare reform and democratic identity in Russia and other post-communist countries', *Global Social Policy*, 1: 310–337.

Collier, S. 2011. *Post-Soviet Social. Neoliberalism, Social Modernity, Biopolitics.* Princeton, NJ: Princeton University Press.

Cotterrell, R. 1992. *The Sociology of Law: An Introduction.* London: Butler & Tanner.

Drechsler, W. 2005. 'The rise and demise of the New Public Management', *Post-Autistic Economics Review*, 33(14): 17–28.

Friman, H. R. 2004. 'The great escape? Globalization, immigrant entrepreneurship and the criminal economy', *Review of International Political Economy*, 11(1): 98–131.

Gel'man, V. Ya. and A. V. Starodubtsev. 2014. *Vozmozhnosti i ogranicheniya avtoritarnoi modernizatsii: rosiiskie reform 2000-kh godakh.* St Petersburg: Izdatel'stvo Evropeiskogo universiteta v Sankt-Peterburge.

Gerxhani, K. 2004. 'The informal sector in developed and less developed countries: A literature survey', *Public Choice*, 120: 267–300.

Heusala, A.-L. 2013. 'Changes of administrative accountability in Russian transitions', *Review of Central and Eastern European Law*, 38(3–4): 267–293.

Ioffe, G. and Z. Zayonchkovskaya. 2010. 'Immigration to Russia: Inevitability and prospective inflows', *Eurasian Geography and Economics*, 51(1): 104–125.

Ivakhniouk, I. 2004. 'Illegal migration: Russia', *European Security*, 13(1): 35–53.

Kaldor M., M. Martin and S. Selchow. 2007. 'Human security: A new narrative for Europe', *International Affairs*, 83(2): 273–288.

Kar, D. and S. Freitas. 2013. 'Russia: Illicit financial flows and the role of the underground economy', *Global Financial Integrity*, February.

Kubal, A. 2013. 'Conceptualizing 'semi-legality' in migration research', *Law & Society Review* 47(3): 555–587.

Kulmala, M., M. Kainu, J. Nikula, and M. Kivinen. 2014. 'Paradoxes of agency: Democracy and welfare in Russia', *Demokratizatsiya*, 22(4): 523–552.

Laszlo, E. 1999. 'Globalization: The outer and the inner dimensions', *World Futures: The Journal of New Paradigm Research*, 53(2): 95–100.

Lavezzi, A. M. 2014. 'Organised crime and the economy: A framework for policy prescriptions', *Global Crime*, 15(1–2): 164–190.

Legvold, R. 2011. 'Encountering globalization Russian style'. In J. Wilhelmsen and E. Wilson Rowe (eds), *Russia's Encounter with Globalization: Actors, Processes and Critical Moments*. Basingstoke: Palgrave Macmillan, pp. 15–39.

Liebert, S., S. E. Condrey and D. Goncharov. 2013. (eds), *Public Administration in Post-Communist Countries: Former Soviet Union, Central and Eastern Europe, and Mongolia*. Boca Raton, FL: Taylor & Francis.

Mahoney, J. and K. Thelen. 2010. (eds) *Explaining Institutional Change. Ambiguity, Agency and Power*. Cambridge: Cambridge University Press.

Meyer-Sahling, J.-H. 2009. 'Varieties of legacies: A critical review of legacy explanations of public administration reform in East Central Europe', *International Review of Administrative Sciences*, 75: 509–528.

Mugarura, N. 2014. 'Has globalisation rendered the state paradigm in controlling crimes anachronistic?', *Journal of Financial Crime*, 21(4): 381–399.

Nardo, M. 2011. 'Economic crime and illegal markets integration: A platform for analysis', *Journal of Financial Crime*, 18(1): 47–62.

Nonini, D. M. 2002. 'Transnational migrants, globalization processes, and regimes of power and knowledge', *Critical Asian Studies*, 34(1): 3–17.

Randma-Liiv, T., V. Nakrosis and G. Hajnal. 2011. 'Public sector organization in Central and Eastern Europe: From agencification to de-agencification'. *Transsylvanian Review of Administrative Sciences*, pp. 160–175. http://rtsa.ro/tras/index.php/tra s/issue/view/24.

Reeves, M. 2013. 'Clean fake: Authenticating documents and persons in migrant Moscow', *American Ethnologist*, 40(3): 508–524.

Rudolph, C. 2003. 'Globalization and security: Migration and evolving conceptions of security in statecraft and scholarship', *Security Studies*, 13(1): 1–32.

Sakwa, R. 2013. 'The Soviet collapse: Contradictions and neo-modernisation', *Journal of Eurasian Studies*, 4: 65–77.

Schneider, F. 2012. 'The shadow economy and work in the shadow: What do we (not) know?' *IZA Discussion Paper No. 6423*, March.

Schneider, F. and D. H. Enste. 2000. 'Shadow economies: Size, causes, and consequences', *Journal of Economic Literature*, 38(March): 77–114.

Schneider, F. and C. C. Williams. 2013. *The Shadow Economy: The Institute of Economic Affairs*. London: Hobbs.

Stepanov, V. 2000. 'Ethnic tensions and separatism in Russia', *Journal of Ethnic and Migration Studies*, 26(2): 305–332.

Tyuryukanova, E. and E. Kostyrya. 2008. 'The socio-economic and criminal effects of contemporary migration in large Russian cities'. In R. Orttung and A. Latta (eds), *Russia's Battle with Crime, Corruption, and Terrorism*. Abingdon: Routledge, pp. 11–35.

Van Aerschot, P. and P. Daentzer (eds). 2014. *The Integration and Protection of Immigrants. Canadian and Scandinavian Critiques*. Dorchester: Dorset Press.

Yuval-Davis, N. 2011. *The Politics of Belonging: Intersectional Contestations*. New Delhi: Sage Publications.

Zabyelina, Y. 2012. 'Costs and benefits of informal economy: Shuttle trade and crime at Cherkizovsky market', *Global Crime*, 13(2): 95–108.

Zayonchkovskaya, Z., N. Mkrtchyan and E. Tyuryukanova. 2009. 'Rossija pered vyzovami immigratsii'. In Z. Zayonchkovskaya *et al.* (eds), *Postsovetskie transformatsii: otrazhzenie v migratsijah*. Moskva: Adamant, pp. 9–62.

2 Migration policies in Russia

Laws and debates

Sergey Abashin

International migration is today one of the key processes and most important discussion topics in Russia. According to the official data, from 1991 to 2000, after the collapse of the USSR, 8.4 million people immigrated to the country (Heleniak 2008; Karachurina 2012). From 2001 to 2013, there were 3.3 million immigrants (Federal State Statistic Service 2015). Thus, within two decades almost 12 million immigrants (8–9 per cent of the country's permanent population) moved to Russia in order to live there permanently; the vast majority of them came from the former Soviet republics. Almost the same number, approximately 11 million, of foreign nationals have been found to reside in Russia every year in recent years (Federal Migration Service 2015). Many of them live there permanently, but do not apply for a residence permit or citizenship. Moreover, a significant proportion of this category of migrants is on rota, i.e. those leaving the country are replaced with new foreign nationals. These migrants are also predominantly either former Soviet nationals or descendants thereof.

Had the USSR continued to exist, the vast majority of these 20 to 25 million people would not have been regarded as international migrants, and resettlement processes, regardless of their scale, would have been regulated by normal interior legislation (Siegelbaum and Moch 2014). The collapse of the USSR certainly provoked an increase in mobility, but it also changed the statuses of people, turning former nationals of one country into foreign nationals in relation to each other, i.e. it created entirely new ways of talking about migration. This process coincided with different tendencies: a transformation from a planned economy to a neo-liberal one, from a multinational empire to several states in the process of building a nation, from friendship among peoples to postcolonial divisions. Many questions arose in the new post-Soviet reality about what kind of a mobility policy should exist between the former administrative boundaries that had become state borders, how to name and identify the status of people who cross them, and whether this mobility is advantageous or, conversely, dangerous, and what kind of institutions and rules should control and regulate this mobility and these people.

A debate on all of these issues has been ongoing during the whole post-Soviet period and has been accompanied by frequent changes in migration

DOI: 10.4324/9781315657424-2

policies. At the same time, academics studying migration processes in Russia point out that migration policy has a cyclical character, related to elections, and an inconsistent character, related to conflict between different lobbyists (liberals, conditional siloviks, nationalists and neo-imperialists) (Mukomel' 2005: 153; Zaionchkovskaya *et al*. 2009: 55–61). Experts talk about discourse segmentation in different areas (journalists, officials, politicians, experts) (Mukomel' 2005: 80) and about strong ideological polarisation in this topic area (Mukomel' 2008). All of these issues mean that reactions, solutions and rhetoric on migration are very contradictory and rapidly changing. Moreover, the mobility processes themselves are also constantly developing, not always predictably; they react to economic and political crises and create new topics for debate all the time.

In this chapter, I will try to outline the main tendencies and milestones of migration policy in Russia in the 2000s. I will describe the search for and shift in basic conceptual foundations of migration policy that took place in this period. I will briefly look into the establishment of the Federal Migration Service (FMS) as a major institution responsible for mobility regulation. I will give an overview of the main documents that were developed in 2012 and defined the way in which the migration interests are seen by the current Russian authorities. I will consider political debate on migration issues using examples of the election agendas of candidates in the mayoral election in Moscow in 2013. Finally I will analyse the main directions and the first results of the changes in migration legislation in 2014 and 2015.[1]

Ours or others

Russian migration policy went through a number of significant transformations between 1991 and 2015 (Malakhov 2014: 1065–7). The gist could be described as a transformation from a single Soviet citizenship and identity to a more differentiated definition of inhabitants of the former Soviet republics as 'our vs alien' and 'preferred vs non-preferred migrants' in Russia. This process has evolved controversially, because for a very long time politicians could not decide what kind of state Russia should be – a national state or a unique 'civilisation' – and what kind of relationship it should have with the different former Soviet republics that became independent countries: an open and associated one or a distanced one.

The first migration laws in the post-Soviet Russia were the Federal Refugees Act and the Act on Forcibly Displaced Persons (Zakon 'O bezhentsakh', Zakon 'O vynuzhdennykh pereselentsakh').[2] They were adopted in 1993 as a reaction to the mass resettlements of people caused by the collapse of the USSR (Robarts 2008). These laws defined the statuses and conditions of post-Soviet migration, at the same time characterising it as extreme. The laws defined the difference between a refugee and a forcibly displaced person, for the first time showing the degree of affinity and desirability of former Soviet people for the new Russia. Foreign nationals who arrived in the country were denominated as refugees, while Russian citizens who acquired Russian citizenship outside Russia or while arriving in Russia were denominated as forcibly displaced persons ('Zakon "O gosudarstvennoi politike ...'; 'Zakon "O pravovom polozhenii...'). Later these laws were amended, and new conditions were introduced for awarding particular statuses (in particular, a list of circumstances that gave the right to refugee status or a permanent residence permit in Russia, and a desire to receive Russian citizenship for displaced persons).

In 1994, President Boris Yeltsin issued a decree 'On the Main Directions of the Russian Federation's State Policy toward Compatriots Residing Abroad', which was followed by the government regulation 'On Supportive Measures to Compatriots Abroad'. In 1995 the State Duma adopted a 'Declaration on Support for Russian Diaspora and on Patronage for Russian Compatriots' (Government 1995), where 'everyone coming from the USSR and Russia and the direct descendants thereof, regardless of their national and ethnic origin, language, confession, occupation, place of residence, and other circumstances, not holding a Russian citizenship and declaring in an unambiguous way their spiritual, cultural, and ethnic ties with the Russian Federation or any federal subject of the Russian Federation and having confirmed these ties' were declared to be 'compatriots'. In 1999, the 'Act on the Russian Federation's State Policy toward Compatriots Abroad' (Zakon 'O gosudarstvennoi ... 2015) was adopted. There, compatriots were denominated, in particular, as 'individuals, who used to hold USSR citizenship, are residing in the states that used to be a part of the USSR in the past and hold the citizenship of the aforementioned states'. However, their descendants, if they belonged to 'the titular nationality of foreign states', lost this status.

'Compatriot' became a basic concept for describing former Soviet citizens who wanted to keep their ties and stay loyal to post-Soviet Russia. Moreover, the concept was interpreted very broadly, which allowed anyone who lived in the post-Soviet space to be included in it. All decisions concerning compatriots were built in the first instance around the logic of supporting their status abroad and secondly as a support for compatriots who decided to move permanently to Russia. In the 1990s, a simplified procedure for acquiring Russian citizenship was available for the latter category.

However, at the beginning of the 2000s, the policy towards former Soviet citizens started to go through significant changes. The Russian authorities decided to draw a clear line between 'ours' and 'aliens' and between 'preferred' and 'non-preferred'. First of all, a divisive line was drawn between those who arrive to get permanent residency and Russian citizenship, and foreign nationals ('labour migrants'), who receive a 'temporary' or 'permanent' residence status. This was written down in detail in the 'Federal Law on Legal Status of Foreign Citizens in the Russian Federation' that was adopted in 2002 ('Zakon "O pravovom polozhenii ...' 2002).[3] The latest versions of the law on compatriots outlined cultural requirements for migrants who would like to become Russian citizens, and strengthened ethnic selection in attracting immigrants from other countries.

Officially the concept of 'compatriots' was interpreted and continues to be interpreted very broadly, embracing Russian citizens living abroad and individuals who used to have USSR citizenship as well as everyone who comes from Russia and the USSR and their descendants. This definition excluded a purely ethnic approach to migration policy, underlined the multinational character of Russian society, and opened the doors for non-ethnic migration from the post-Soviet space. However, the concept of 'compatriot' was gradually linked to someone's plans to move to Russia (Heleniak 2001: 546). In 2006, a 'State Programme to Support Voluntary Resettlement to the Russian Federation of Compatriots Living Abroad' ('Ukaz Prezidenta...' 2006) was revealed. The programme stated that the socio-economic development of the country requires 'a stabilization of population size', and, subsequently, a migrational input into the population of Russia. Moreover, compatriots 'raised in the traditions of the Russian culture, speaking Russian and willing to maintain their ties to Russia', were considered the most desired category of these resettlers. At the same time, the definition of compatriots was given in the law in 1999.[4] They were entitled to different financial privileges and compensations. The programme was planned to operate until 2012.

In 2012 the resettlement programme was continued and declared indefinite, but it was significantly adjusted so that the concept of 'compatriot' became even narrower. The main adjustment consisted of amendments to the 'Act on the Russian Federation's State Policy toward Compatriots Abroad' that radically narrowed the definition of a compatriot (Zakon 'O gosudarstvennoi...' 2015). The new version regarded as compatriots 'individuals and their descendants, living outside of Russia and belonging, as a rule, to ethnicities that historically live on the territory of the Russian Federation, and who made a free choice in favour of spiritual, cultural and legal ties to the Russian Federation, whose direct ancestors lived in the past on the territory of the Russian Federation'.

The narrowing of the 'compatriot' concept cleared a space for the legal and rhetorical institutionalisation of other statuses and definitions in respect to migrants from the post-Soviet space. Gradually, media and politicians filled this niche with concepts of 'migrant' and particularly 'gastarbeiter' that are used predominantly for labour migrants from the countries of the former USSR that do not have a visa regime with Russia. Thus, a division between the categories of 'good compatriots' and 'bad gastarbeiters' occurred. In practice, however, these concepts are mixed, and placement into one category remains arbitrary and dependent on many factors, including bureaucratic and administrative interests. Migration policy in the 2000s was built up around the topic of how to separate one from the other. This formation was taking place simultaneously in institutional, ideological, political and legal modes, each of which has its own specialities and background. As a result, there are plenty of legal statuses and legality modes (Reeves 2013).

Federal Migration Service

An independent FMS was founded in 1992 on the basis of what used to be the Soviet Committee for Migration Affairs at the Ministry of Labour and Employment. The FMS had a rather modest complement of civil servants (a few hundred) and its tasks included the accommodation of refugees and forcibly displaced persons from the former USSR republics. However, by the end of the 1990s, when the influx of Russian-speaking resettlers started to decrease and was replaced by the growing influx of foreign-language-speaking migrants, a decision was made to unite migration and nationality issues under one single authority. In 2000, the FMS apparatus was integrated into the Ministry for Federal Affairs, and National and Migration policies. Then, one year later, this ministry was dissolved and the main tasks of immigration control were given to the Ministry of Internal Affairs, where the migration service became a separate department, the head of which received a post of deputy minister. Simultaneously, in 2001 an interdepartmental working group was created whose task was to prepare proposals for an update of migration legislation; the then deputy head of the President's Administration, the former secret service officer Viktor Ivanov, led the group.

Several processes were taking place in the background of the debate on migration policy at the beginning of the 2000s: the activation of the fight against terrorism and rebellion in the North Caucasus, the centralisation of the management system, and the strengthening of federal institutions, including law enforcement agencies. In the laws on citizenship and the legal status of foreign nationals adopted in 2002, the procedure for acquiring a permanent residence permit and the Russian citizenship was seriously restrained. New migration control mechanisms were introduced, such as a migration card, a registration procedure at the address of accommodation/ residence. A new article covering crimes of 'illegal migration organisation', complemented the Criminal Code, and administrative punishment in migration cases was hardened. In 2003 the government adopted 'The Conceptual Foundation for Regulating Migration Processes in the Russian Federation' developed in the Ministry of Internal Affairs ('Kontseptsiya regulirovaniya' 2003). The document states a need for 'a strong will of the state' and 'a solid law and order in the area of regulating migration processes', and discusses an elemental and uncontrollable 'population growth' and 'worsening crime situation', a threat of 'penetration of terrorist organisations', and a mass and illegal residence in Russia of Transcaucasia, Central and Eastern Asian states' nationals, that 'creates a threat to the national labour market and fosters a shadow economy'. The conceptual foundation also laid out a plan for the development of a single immigration control system in the Russian Federation and for regulating international labour migration.

The decision to recreate the FMS was made in 2004. This time, the service would have an extended array of functions: in particular, it would be responsible for passport and visa procedures. During the period from 2004 to 2012, the FMS officially remained a department of the Ministry of Internal Affairs, and militia/police officers were attached to the service while keeping their ranks and military benefits. However, in reality the service gained an autonomous status – it was financed as a separate expenditure in the state budget, and its work was regulated by separate legislation and regulations. Several former KGB and FSB officers joined the management of FMS: specifically the post of the head of the service was given to the representative of this agency, Konstantin Romodanovsky. This also underlined a certain independence of the new institution.

The FMS was allocated significant organisational and monetary resources that far exceeded those that the agency had in the 1990s. In 2004, the agency employed around 20,000 people, and by 2014 the number of staff had doubled, to 40,000. Among them, the number of federal state officials, the most privileged group of civil servants, increased from 3,000 to 12,000, and the central administration grew from 400 to 700 people. In the ten years of the agency's existence from 2005 to 2014, its funding increased tenfold, from 3.5 billion roubles to 36.1 billion roubles (Government 2005, 2014).

This concentration of resources and power to manage migration processes in one institution had several important and at the same time controversial impacts. A rather powerful bureaucratic structure was created, with its own hierarchies, centre, and regional offices, daily routine activities and a number of services that could generate income for the state and at the same time offered opportunities for shadow earnings. This institution could actively interact not only with the president's administration and the government, but also with regional governments, via the regional offices of the FMS. The FMS also received the possibility and right to cooperate with other countries on issues of migration, as well as with international organisations dealing with this issue. All this made the service an important place for negotiation and lobbying.

The recreation of the FMS allowed the consolidation of migration policy, although leaving some of the functions to other agencies.[5] A cohort of state officials specialised in migration, collecting and manipulating migration statistics, creating their own group of official and unofficial experts. The dissolution of the interdepartmental group for developing migration legislation made the service a main institution where the ideas of migrations policies are developed. Moreover, due to the bureaucratic logic of increasing its weight and funding, it is important for the FMS that the 'migration problem' is constantly on the informational and political agenda and that state officials are seen to be 'dealing with' this problem, 'solving' it and performing an important state task.

Yet another impact, partly unexpected, was that, contrary to the original logic of strengthening force mechanisms for managing migration, the formation of the separate institution responsible for migration control allowed the topic of migration to be detached into a separate object of concern, slightly distancing it from a purely repressive perspective, to create conditions for reviewing legalisation issues from a more liberal point of view.[6] This was caused, in particular, by the fact that liberal experts could have more influence on the decision-making within the frames of this institutional format, that business dependent on foreign labour could negotiate faster to resolve its difficulties, and that the state officials themselves were more interested in the different indirect mechanisms impacting on migration when it was possible to act without direct subordination to the force agencies.

Not without the participation of the FMS, it was decided in 2007 to simplify access to the labour market for migrants without visas (application process and work permit, notification-based procedure for the employers, high quotas, notification- rather than permission-based migrant registration, work permits being given to employees and not to employers). In 2009, another liberal decision was made: that labour migrants from visa-free countries could receive a work permit in Russia by purchasing a special paid document (patent), which however concerned only the work of individuals, but in fact gave an opportunity to for all foreigners to have some legal status. In 2012, the FMS actively took part in formulating the new migration policy, and 2013–15 saw the beginning of the implementation of the new migration regulations that contained more flexible and liberal formulations and norms, which I will discuss later.

In other words, the separate migration agency that was created deep inside the secret service turned out to be a monopolist in the formulation of migration policy independently of repressive institutions. This trend eventually led to the situation where in 2013 the head of the FMS Konstantin Romodanovsky received the rank of federal minister directly subordinate to the government, and the migration service was officially released from the subordination of the Ministry of Internal Affairs, and became a civil institution. We cannot say that this process has taken place without an internal struggle: on the one hand, there are ideas to make migration policy less strong-arm, to shift the accent towards problems of integration and give part of the functions to the Agency of Nationality Affairs that was created in 2015 (from 2004, the government had no institution dealing with nationality issues), and on the other hand, there are proposals to strengthen the control element again by returning the FMS back to the Ministry of Internal Affairs (MIA) or giving the service some policing and investigative functions.[7]

The end result has been an unexpected presidential edict in April 2016 concerning the abolishment of the FMS and transferal of its functions to the Central administration of migration in the MIA. In the process, the status of the organisation of migration questions fell below the 2013 decision, and even below its position in 2004. Migration policy again lost its independent status as a unified point of accumulation of ideas and authority.

Policy concept of 2012

The new version of the migration policy was declared in 2012, when Vladimir Putin formally returned to the post of president. I would like to draw attention to two texts where the main principles of the new policy were laid out: the first is a pre-election newspaper piece by the then still Prime Minister Putin, 'Russia: the national issue' published on 23 January 2012 in the *Nezavisimaya Gazeta*; and the second is 'The concept of the state migration policy for the RF during the period till 2025', also signed by Putin as the new-old president on 12 June 2012 (Putin 2012, Kontseptsiya gosudarstvennoi).

In the article, the prime minister talked about the cultural diversity of Russia and the 'risks' of inter-ethnic and inter-confessional 'tensions' related to this. He linked these risks, in particular, to the migration that will inevitably grow everywhere in the world. Putin criticised attempts to integrate 'minorities' through assimilation in the 'melting pot' saying that the pot is 'knocking and reeking'. He also criticised the idea of 'multiculturalism' and 'tolerance', which in his opinion are leading to minorities' isolation and to their reluctance not only to assimilate, but also to 'adapt', which as a 'responsive reaction' causes an increase of xenophobia 'amongst the local population'. Melting pot and multiculturalism failures, in Putin's opinion, are related to the crisis of the 'very model of the national state' in Europe and he counters it with the Russian model of a 'multinational state' evolved over centuries, where 'a process of mutual accustomization, mutual penetration, and ethnic mixing on the family, friendship and collegial level was constantly going on'. What is more, the core, the 'binding tissue of this unique civilization' is the Russian people and Russian culture.

A separate part of the article dedicated to the 'migration problem' and 'our integration project'. There Putin admits that 'illegal immigration could never and nowhere be eliminated completely, but it, definitely, should be and can be minimized' by the law-enforcing functions of the migration services and through tightening punishment for the violation of migration rules. However, besides repression, the text discusses the need to divide 'favoured treatment modes' for different migrant categories: priority in selection and qualifying for residence and work permits should be given to those whose 'qualification, competence, competitiveness, and cultural and behavioural compatibility' match the Russian conditions best. The article mentions 'respect towards local traditions', a necessity to avoid an occurrence of 'closed, isolated ethnic enclaves' and a need for 'civilized integration and socialization of migrants'. In this regard, an innovative proposal was articulated to make tests in Russian language, Russian history, Russian literature, and the foundations of the state and the law obligatory for gaining and extending migration status. Finally, Putin mentions 'Eurasian integration' as a means of reducing inequality in the post-Soviet space and consequently 'at least minimization of migration flows'.

Adopted in the same year 'The Concept of the State Migration Policy' was slightly different from the article. It was not aimed at a broad audience and did not pursue populist pre-election objectives, but its accent shifted from the national issue to economic and demographic problems.

The concept, just like the article, does not begin with threats and negative consequences, but with the inevitability and possible benefits of external migration. It says that migrants should be welcomed as 'one of the sources to increase population size' in the country and particular regions, and as a source of fulfilling 'the needs of the Russian economy' in 'labourers in priority professional and qualification groups'. Also it says that 'experience of countries that practice an active migration policy shows that migration processes accelerate socio-economic development and ensure population prosperity growth'. However, the list of tasks for migration policy is reshuffled: first 'ensuring the national security of the Russian Federation', and 'maximum protection, comfort, and well-being of the Russian Federation's population' is listed, and only then population growth and economic needs.

The concept mentions risks and problems, among which is 'illegal migration' that 'feeds the shadow economy' and 'worsens negative attitudes towards migrants'. At the same time, among the problems is mentioned the fact that migration policy is orientated towards 'bringing in temporary foreign labourers and does not include measures that would facilitate resettlement to the place of permanent residence, or the adaptation and integration of migrants'. The document discusses 'incentives' for moving permanently to the Russian Federation intended for certain groups of foreigners, and differentiation mechanisms for these groups, such as a definition of 'compatriots', and 'highly skilled' and 'in-demand' workers, as well as a division into categories of 'short-term and long-term labour migration'.

For 'the support of adaptation and integration of migrants', the concept suggests that 'both migrants and host society should develop skills of intercultural dialogue and actions against xenophobia, and national and racial intolerance', separately mentioning the need for teaching Russian, providing 'legal education, and awareness about cultural traditions and behaviour norms', 'ensuring access for the foreign nationals and members of their families to social, medical and educational services dependent on their legal status', 'measures against the social exclusion of migrants, space segregation, and ethnic enclave formation', and the 'development, introduction, and implementation of programmes aimed at the adaptation and integration of migrants, including opening centres of informational and legal support for migrants, and Russian language, history and culture courses'.

The document also mentions the fight against 'illegal migration', in support of which it suggests a 'refinement of penalties for migration legislation violations' and 'a refinement of the immigration control system', and the 'creation of infrastructure for readmission procedures and ensuring the operation of special institutions to detain foreign nationals and stateless persons'.

Both documents dealing with the new migration policy and signed by Putin are controversial. First of all, they are not of a binding nature and, as such, are first and foremost political statements. Second, even if these texts are not in conflict with each other, they nonetheless describe the migration problems differently: either as a national issue, or as an economic and demographic one. This difference allows the discussion of migration to be switched from one register to another and the arguments to be manipulated from various discourses. Third, each of these texts contains a very diverse set of points: on the benefits and disadvantages of migration, on security and development, on prohibitions and encouragement. In this set, everyone can see and read whatever is closest to their own ideological point of view. This is a peculiar compromise of several lobbying forces that does not close the discussion, but rather opens it up in very different areas.

The Moscow mayoral election in 2013

In the public domain, the controversial nature of the Russian migration policy, normally not very obvious in the official statements, gains features of an open political battle (Mukomel' 2005: 86–103, Mukomel' 2011: 86–108, Malakhov 2014: 1070–5). This was most clearly seen during the Moscow mayoral election in 2013.

The capital has a special status in Russian society. Moscow is not just the largest megalopolis, with 12–14 million registered and unregistered inhabitants, but has an over-concentration of finances, state institutions and political forces, as well as information resources. Many local events taking place in this city attract all-Russian coverage and have all-Russian significance. Specifically Muscovite problems and concerns very much influence the language of power and ideology, and this language is transmitted to other regions, where local officials, politicians and journalists reproduce Moscow clichés and questions in their home territory. The attitude towards migration is to a great extent formulated precisely in the Moscow region, where the concentration of foreigners is very high (an estimated 25–30 per cent of all of the foreigners in the country), and this purely metropolitan attitude, aggravated by dismal traffic problems, high prices, poor ecology, etc. is then spread across the country.

It is no coincidence in this regard that the election of the head of the city of Moscow in 2013 sharply exacerbated political and public debates about migration in Russia in general. Attitudes towards migration became one of the key elements of the politics in the country. This topic gained a significant public nature and all politicians, all parties, and all public persons expressed their opinion. Numerous phobias that had been previously morally or politically censored gained in this debate a rather legitimate, politically acceptable and even, in some senses, approved nature.

The election was due on 8 September, so the pre-election campaign occurred over three summer months. A rather broad spectrum of political forces was present at the elections, which dramatically sharpened the pre-election debate and strengthened the populist element of all of the agendas. The opposition used the topic of migration, regarding it as a weak spot of the current management system, while the powers in response tried to demonstrate that they were dealing with the problem. The result was a mutual escalation of anti-migration panic. What is more, the arguments and rhetoric of the pre-election campaign matched the language of the texts signed by Putin in 2012 very little, and created an entirely different set of questions and topics.

Pre-empting criticism of condoning foreign migration, the incumbent and the candidate from the ruling United Russia party, Sergey Sobyanin, from the very beginning of his campaign, in fact even before he officially declared it, began to demonstrate a strict attitude towards the newcomers. He said that Moscow needs migration, because the city is experiencing a shortage of labour. However, in his opinion, this need could be satisfied with people coming from other regions of Russia, Russian citizens, while it was necessary to reduce the number of foreign migrants, particularly, as Sobyanin casually mentioned, the number of newcomers from Central Asia, whose culture is 'inadequate with our traditions'. Sobyanin also suggested keeping migration seasonal, i.e. not to motivate migrants to 'adapt', but to motivate them to leave after finishing their work. 'In my opinion Moscow is a Russian city and it should remain like that. Not a Chinese, not a Tajik and not an Uzbek city,' he said in one interview, clearly exaggerating the threat of the capital turning into a 'non-Russian' city. The acting head of the city, however, spoke out against the introduction of visas with countries from which the main migrant influx originates, but he emphasised the fact that rules for foreigners would be hardened in Moscow.

Sobyanin could not confine himself to rhetoric: he had to demonstrate his determination and ability to solve the migration issue. On 27 July, at the height of the official pre-election campaign, a rather ordinary incident happened at Matveevsky market in Moscow: during an identity check, a local merchant from Dagestan, Russian citizen Magomet Rasulov, hit a policeman several times. Someone filmed it, and the video was quickly distributed on the Internet and TV. Immediately, police raids started, which were shown on all state TV channels in news programmes. Naturally, demonstrative violence shifted from Caucasians, who are Russian citizens, to foreign migrants, who were easier to declare as lawbreakers, because many of them indeed do not have all of the documents required for residence and work. Within the frames of the same campaign, a detainment camp for foreign nationals who violated administrative rules and were to be deported was opened on 1 August in Golyanovo, the northern district of Moscow. The camp had 900 places and quickly filled with several dozen and later several hundred foreigners, most of whom were Vietnamese citizens.

Regardless of Sobyanin's attempts to look like a person who is solving the migration issue, it was much too attractive for criticism from the opposition. The new candidate, Alexei Navalny, who of course needed to find new topics and a new language to position himself as a 'new politician', criticised him especially actively.

Navalny positioned himself as a moderate nationalist, a European-type national-democrat, and used as an example Le Pen's party in France and Wilders' party in the Netherlands. Navalny tried to include the topic of migration in the anti-corruption rhetoric. First, he accentuated the fact that there are too many foreign migrants, and their arrival in Moscow is related to the financial interests of civil servants and corruption. In his opinion, migration on this scale is not needed and only maintains an inefficient economy in the capital. He also actively elaborated upon the theme that the fast-growing number of crimes is related to migrants. At the same time, Navalny underlined that he was talking exclusively about the inhabitants of Central Asia and the North Caucasus, because, in his opinion, it was migrants from these regions who cause most of the problems, whereas those coming from Ukraine, Belarus and Moldova are law-abiding people and better qualified. As a solution to the problem of excess foreign migrants, Navalny suggested the introduction of a visa regime with Central Asian states.

The other four candidates also actively participated in the migration debate. The strictest position, close to the position of Navalny, was held by the representative of LDPR (the party of Vladimir Zhirinovsky), who iterated his agenda concerning migration very laconically and unequivocally: 'First of all we should prohibit any migration. Secondly, we should catch and deport all illegals. Thirdly, all legal migrants should be proofed in terms of professional qualifications'.

The liberal Yabloko party leader Sergey Mitrokhin in some of his speeches criticised his competitor Navalny for an alliance with nationalists, condemning the 'concentration camps', 'raids', 'deportations' and the idea of visa introduction. On other occasions he himself talked and wrote about epidemics as a threat caused by migrants, about an increase of conflicts, and about ousting local workers out of the labour market due to the influx of cheap labour. Mitrokhin suggested hardening measures that should result in the reduction of foreign migrant numbers. Mitrokhin also implied that Moscow is a more preferable place for migrants with 'Slavic faces'.

Ivan Melnikov, a party functionary since Soviet times, a candidate from the Communist party, did not make migration a main topic of his pre-election campaign. He, however, also inevitably expressed his opinion on this topic and in a very soft way repeated the general ideas, roughly in the same spirit as Sobyanin: there are a lot of migrants in Moscow, there should be fewer of them, migrants should stay here legally and should arrive on a working visa, but we do not need to introduce visas with CIS countries, and illegal migrants are a 'concern of the law enforcement agencies'. The candidate from the A Just Russia party, also a functionary since the Soviet period, Nikolay Levichev, following Sobyanin and Melnikov, tried to find a position of moderate criticism of the migration situation. He repeated the whole array of anti-migrant arguments that mass migration, especially illegal migration, creates the danger of an increase in criminality, leads to the formation of uncontrolled 'ethnic enclaves', where migrants poorly integrate into the Russian society, leads to changes in the ethnic balance of the city, 'corrupts business', etc. At the same time, he admitted that the Russian economy needs migrants, therefore it is necessary to legalise them.

The mayoral election in Moscow in 2013 became the first political event in Russia where migration as a theme was not only publicly discussed, but also became probably one of the most-discussed topics in the pre-election campaign. The opposition participated in the election to some extent and actively used the topic of migration, and largely thanks to their campaigning, this topic was put at the core of the political debate. All political parties and forces, from the right to the left of all kinds, discussed and criticised migration policy during this campaign. All six candidates focused on describing the threats and dangers caused by migrants. Most of the expressed proposals had a repressive and to different extents limiting nature, and the rhetoric of all of the participants had elements of ethnic phobias, so it is not a coincidence that in all debates names and images of predominantly Central Asian and partially Caucasian migrants were used. All of this created a wave of really rather openly racist statements in the media and on the Internet that now was somehow being legitimised by the political discussion of migration.

Even though emphasising the topic of migration did not bring any tangible benefit to any of the candidates in the elections, not least because all of them were saying the same thing, still the general level of the negative perception of foreigners, migrants, aliens in Russian society dramatically increased as a consequence of the elections. An opinion poll undertaken by the Levada Centre between 4 and 8 July, i.e. during the first half of the pre-election campaign, showed that the main problem for Muscovites at that point was that there were 'many migrants from former southern Soviet republics and the North Caucasus'. Fifty-five per cent of the interviewees placed this in first place. Interestingly, in February 2013, five months before the elections, the number was 44 per cent and the migration issue was less important than traffic jams and high prices, only significant at the level of utility bills.[8]

New migration rules 2014–15

The conceptual ideas recommended by the experts in 2012 and the public discussion in 2013 defined the nature of the new developments in migration policy in 2014–15. These developments had several directions and were supposed to ensure the solving of various tasks.

First of all came a limitation of the number of foreign nationals in Russia. At first two restrictive measures were adopted, valid from 2013–14: a rule for three-month stays of foreigners from visa-free countries in Russia within a six-month period, and an introduction of exclusion for three or five years for minor administrative infringements (even traffic regulation infringements). Practices of foreigner deportation were extended. Notwithstanding that the concept of the new migration policy rather talked about attracting foreigners, and about their legalisation in order to solve economic and demographic problems, in reality the policy and the public rhetoric emphasised the ousting of migrants, especially those from Central Asia.

Second, there was the idea of legalisation of foreign workers from visa-free countries. To solve this problem, starting from 2015, instead of the double system with quota permits and working patents for individuals, it was decided to introduce a single patent system for individuals, legal entities and sole traders. Permits remained only for countries with visa regimes, from where migration does not have a mass scale and which were easy to regulate by means of visas. Simultaneously, this new rule was supposed to solve the issue of increasing tax collections from foreign workers via payments for patents and the social security issue for foreign workers by means of acquiring health insurance, an obligatory condition for patent granting. It was also envisaged that with a flexible patent price, and the right to introduce and stop giving quotas, the regional authorities would receive a tool for regulating migration flows in their territories.

The third direction suggested a division of foreign nationals into those who are invited temporarily, and those who are invited to live in Russian with the prospect of Russian citizenship. In particular, norms were introduced according to which 'Russian native speakers', 'entrepreneurs and investors' and experts in certain professions, including blue-collar workers (lathe operators, nurses, electricians, etc.) could receive a residence permit and Russian citizenship more easily. For the rest of the foreigners working on a patent basis, the regime of the more complicated residence permit procedure was kept in place and an additional condition of patent renewal after one year was introduced; after two years they would have to leave Russia.

The fourth direction is an activation of integration mechanisms for foreign nationals. In 2014, the FMS prepared the draft of the law 'On Social and Cultural Adaptation and Integration of Foreign Nationals in the Russian Federation' ('Proekt zakona ...' 2015). Its main idea was to link the granting of a working patent and a residence permit in Russia to certification at a certain level in Russian language, history and legislation. The law was not adopted, and the 'integration' department of the FMS itself was abolished following the agency structure's optimisation. However, the requirements for the successful passing of the paid examination in the aforementioned three disciplines by foreign nationals as prerequisites for patent and residence permit granting were added as amendments to the fundamental law on foreigners in Russia.[9] These requirements will be valid from 2015.[10]

At first sight, the implemented measures immediately brought the results that the management of the FMS is now presenting as its own achievements. For instance, the number of exclusions and deportations increased dramatically: from approximately 73,000 and 35,000 people in 2013 to 645,000 and 139,000 people in 2014 (in nine months of 2015, 380,000 and 85,000 respectively) (Ofitsial'nye statisticheskie dannye). The number of foreign nationals from Central Asia and North Caucasus residing in Russia decreased by about 15 per cent from 2014 to 2015. At the same time, the FMS's revenue in the first nine months of 2015 was 20 per cent higher than in the same period of 2014 and reached 42 billion roubles, without including the earnings of insurance companies and education institutions.

However, in reality the picture is more complicated. Some of the decrease in the number of foreigners is rather a result of the economic crisis of 2014–2015 and the drop in workplaces and income than proof of the efficiency of the prohibitive measures. In fact migrants have learned to evade them by changing passports at home and replacing some migrants with others. Moreover, due to the decrease in migrant numbers the total amount of revenue of the FMS is less impressive than it could have been, taking into account the threefold increase in patent prices. The process of getting the new patents turned out to be very complicated, and as a result, the number of foreigners from visa-free countries legally working and residing in Russian has decreased: within seven months of 2015 only 1.2 million people managed to receive the new patents in comparison to 1.6 million in 2014 (excluding 0.8 million work permits). The integration examination procedure that was supposed to become obligatory for several million people in reality turned out to be a formality incomprehensible for migrants who come to Russia for temporary work.

The situation in 2015 was in fact evolving as a catastrophe, as several million migrants could have become outlaws and created legal chaos. To avoid this situation, several regulations were introduced that functionally ceased the use of the new migration rules for a large number of foreigners. In particular, the decision was made to prolong the validity of the old patents, with an increase in their price; this was made in Moscow, where approximately a quarter of all labour migrants reside. The old patents were intended for those working for individuals, but the authorities effectively closed their eyes to law violations and migrants working for legal entities, which makes their status semi-legal. In 2015, the citizens of Belarus, Kazakhstan, Armenia and Kyrgyzstan (in total two million people residing in Russia), i.e. those countries which joined the Eurasian Economic Union, were exempt from the new migration rules. They were allowed to apply for work without patents, and Kyrgyzstan nationals, who were previously excluded from entering Russia, were granted amnesty. In addition, 0.6 million Ukrainian nationals received a status of temporary exile for a year and the possibility to work in Russia without permits. The foreign nationals who apply for work at the construction sites of the 2018 World Cup (this exemption also existed in the old system of 2013) were also exempt from the new migration rules: they can sign a contract directly with the organisations who hold the assignment.

In general, the new reforms of the migration policy in 2014 and in particular in 2015 give the impression of being a chaotic rather than a strategic sequence of actions. The task of attracting foreign labour migrants and the simplified legalisation of their residence and work in Russia, which was the idea of the single patent system, is actually blocked on the one hand by the massive and unclear use of prohibitive measures, and on the other hand by the complicated and for migrants rather expensive bureaucratic legalisation procedure. The task of creating a unified migration system that would minimise corruption and clearly divide migrants into several main categories was dented by the will of state officials immediately reacting to current events such as the war in Ukraine, the World Cup and negotiations over the establishment of the Eurasian Economic Union, bypassing the main goals. All of this is creating an extremely confusing legal situation with a large number of grey and shadow areas and non-transparent interests of various lobbyists.

Conclusion

In the 2000s, an institutional and ideological space was created in Russia that made cross-border mobility an official and public 'problem' and 'agenda'. There are plenty of various bureaucratic, financial, political (including foreign politics) and informational interests around this topic. As a result of multilateral negotiations and sometimes collisions, of taking into account different lobbyist interests and of a search for balance between them, a very cumbersome and controversial, multilayer and constantly self-correcting complex of regulations and actions has been formed that is called 'migration policy'.

By the beginning of the 2000s, two radically opposite poles of attitude towards international migration, mainly consisting of people coming from the former Soviet republics, were formed in the Russian political and ideological debate. On the one hand, it is regarded as inevitable and even necessary for resolving economic and demographic difficulties, while on the other hand, it is seen as dangerous and undesirable from points of view of security and cultural unity, as well as the possible negative economic consequences. At the same time, the migration policy is trying to simultaneously take into account arguments from both sides. In particular, by combining cultural, professional and other attributes, state officials have attempted to design images and categories of 'preferred' and 'non-preferred' migrants out of the former Soviet citizens and descendants thereof, for which different favour regimes are suggested: the former should be motivated to resettle, while the latter should be restricted and ousted by all available means.

In reality, however, the line-up of clear legal norms and a bureaucratic procedure that would allow an unambiguously divide between the 'benefits' of migration and its 'disadvantages', and between the 'preferred' migrants and the 'non-preferred' ones, is working badly. The reason for this is not only that prepared decisions do not work the way they should do, because of the weakness of institutions and lack of knowledge, and that the management system failures are corrected in the process, making the situation even more complicated, and that it is necessary to react to different emergency situations that require temporary and exceptional regulations and procedures of different kinds. These circumstances are important factors of opportunities and abilities to implement ideas and plans in reality. But also very important, in my opinion, is an overly radical division of notions and expectations in Russia related to migration and migrants; a lack of a more or less consolidated position on this topic. All administrative efforts have aimed at a search for some balance between very different desires: from the creation of the 'Russian' state to consolidation of the 'Eurasian' block with other former Soviet republics; from liberal competition on the labour market to protectionism and isolationism that in the end block each other. Here a temptation to use the topic of migration for populist purposes is added, which begins to subordinate the logic of decision-making to rhetoric benefits and selective objectives. 'Migration policy' becomes a field of political fight and ministerial game, whereas resettlements of people follow their own logic.

Notes

1 The study was conducted within the project No 14-18-02149 of the Russian science ('Transnational and trans-local aspects of migration in modern Russia'), at the European University, St Petersburg.
2 Zakon 'O bezhentsakh', No. 4528-I and Zakon 'O vynuzhdennykh pereselentsakh', No. 4530–1.
3 Zakon 'O pravovom polozhenii inostrannykh grazhdan v Rossiiskoi Federatsii, No. 115-FZ.
4 Zakon 'O gosudarstvennoi politike Rossiiskoi Federatsii v otnoshenii sootechestvennikov za rubezhom', No. 99-FZ .
5 There are also other lobbyists in the government, for example the Ministry of Heath and Social Security (from 2012 the Ministry of Labour and Social Security), that are responsible for defining quotas for the foreign labour force and the list of professions exempt from quotas, or who could follow the simplified procedure for a residence permit. The FSB (the frontier service in particular) and the Ministry of Heath and Social Security can also still have an impact on the migration debate.
6 This policy was supported by many liberal economists (Andrienko and Guriev 2005).
7 The story of two former high-ranking FMS officials could be regarded as evidence of internal conflicts. In 2008, Romodanovskiy's deputy, Vyacheslav Postavnin, a former KGB and MIA officer, resigned from his post, and in 2011 Konstantin Poltoranin, the FMS press secretary and a former MIA officer, left office following a row. Moreover, the latter, who was previously all for the softening of the migration regime and patents, started to criticise the migration policy for an excess of migrants and for corruption (saying, 'at stake is the survival of the white race' and 'blood mixing was happening in the correct regime' in a BBC interview), while the former, in contrast, turned into a critic of migration policy from the liberal point of view and became president of the 'Migration – XXI century' foundation.
8 See the article 'Muscovites mostly concerned about the migrants' (*Moskovskie novosti*, 17 July 2013).
9 Interestingly, all problems are regulated as a matter of fact by one law 'On Legal Status of Foreign Nationals in the Russian Federation'. The law was adopted in 2002, but later constantly amended. The law was significantly changed several times: it was in fact a series of laws replacing each other, but remained one law uniting all regulations concerning all foreigners' categories and regulating their activities.
10 It is curious that the state grant for writing a textbook for these exams was given to the Russian Orthodox Church, and the leading organisation for the project was the University of Peoples' Friendship, whose rector is former minister of education Filippov. The questions in the Russian history examination refer to Sovietness, Russianness, and orthodoxy, as well as to loyalty towards the current regime. All this looks like a mix of imperial and nationalistic logics with strong bureaucratic lobbying of separate agencies that are trying to gain financial and other benefits from this innovation.

References

Andrienko, Y. and Guriev, S. 2005. *Understanding Migration in Russia: A Policy Note*. Moscow: World Bank.

Heleniak, T. 2001. 'Migration and restructuring in post-Soviet Russia', *Demokratizatsiya* 9(4): 531–549.

Heleniak, T. 2008. 'An overview of migration in the post-Soviet Space'. In C. Buckley, R. Blair and E. T. Hofmann (eds), *Migration, Homeland, and Belonging in Eurasia*. Baltimore, MD and Washington, DC: Woodrow Wilson Center Press and John Hopkins University Press, pp. 29–67.

Karachurina, L. 2012. 'Postoyannaya migratsiya mezhdu Rossiei i stranami SNG i Baltii', *Demoskon-Weekly*535–536. Retrieved 2 October 2015 from www.demoscop e.ru/weekly/2012/0535/analit05.php.

'Kontseptsiya gosudarstvennoi migratsionnoi politiki Rossiiskoi Federatsii', *Prezident Rossii*. Retrieved 5 September 2015 from http://kremlin.ru/events/president/news/ 15635.

'Kontseptsiya regulirovaniya migratsionnykh protsessov v Rossiiskoi Federatsii'. 2003. *Demoskon-Weekly*. Retrieved 4 October 2015 from www.demoscope.ru/weekly/ knigi/zakon/zakon022.html.

MalakhovV. 2014. 'Russia as a new immigration country: Policy response and public debate', *Europe-Asia Studies*, 66(7): 1062–1079.

'Mezhdunarodnaya migratsiya', Federal'naya sluzhba gosudarstvennoi statistiki. Retrieved22 October 2015 from www.gks.ru/wps/wcm/connect/rosstat_main/rosstat/ ru/statistics/population/demography.

Mukomel', V. 2005. *Migratsionnaya politika Rossii: postsovetskie konteksty*. Moscow: Dipol'-T.

Mukomel', V. 2008. 'Novaya migratsionnaya politika Rossii: izderzhki ideologii', *Moldoscopie (Probleme de analiza politica)*, 42(3): 93–110.

Mukomel', V. 2011. 'Rossiiskie diskursy o migratsii: "Nulevye gody"'. In M. Gorshkov (ed.), *Rossiiya reformiruyushchayasya: Ezhegodnik-2011*. Moscow: Institut sotsiologii RAN, Nestor-Istoriya, pp. 86–108.

'Ofitsial'nye statisticheskie dannye', *Federal'naya migratsionnaya sluzhba*. Retrieved 27 August 2015 from www.fms.gov.ru/about/statistics/data.

'Postanovlenie "O Deklaratsii o podderzhke rossiiskoi diaspory i o pokrovitel'stve rossiiskim sootechestvennikam', *Informatsionno-pravovoi portal BestPravo*. Retrieved 19 October 2015 from www.bestpravo.ru/rossijskoje/er-normy/m3w.htm.

'Proekt zakona "O sotsial'noi i kul'turnoi adaptsii i integratsii inostrannykh grazhdan', Federal'naya migratsionnaya sluzhba. Retrieved 24 August 2015 from www.fms.gov. ru/documentation/865/details/81610.

Putin, V. 2012. 'Rossiya: natsional'nyi vopros', *Nezavisimaya Gazeta*, 23 January.

Reeves, M. 2013. 'Clean fake: Authenticating documents and persons in migrant Moscow', *American Ethnologist*, 40(3): 508–524.

Robarts, A. 2008. 'The Russian state and migration: A theoretical and practical look at the Russian Federation's migration regime'. In C. Buckley, R. Blair and E. T. Hofmann (eds), *Migration, Homeland, and Belonging in Eurasia*. Baltimore, MD and Washington, DC: Woodrow Wilson Center Press and John Hopkins University Press, pp. 99–121.

Siegelbaum, L.H. and L. P. Moch. 2014. *Broad Is My Native Land: Repertoires and Regimes of Migration in Russia's Twentieth Century*. Ithaca, NY and London: Cornell University Press.

'Statisticheskie svedeniya v otnoshenii inostrannykh grazhdan, nakhodyashchikhsya na territorii Rossiiskoi Federatsii', *Federal'naya migratsionnaya sluzhba*. Retrieved 22 October 2015 from www.fms.gov.ru/about/statistics/foreign/details/54891/.

'Ukaz "O merakh po okazaniyu sodeistviya dobrovol'nomu pereseleniyu v Rossiisuyu Federatsiyu sootechestvennikov, prozhivayushchikh za rubezhom', *Informatsionno-pravovoi portal Konsul'tantPlyus*. Retrieved 16 October 2015 from www.consultant.ru/law/doc/ukaz637/;http://base.garant.ru/189653.

'Ukaz prezidenta RF "O merakh po okazaniyu sodeistviya dobrovol'nomu pereseleniyu v RF sootechestvennikov, prozhivayushchikh za rubezhom"', 22 June 2006. Retrieved 19 October 2015 from www.consultant.ru/law/doc/ukaz637; http://base.garant.ru/189653.

'Vedomstvennaya struktura raskhodov federal'nogo byudzheta na 2005 god', *Informatsionno-pravovoi portal Garant*. Retrieved 21 September 2015 from http://base.garant.ru/12138196.

'Vedomstvennaya struktura raskhodov federal'nogo byudzheta na 2014 god', *Informatsionno-pravovoi portal Garant*. Retrieved 21 September 2015 from http://base.garant.ru/70525334/7/#block_6000.

Zaionchkovskaya, Zh., N. Mkrtchyan and E. Tyuryukanova. 2009. 'Rossiya pered vyzovami immigratsii'. In Zh. Zaionchkovskaya and G. Vitkovskaya (eds), *Postsovetskie transformatsiii: otrazhenie v migratsiyakh*. Moscow: Tsentr migratsionnykh issledovanii, Institut narodokhazaistvennogo prognozirovaniya Rossiiskoi akademii nauk, pp. 9–62.

'Zakon "O bezhentsakh"', *Informatsionno-pravovoi portal Garant*. Retrieved 19 October 2015 from http://base.garant.ru/10105682.

'Zakon "O vynuzhdennykh pereselentsakh"', *Informatsionno-pravovoi portal Garant*. Retrieved 19 October 2015 from http://base.garant.ru/10105693/#block_1.

'Zakon "O gosudarstvennoi politike Rossiiskoi Federatsii v otnoshenii sootechestvennikov za rubezhom"', *Informatsionno-pravovoi portal Garant*. Retrieved 19 October 2015 from http://base.garant.ru/12115694/#block_8.

'Zakon "O gosudarstvennoi politike Rossiiskoi Federatsii v otnoshenii sootechestvennikov za rubezhom"', *Informatsionno-pravovoi portal Konsul'tantPlyus*. Retrieved 16 October 2015 from http://base.consultant.ru/cons/cgi/online.cgi?req=doc;base=LAW;n=150465;fld=134;from=89945-266;rnd=0.8757458364747098.

'Zakon "O pravovom polozhenii inostrannykh grazhdan v Rossiiskoi Federatsii"', *Informatsionno-pravovoi portal Garant*. Retrieved 19 October 2015 from http://base.garant.ru/184755.

3 Russian foreign policy and migrant workers

Markku Kangaspuro and Anna-Liisa Heusala

Introduction

Since the fall of the Soviet Union, Russian foreign policy has constantly been attempting to balance cooperation with the West, the promotion of integration in the former Soviet economic space and cooperation with China and other Asian countries. In this vein, the establishment of the Eurasian Economic Union and its enlargement, has probably been the most ambitious political initiative of President Vladimir Putin. In the Russian Foreign Policy Concept (Kontsepsija vneshei politiki Rossijskoi Federatsii 12 February 2013), the primary strategic aim is to strengthen Russia's influence over the former Soviet area and its sphere of interest, and increase Russia's globalised competitiveness through this regional integration process.

The history of the official Eurasian integration began in 1995 when the Agreement on the Creation of the Customs Union between Belarus and the Russian Federation was signed. After Kazakhstan joined, these countries established the Treaty on Enhancing Integration in Economic and Humanitarian Spheres in 1996, also signed by Kyrgyzstan. In 1999, the Agreement on the Customs Union and Common Economic Space[1] was signed, with the additional membership of Tajikistan. A series of legal changes were set in motion in the member states.[2] The Agreement stipulates that the single economic space creates an area which is formed on shared regulative economic mechanisms based on market principles and the application of harmonised legal rules, and that there is a single infrastructure and coordinated fiscal, monetary, foreign exchange, financial, trade and customs policies, which are implemented to ensure the free movement of goods, services, capital and labour force.

In 2000, a new organisation was created with the signing of the Treaty on the Creation of the Eurasian Economic Community (EurAsEC). This development was accompanied by the work of such institutions as the Interstate Council, consisting of heads of state and governments, and the Integration Committee. On 1 January 2012, the Eurasian Economic Space began functioning to promote the free movement of goods, services, labour and capital as well as the harmonisation and unification of industrial, financial, tax and

DOI: 10.4324/9781315657424-3

investment policies (Galiakberov and Abdullin 2014: 118).[3] On 29 May 2014, the heads of state of the Russian Federation, Belorussia and Kazakhstan signed the Treaty of the Eurasian Economic Union[4] (hereafter, the EEU), which forms the final end result of the multi-stage structure of agreements. The members of the EEU pursue a harmonised policy in the key areas of integration, the energy, industry, agriculture and transport sectors (Kansikas and Palonkorpi 2015: 204). The EEU has been officially functioning since 1 January 2015. The Ukrainian crisis put an end to the goal of having Ukraine as one of the key members in the EEU, which underlined the symbolical importance of including Kyrgyzstan[5] and Armenia.[6]

Our chapter focuses on the conflict between Russia's foreign policy goals in Eurasian economic integration and its labour market conditions, particularly with regard to organised interest representation and positions taken on the diminishing of the shadow economy. The political connotations of the EEU have received quite a bit of attention both as a regional and interest-based[7] counter-force to European Union enlargement and as a manifestation of Russia's Great Power identity and civilisational geopolitics.[8] In the first case, Russia's foreign policy challenges to Eurasian integration are most of all shaped by pragmatism and globalisation. They can be interpreted as an attempt to define and consolidate the contours of Russian national sovereignty in a 'borderless' world and advance its legitimate international interests. In the latter case, the Russian foreign policy is defined by a search for Russia's historical place and mission in the post-Cold War world (see Morozova 2009: 676). We present a view in which the shadow economy is one of the main practical challenges to both versions of Russia's regional geopolitical ambitions.

Since November 2014, the shadow economy in Russia is estimated to have increased by 3–4 million persons, mostly because of layoffs in small businesses. According to Rosstat, there were 5.4 million individual entrepreneurs in the Russian Federation in 2013. Between 2013 and 2015 over 600,000 individual entrepreneurs have lost work and many more are in danger of losing their official registration because of strict credit and fiscal policies. In 2015, the number of the unemployed grew by 19,000–20,000 persons each week. Altogether, the shadow economy may have reached 40 per cent of the Russian economy, because of the ongoing economic crisis.[9] Against this backdrop, there is increased official attention to the modernisation of the Russian labour market and migration policy, including work-related migration. Thus, two parallel and contradictory processes are currently taking place in Russia.

In this chapter, we will look at these processes with the aim of outlining the dynamics between the EEU, domestic discussions on migration and attempts to modernise the Russian labour market. We aim to answer the questions: what is the significance of regional integration in the formation of policy on labour market modernisation? And what perspectives do public organisations bring to the discussion on the shadow economy? The chapter is structured in the following way. First, we look at the Russian foreign policy goals in the EEU process and evaluate this against domestic sentiments about migration and the 'borderless world'. Second, we outline some of the main elements related to the shadow economy in the Concept of Migration Policy until 2025 and examine the viewpoints of two labour market organisations with regard to Russia's economic modernisation. Finally, we compare the complicated and ambitious plans to change Russian migration policy in the EEU with the policy recommendations of these organisations.

Foreign policy goals of regional integration and domestic anti-migrant sentiments

Eurasian integration has been one of the key foreign and economic policy goals of Putin's third presidential term. Just before the United Russia party meeting at which his presidential candidacy was announced, an article was published in which he outlined Russia's integration policy. It consisted of economic integration in the sphere of the former Soviet Union, a post-Cold War world Gaullist idea of Greater Europe and its multiple centres and Russia's role and identity in Eurasian as a 'European power in Asia, not a Eurasian power in Europe' (Sakwa 2015: 18–19).

The loose ideological background[10] behind the Eurasian integration process is Eurasianism, which can be interpreted as a civilisational world-view, or as a political justification of Russia's foreign policy, or as economic policy in terms of a Custom Union and wider Eurasian economic cooperation comprising Chinese economic initiatives (Silk Road) and Russia's initiatives to establish a common economic space from Lisbon to Vladivostok. The president of Kazakhstan, Nursultan Nazarbayev, is often mentioned as the founding father of the ideational justification of Eurasian integration because of his 1994 speeches referring to Lev Gumilev's (1912–92) Eurasianist ideas. The establishment of the EEU consolidated the foreign policy framework that President Putin outlined with regard to Eurasian integration during his election campaign in 2012.[11] In the EEU, answers to the questions of Russia as an imperial state versus a nation state, Russia as a Eurasian versus a European state, and Russia's response to the challenges of globalisation in the frame of post-Cold War international relations are sought at a very practical level.

The EEU's political reasoning can be found in various sources. Richard Sakwa (2015: 12–13) approaches the Eurasian Union in the framework of 'regionalism'. He sees that regions are potentially becoming the successors to traditional nation-states and a way for them to response to the pressure of globalisation. He points out that there are three 'dominant forms of regionalism in the world today – micro-regional economic integration, meso-regional political integration and macro-transcontinental security regionalism'. The EU represents micro-regional integration overlapping with both the meso-political regionalism of the Council of Europe (CoE), encompassing a number of countries stretching through Europe to Asia. In security politics, the North Atlantic Treaty Organization (NATO) embodies macro-regionalism. Sakwa claims that there is not only one normative form of regionalism, as we often see it from a Eurocentric perspective, drawing on the EU experience. He claims that 'there are diverse forms of regionalism, each with its normative logic combining political, security, economic and identity dynamics'.

The dynamics connected to Russia's regional ambitions have also received some attention at the official level from the presidents of both Kazakhstan and Belorussia, who have underlined that they favour economic integration but are hesitant to advance a political integration that would diminish the political sovereignty of their states. In his interview in *Izvestiya* (26 October 2011) President Nazarbayev emphasised his consistently repeated statement that Eurasian economic integration does not mean any restoration or reincarnation of the Soviet Union. This point of view was again restated by him and also President Lukashenko during the Ukrainian crisis. The Western reaction to President Putin's initiative has for the most part considered it not just as a form of rational regional integration, but as a hegemonic power politics on a collision course with the interests of the West.[12]

Sergey Markedonov (2012) and David Lane (2015a) take a different view and point out that this interpretation might be an oversimplification. Eurasia is crucially important for Russia's policy not due to its past but primarily because of issues of the present globalisation. Lane sees the Eurasian Union as a complementary regional capitalist economic formation in the world economic system and as an attempt to construct a new pole in the multipolar world order preferred by Russia's foreign policy. He assesses that the objective of a regional bloc is to 'reverse the effects of globalisation, particularly to ensure the sovereignty of the nation state'. The dominant feature of the post-Cold War world has been international borderless trade and the deterritorialisation of politics, and in this vein regional forms of association have become major components of international political and economic organisation (Lane 2015a: 4–6, also Cooper 2013).

Sakwa points out that the Eurasian Union is a strategy to meet global economic competition by taking advantage of Russia's historical ties with the former Soviet Union. Like Lane, he also emphasises that in economic terms, the EEU does not challenge the principles of a capitalist economy: free trade and movement of capital and workforce. As a response to hesitant current and potential member states of the Eurasian Union and to Western sceptics and critics, Putin has assured that the integration project in Eurasia relies on all-European values of freedom, democracy and market rules and has nothing to do with re-establishing the past Soviet Union (Sakwa 2015: 18).

But Russia's foreign policy choices in regional integration can also be seen in the framework of an alternative strategy of right-wing anti-globalism.[13] Mikhail Remizov holds that this alternative is not only acute in Russia but claims that it has 'particularly good chances for success'. While President

Putin defines the disintegration of the Soviet Union as the geopolitical catastrophe of the millennium, for Russian 'nationalists' it represents a chance to consolidate the Russian territory on a national foundation. Remizov claims that what Russia needs and what makes it strong is its already now prevailing high cultural and ethnic homogeneity. He ends up counting Russians, Ukrainians and Belarusians living in Russia as belonging to a single ethnic entity (Remizov 2012: 4, 6).

Yet another perspective is to see the EEU in connection to Russia's role in Asia, particularly with regard to China. Chinese migration and the role of the Chinese in Siberia have been long-lasting topics in Russian discussions on the future. China has penetrated deeply into the Russian economy and the total number of Chinese immigrants in Russia – both legal and illegal – is variously estimated to be several millions. Some analysts have therefore paid attention also the influence of the EEU on relations with China. It is suggested that the EEU is also an attempt to establish a stronger economic bloc to counter the effects of China in Central Asia. Apart from everything else, the creation of the EEU is hoped to slightly balance the asymmetric size of the Russian and Chinese economies and the Chinese influence over member states of the EEU and the Central Asian region (Krichevsky 2011).

Eurasian integration has contributed to the tensions in Russian domestic identity politics, which reflect the universal discussions about the effects of large-scale migration. For some Russians, the EEU signifies Russia's cultural and political diversion from Europe towards Asia and a weakening Russian (Russkii) ethnicity due to the influx of Muslim migrants from Central Asian states. For others, migrants represent a concrete social and political threat in their communities, and the deterioration of social and legal order.

However, the EEU has received wide acceptance across all major political parties in Russia. The dominant 'United Russia' has favoured the economic dimensions of this process, while the Communists, for instance, have welcomed attempts to draw the former Soviet republics into closer alliance with the Russian Federation (Cooper 2013: 89). Migration policies are at the heart of various questions, including technical ones, which influence public attitudes towards the EEU. As Kazantsev points out, the challenge for the Russian government lies in the attempts to simultaneously foster integration through common labour markets with the Central Asian states and to manage the consequences of work-related migration (Kazantsev 2015: 212).

According to the Levada Centre's recent surveys, there is room and support for the idea of the EEU among the Russian public. A rapidly increasing portion of respondents support the statement that Russia has its own specific way of development (55 per cent in a 2015 survey), compared to the diminishing portion of those who hold that Russia's way is European civilisation (17 per cent of respondents), even though as recently as 2013, 31 per cent still supported the 'European way' as a good choice for Russia. Moreover, in 2015, 19 per cent of respondents supported the statement that Russia should turn back to the development of the Soviet Union (Levada Centre 2015a).

Although the Ukrainian crisis and economic sanctions have certainly affected this change in opinions, the results can also be interpreted as showing public responsiveness to the idea of Russia-led regional development.[14]

The disagreement on Russia's imperial future lies on the common interpretation that in the Soviet Union (ethnic) Russianness (*Russkii*) remained unclear and only after the fall of the Soviet Union did this suppressed identity start to blossom. The Eurasian integration project has provided a major political platform for the reassessment of what 'identity' signifies in real foreign policy terms. As Marlene Laruell points out, 'a political project always mobilises some kind of identity and no political objective can be achieved without reference to specific cultural symbols' (2009: 7). According to Serguei Oushakine, in the Soviet Union, 'the Russian dominance in political, social, and cultural areas was widely practiced but rarely acknowledged in any explicit way'. The Soviet model of nation-building allowed Russian ethnicity to persist as an indeterminate source of power (Oushakine 2009: 10).

The fall of the Soviet Union gave birth to a demand for a new definition of a Russian ethnically defined state identity, clearly separate from the former Soviet imperial identity (Oushakine 2009: 89). This ongoing discourse on ethnicity and Russia's identity is intertwined with the discussion of Russia's future and role in the former Soviet space. Essentially, Russian discussions on migration and the Eurasian integration process have used similar arguments to those found in other industrialised societies faced with globalisation and rapid societal transformation. In the Russian case, the culture threat hypothesis, the core (national) values hypothesis, the cultural affinity and race hypothesis (Buckler 2008) seem to have captured the imagination of the political elite as well.

Ethnic nationalism (support for the statement 'Russia for Russians') and xenophobic or reluctant attitudes towards immigrants from southern republics and Central Asia has been a widely accepted position in Russia. In a 2012 Levada Centre survey, the majority of Russians (56 per cent) agreed with the statement 'Russia for ethnic Russians' and no less than 70 per cent of respondents answered that government should restrict the influx of migrants. In a similar vein, a clear majority of respondents supported the statement that illegal migrants from CIS countries should be expelled from Russia (Levada Centre 2013: 157–9).

From September 2012 to June 2013, popular opinion turned against even internal migration. The proportion of respondents in favour of limiting migration for permanent work or residence from other parts of Russia to their home regions or cities increased from 57 per cent to 65 per cent. A devastating majority, 71 per cent of respondents, agree with the statement that immigrants increase the crime rate, and 67 per cent think that immigrants take jobs from Russians. Only 24 per cent see migration in an economically positive light when answering the statement 'immigrants generally facilitate Russian economic growth' (Levada Centre 2013: 158–9).

With regard to the dispute of Russia's favourable development as a multicultural state versus a culturally and ethnically homogeneous state, popular support for the official definition of Russia as a poly-cultural state is rather low. As many as 46 per cent respondents agree with the statement that 'immigrants destroy the Russian culture', and only 23 per cent clearly oppose this idea. The slogan 'Stop feeding the Caucasus' increased in popularity from 55 per cent to 62 per cent of respondents between 2011 and 2013 (Levada Centre 2013: 155–7).

These sentiments have caused a political response at the highest level. In Putin's article, 'The national question', written for the presidential election campaign in 2012, he underlined the role of the EEU in controlling migration policy. Putin saw the role of the EEU as 'curbing chaotic migration from post-Soviet states by means of regional integration'. Following an international trend, he furthermore connected migration and the integration of migrants to national security, the rule of law, corruption and criminality. In this manner, Russia's institutional problems and various aspects of migration were 'securitised' as a problem demanding a law-and-order response.

The article was also a response to the Russian nationalistic opposition, as Putin emphasised the dangers of nationalism, which threaten the stability and peaceful relations between different ethnicities and religions. Nonetheless, as a concession to critics of migration, much attention was also given to improving the work of law enforcement agencies. In particular, Putin underlined the fight against corruption and demanded better control of the implementation of laws and regulations, such as registration rules and penalties for their violation (Putin 2012). Within the framework of domestic politics, his article is interpreted as a response to the liberal–nationalistic opposition (see Chapter 4 on Alexey Navalnyi's role) and its critics of corruption, the wrongdoings of the current regime and social problems, which the opposition has connected to the 'Asian influence' and migration in general.

'Decent work' and EEU integration

In 2012, a new Concept for State Migration Policy until 2025 was enacted in Russia. The concept is based on an emphasis on integrative policy measures, the differentiation of various groups of immigrants and modified rules for each group, the increased effectiveness of the implementation of regulations and the curbing of the shadow economy. According to the Concept, the legislation of the Russian Federation does not meet the demands of economic growth and industrial development, nor does it sufficiently support the demographic and social requirements of Russian society. Migration legislation is evaluated as attracting temporary workers and not facilitating their transition towards permanent stay, adaptation and integration into their surrounding communities. As an addition to the challenges of integration, the Concept mentions that the new – post-Soviet – generation of migrants from Russia's southern neighbours have a lower level of education and professional qualifications and less knowledge of the Russian language.

The Concept brings out the large number of illegal migrants, from 3 to 5 million each year, who work in the shadow economy, which mainly contributes to the negative sentiments among Russian citizens. This document states that difficulties in obtaining permits to stay and housing slow down the process towards citizenship among law-abiding immigrants. The lack of programmes for integrating migrants into Russian society has led to their isolation and increased negative attitudes towards them. To change the situation, Russian policymaking should be inclusive and also use the resources of the mass media.

Migrant workers have already been necessary for Russia's economy for a long time, with an estimated 10–11 million foreigners working in the Russian Federation. Of these, around 75 per cent have stayed in Russia for longer than three months (Virkkunen and Fryer 2015: 56). Immigration has played a major role in preventing Russia falling into an even deeper demographic disaster than the one it experienced in the 1990s. The flow of Russian immigrants returning from the former Soviet republics has compensated for the population losses caused by the drastically increased mortality rate after the fall of the Soviet Union. During the 21 years between 1992 and 2013, the natural death rate of Russia gave a loss of 13,200,000 people, which the immigration of 8,400,000 people compensated by 63 per cent. A larger majority of immigrants were returnees (1997: 70 per cent) and ethnic Russians (62 per cent) from the former Soviet republics. Ten years later, the turnover was respectively 35 per cent and 30 per cent (Mezhevovo 2015: 25–6). In 2010, the population of Russia was 142,800,000. Without migration, the figure would have been 130,000,000 (MPC 2013: 3).

In spite of the improvements, the future of Russia's demographic development in a ten-year perspective presents a challenge for the government. The mortality rate is high by world standards, the 22nd highest in the world, despite the decrease in mortality in 2005–12. On one hand, Russia cannot solve its demographic crisis with migration alone, but on the other, it cannot meet the demands of its labour market with the insufficient birth rate in coming years (Critical 10 Years: 7). The labour market conditions are intertwined with the modernisation and diversification of the Russian economy. Before the current crisis, the economic structures and management models did not encourage companies to modernise their production processes (Remizov 2012: 29) and thus improve their world market competitiveness.[15]

To guarantee employment opportunities to Russian citizens, the government has limited the number of foreign workers employed in Russia using quotas, which in recent years have not exceeded 3 per cent of the entire labour force. Additional medical examination requirements and a ban on participation in certain types of activities have been introduced with regard to foreign workers. A mandatory Russian language examination and a test in Russian history and the principles of Russian legislation is required, although this is not applicable to that section of the workforce labelled highly qualified specialists. In the Eurasian integration, Russia will not only lose the possibility of imposing any institutional restrictions on immigration within the common free market zone, but it will also have to take the obligation to ensure equal rights with regard to employment, wages and other social and legal guarantees to the citizens of the member states (Troitskaya 2012).

Drawing from the research undertaken by the Eurasian Development Bank (EDB), a picture emerges where migrant communities are in practice living completely outside the official society, as is also pointed out in the Concept of Migration Policy. When migrants were interviewed for the research and asked about their channels for assistance and support in social and legal rights and finding work and accommodation, none of the respondents mentioned state structures, while 81 per cent answered that they get help from their expatriate community and 9 per cent from the local population (Vinokurov and Pereboyev 2015: 73).

The Concept of Migration Policy until 2025 lays out the key areas of comprehensive modernisation of Russia's immigration policy, based on thinking on national security. Among these are the protection of the national labour market; the differentiation of the control of migration flows according to length of stay, social demographics and professional qualifications; the facilitation of the adaptation and integration of migrants into the surrounding Russian society; and the development of reliable statistical information on developments in the market and the flows of migrants (*Konseptsija gosudarstvennoi migratisionnoi politiki Rossijskoi Federatsii na period do 2025 goda*).

As these lists of policy goals demonstrate, the development of the Russian migration administration, as well as thinking on the relevance of coherent migration policy in the Russian Federation, have increased in significance over the years. The Concept consolidates the official learning process of 20 years of developments in the Russian labour market. The national security framework in particular underlines the significance of the stated goals, as national security is currently the dominant mode of reasoning in the Russian government's decision-making. The Concept lays out a breath-taking number of questions which need to be resolved in the next ten years, paving the way towards regional integration and Russia's competitiveness in the global market.

A significant question regarding harmonisation in Eurasian economic integration is labour law and particularly regulations concerning labour organisation and protection, which have a direct impact on attempts to curb the shadow economy. The Russian Labour Law of 2006 stipulates that labour protection services should be set up in all organisations of over 50 persons, by either the employer or the employees. In smaller organisations, a labour protection expert should be established at the discretion of the employer regarding the forms of labour protection services. The goal of these measures is to observe labour protection requirements and prevent industrial accidents and occupational diseases. The cooperation of employees and employers can be carried out through collective bargaining, mutual consultations, the participation of employees or their representatives in the running of the enterprise and the participation of employees in solving labour disputes (Gorbacheva 2011: 160).

In anticipation of the Eurasian integration processes, both the employer organisations and the largest trade unions in Russia have been active in offering policy recommendations and participating in legislative development. Here, we wish to briefly look at two examples of interest representation in the Russian Federation: the National Association of Builders[16] (Natsionalnoye obyedenenii stroitelee, NOSTROI) and the Federation of Independent Trade Unions in the Russian Federation (Federatsiya Nezavisimykh Profso-juzov Rossii, FNPR). Both organisations have a well-established position and some considerable political clout as participants in legislative processes and direct lobbyists with the Russian government.

The concept of 'decent work', introduced in the ILO Decent Work Agenda of 1999 forms the core of the programme of the Federation of Independent Trade Unions in Russia (FNPR). The programme, which presents the political and societal aims of the Federation, starts with an analysis of globalised economic conditions and their impact on national sovereignty and social stability. The critique is directed at the neo-liberal economic policies also supported by the Russian business sector. This policy is described as resulting in growing numbers of unemployed, unofficial employment and the overall degradation of the quality of life and social guarantees for workers (Programma FNPR 'Dostoinii trud- osnova blagosostayanii tseloveka i razvitiya strani).

The most important hindrances to Russian economic modernisation, however, are found in the old-fashioned management style and economic model, as well as the dependence on imports. According to the FNPR, attempts to modernise Russian production have been overrun by new methods to take advantage of workers and diminish their earnings. The tax system (based on the 13 per cent flat tax) is seen as a major obstacle to strengthening social equality and increasing state funds. In addition to these structural problems, the Trade Union movement is under pressure, as activists are laid off and labour and other laws are broken (*Programma FNPR 'Dostoinii trud- osnova blagosostayanii tseloveka i razvitiya strani*).

In this situation, the FNPR's list of recommendation includes the overall modernisation of employment positions, emphasis on creating high productivity work, as well as paying attention to workplace safety and effective state control of the implementation of legal rules and regulations. In addition, the Federation advocates raising the medium income level and guaranteeing the timely payment of salaries. It wishes to bring attention to the qualification of workers, the professionalism of management, and the ageing equipment in Russian industry. The Federation promises to take a more active role in fighting the shadow economy, and urges the state control agencies to pay more rigorous attention to curbing the shadow economy in the future. In more concrete terms, the Federation advocates a viewpoint according to which the flow of foreign migrants to Russian should be regulated on the basis of regional economic needs and that social benefits should be provided to those migrants working in the Russian labour market legally (*Programma FNPR 'Dostoinii trud- osnova blagosostayanii tseloveka i razvitiya strani*, 9 February 2015).

At the beginning of 2016, NOSTROI held a round-table meeting entitled 'The formation of a common market for services in the construction sector in the EEU'. The aim was to discuss the implementation of decisions made by the Economic Council of the EEU in the sphere of construction through the integration of this specific market and harmonisation of relevant legislation. Criticism was directed towards the passiveness of the authorities in all member states in providing a normative–technical basis for the operation of services in the construction sector in the common market. In addition, the point was made that the Russian position with regard to the safety of buildings and materials in the EEU was put together without consulting the expertise of construction sector professionals (Natsionalnoye obyedenenii stroitelee, NOSTROI).[17]

NOSTROI strongly underlines the significance of standardisation in the EEU. Standardisation concerns technical requirements for the rules and standards of building materials, constructions and parts, and for the use of these objects. Included in the standardisation is also the organisation of the construction work, which should lead to the evaluation of the qualification of actors in the construction sector. The goal is to establish a register of reliable providers of building services (Natsionalnoye obyedenenii stroitelee, NOSTROI).[18]

The two approaches with regard to the challenges of the labour market and Russian industry are different, but have some important points of common interest. The trade union perspective bases its recommendations on an assessment of the negative influences of neo-liberal globalisation, which an open-border policy will most likely increase. Considerable modernisation of Russian workplace culture and management is underlined as the key to industrial modernisation and curbing of the shadow economy. The essential question in this regard is investment on human capital, also redefinitions of qualifications and adequate wage levels. The builders' point of view emphasises technical standardisation. However, the goals of the standardisation process include regard for the integrity of business owners, the control of work processes and increasing the qualification of actors in the construction market. Together with the Concept of Migration until 2025, these examples demonstrate the considerable official attention paid to the challenges in the Russian labour market. In this regard, the Eurasian Commission's new Programme for the Development of Integration in the Sphere of Statistical Information for 2016–20[19] can also be seen as one more step towards developing structures which could potentially have a positive effect on regional societal transformation.

The overall picture, which emerges from our outline points to a possible consolidation of a political agenda for and incremental labour market transformation in Russia. Its driving force is a functionalist view on post-Soviet integration and ambitious goals for legal and institutional development. The implications for Russia's welfare and educational policies are considerable. However, it is possible that the geopolitical goals of the EEU integration are overshadowed by implementation of changes in Russian institutions. At the same time, the welcomed consequences of labour market transformation should also reinforce the interest-based thinking in Russia's foreign policy.

Conclusions

The ethnic groups from the areas and cultures of the EEU have been and will again be pivotal for the future of Russian regional integration policies. Free movement of labour, which means a continuous influx of migrants to Russia, and enlargement of the member and associate states are currently met with mixed sentiments in the Russian domestic policy arena. Key political parties have promoted the integration process, which is viewed more critically by interest representatives in Russian labour market. We can conclude that Russia's foreign policy goals with regard to the member states in Central Asia, are challenged by a deeply embedded nationalistic and anti-migration popular opinion inside Russia. The anti-Islamist mood, the rejection of Central Asian migrants on the basis of threat to Russian culture and society, and its core (national) values (Buckler 2008) raise potential difficulties for the whole idea of the EEU and in particular the process of deeper integration.

All in all, the Russian labour market actors, the state included, seem to have been activated by the ongoing parallel developments of the economic crises and the integration attempts in the EEU. The modernisation and diversification of the Russian economy certainly depends on the changes advocated by employees and employers alike. The economic crisis has temporarily slowed down massive work-related migration to Russia, thus giving an opportunity to assess the conditions of the Russian labour market. The anti-migration mood among the Russian citizenry may – paradoxically – increase the popularity of policy shifts. The goals of the EEU push forward questions of harmonisation and standardisation, which reveal the loopholes and old-fashioned structural mechanisms upheld by national legislation and administrative rules. Viewed in this way, the current parallel processes may – in the best of cases – provide the necessary motivation for the long-overdue changes in the shadows of the Russian labour market.

It is our conclusion, that the current labour market conditions and the shadow economy pose a serious challenge to Russia's regional ambitions in the EEU process. The achievement of Russian geopolitical goals in the EEU is affected by practical challenges to Russian institutions. Considerable investment on human capital is required to implement real change in practices and ways of thinking. Russian foreign policy goals are thus linked with the overall development of welfare and educational opportunities in the society. The shadow economy reproduces structural corruption, from street level to corporate decisions and public procurement procedures. In this vein, the shadow economy remains a major stumbling block in the path of Eurasian integration. Finally, the prospect for further political integration is under question, given the negative consequences of the Ukrainian crisis among the member states. Taking into account these factors, the pragmatist, interest-driven thinking should remain a necessary component of Russia's foreign policy.

Notes

1 Dogovor o Tamozhennom soyuze i Edinom ekonomicheskom prostranstve 26 fevralya 1999, Sobranie Zakonodatel'stva RF. 2001. No. 42 Art. 3983.
2 For instance Ruget and Usmanilieva's (2010) study shows that the Kyrgyz government has passed several important policy initiatives to assist Kyrgyz migrants working in the Russian Federation. Among these are the creation of the State Committee for Migration and Employment in 2005 and a website for Kyrgyzstanis living in Russia; the adoption of a Law on External Labour Migration and in 2006 the principle of dual nationality.
3 The Agreement on the prevention of illegal migration from third countries was signed between Russia, Kazakhstan and Belorussia in 2010 (Soglashenie o sotrudnichestve po protivodeistviyu o nelegal'ney trudovey migratsii iz tretikh gosudarsv, Sankt-Peterburg, 19 nojabrja, 2010 goda).
4 Dogovor o Evraziiskom ekonomicheskom soyuze (Podpisan v. g. Astane 29/05/2014, red. ot 08/05/2015).
5 Dogovor o prisoyedinenii Kyrkyzkey Respubliki k dogovory o Evraziiskom ekonomicheskom Soyuze ot 29 maya 2014 goda, (Moskva, 23 dekabrja 2014 goda).
6 Dogovor o prisoyedinenii Respubliki Armeniya k dogovory o Evraziiskom ekonomicheskom Soyuze ot 29 maya 2014 goda, (Minsk, 10 oktjabrja 2014 goda).
7 Erik Shiraev (2013: 263) points out the shift in Russia's foreign policy thinking in 2000, when a new concept based on three words – predictability, consistency and pragmatism – appeared.
8 Natalia Morozova (2009) has analysed the evolution of geopolitical thinking in Russia's foreign policy and the definitions of Eurasianism in traditionalist, modernist and civilisational Russian geopolitical approaches.
9 www.rbc.ru/economics/26/02/2015/54ef19049a7947453eeb6428, the numbers are from experts at the Higher School of Economics and the organisation of the business ombudsman, Boris Titov.
10 Marc Bassin (2008) describes Eurasianism in the following manner: 'There remains the rich legacy of Eurasianism across the twentieth century: the "classical" period of the interwar years (itself a profoundly heterogeneous and ideologically fragmented movement) and the attempts to sustain Eurasianist perspectives in the Soviet Union itself, most importantly those of L. N. Gumilev. All of these various incarnations were and are crafted to fit highly differing political contexts and advance fundamentally different political and ideological agendas, for which reason it is simply impossible to reduce Eurasianism in any meaningful way to a common set of doctrinal denominators, however limited and rudimentary. At the very most, only two elements may be said to be common to all these versions: Eurasianism everywhere claims to represent some unique synthesis of European and Asian principles, and in the present day, it claims everywhere to be the legitimate heir of the "classical legacy". Natalia Morozova (2009: 676) writes that in

Russia post-Soviet era foreign policy 'the adherents of "traditionalist" and "modernist" geopolitical camps are mainly preoccupied with the question "how?" – how Russia should act in order to preserve territorial integrity and enhance its international standing. The exponents of "civilisational" geopolitics invoke the intellectual resources of classical post-revolutionary Eurasianism in order to answer the question "what?" – what is Russia in the post-Cold War world order and what its post-Soviet identity can be grounded in'. Marlene Laruell (2015: xii, 21–2) points out that today neo-Eurasianism is not as such anti-European, but anti-American, anti-western and anti-liberal. For those supporting the political connotations of Eurasianism, Russia represents the third, conservative way to unite the European and Asian heartlands to resist maritime powers such as the United States.

11 Putin published several articles; the second, on Russia's national question (*Rossia: natsional'nyi vopros*), which is discussed in this chapter, was published in *Nezavizimaya Gazeta* on 23 January 2012.

12 This view has been pronounced clearly by US Secretary of State, Hillary Clinton. She declared that the intention of the US is to slow down or prevent the birth of the Eurasian Union, which the West holds to be a tool of the great power politics of Putin's Russia (Lane 2015b: 2). Sakwa attaches the competitive and antagonist features of the rapidly advanced Eurasian Union to his claim that the current stage of the situation comes as a result of the 'failure of Western leaders in the first two post-communist decades' to respond positively to the dreams and initiatives of Greater European integration. There has not been a proper answer to Mikhail Gorbachev's vision "Europe our Common Home", Nikolai Sarkozy's return to the idea of pan-Europa, and different versions of initiatives of common Europe from Lisbon to Vladivostok and free trade zone from the Atlantic to the Pacific suggested by Vladimir Putin in the EU–Russia summit in Brussels on 28 January 2014. The result has been that we are facing the development in which there emerges geopolitical contestation to the heart of Europe' (2015: 22).

13 The Russian political spectrum quite often overlaps with the agenda of European-minded 'liberal' forces, although we do not perceive the political programmes of both of these groups as identical. Their variation is quite broad.

14 In 2015, 59 per cent of respondents did not agree with the statement that Ukraine is a foreign country, and disagreement concerning Belorussia as a foreign country was even higher, at 67 per cent. The fact that even 50 per cent did not hold even Georgia as a foreign country says something about the deeply rooted feelings of common regional history and cultural bonds among Russians (Levada Centre 2015b). At the same time, the importance of economic integration with the West was still supported by 64 per cent of respondents in March 2015 (Levada Centre 2015c).

15 One explanatory fact for migrants' unwillingness to move back to their home countries is that the economic slump has been steeper in Central Asia than in Russia. Vinokurov and Pereboyev (2015: 71) have calculated that a 1 per cent loss of GNP in the originating country increases emigration by around 0.65 to 0.77 per cent.

16 Of the membership, 7 per cent are large businesses, 23 per cent middle-sized businesses, 70 per cent small businesses.

17 http://nostroy.ru/articles/detail.php?ELEMENT_ID=4173

18 http://nostroy.ru/department/folder_obrazovanie/professional_standarty/sovet-po-p rofessionalnym-kvalifikatsiyam/

19 www.eurasiancommission.org/ru/nae/news/Pages/29-12-2015-1.aspx

References

Bassin, Mark. 2008. 'Eurasianism "classical" and "neo": The lines of continuity', in T. Mochizuki (ed.), *Beyond the Empire: Images of Russia in the Eurasian Cultural Context*. Moscow: Slavic Research Center, pp. 279–294.

Buckler, K. 2008. 'Public opinion on illegal immigration: A test of seven core hypotheses', *Journal of Crime and Justice* 31(1): 113–147.

Clinton, H. 2012. 'Clinton calls for Eurasian integration an effort to re-Sovietise', RFE/RL. Russia Report 9 December. Retrieved 9 December 2015 from www.rferl. org/content/clinton-calls-eurasian-integration-effort-to-resovietize/24791921.html.

Cooper, J. 2013. 'Russia and the Eurasian Customs Union', in R. Dragneva and K. Wolczuk (eds), *Eurasian Economic Integration: Law, Policy and Politics*. Cheltenham: Edward Elgar, pp. 81–99.

Critical 10 Years. 2015. *Critical 10 Years: Demographic Policies of the Russian Federation: Successes and Challenges*. Moscow: 'Delo' Publishing House (RANEPA).

Galiakberov, A. and A. Abdullin. 2014. 'Theory and practice of regional integration based on the EurAsEC model (Russian point of view)', *Journal of Eurasian Studies* 5: 116–121.

Gorbacheva, Z.A. 2011. *Labor Law in Russia*. Alphen aan den Rijn: Kluwer Law International.

Kansikas, S. and M. Palonkorpi. 2015. 'The EEU, the EU and the new Spheres of Influence game in the South Caucasus', in M. Palonkorpi, (ed.), *The South Caucasus Beyond Borders, Boundaries and Division Lines*. Turku: Juvenes, pp. 197–229.

Kazantsev, A. A. 2015. 'Eurasian perspectives on regionalism: Central Asia and beyond', in P. Dutkiewicz and R. Sakwa (eds), *Eurasian Integration – The View from within*. London and New York: Routledge, pp. 207–25.

Krichevsky, N. 2011. 'Eurasian economic union is a barrier against China', *Russia Beyond the Headlines*. December 5, ITOGI MAGAZINE. Retrieved 9 December 2015 from http://rbth.com/articles/2011/12/05/eurasian_economic_union_is_a_ba rrier_against_china_13903.html.

Lane, D. 2015a. 'Eurasian integration as a response to neoliberal globalization', in D. Lane and V. Samokhvalov (eds), *The Eurasian Project and Europe. Regional Discontinuities and Geopolitics*. Basingstoke: Palgrave Macmillan, pp. 3–20.

Lane, D. 2015b. 'Is the Russian Federation a threat to the international order?' *Valdai Discussion Club* 9(6). Retrieved 16 December 2015 from http://valdaiclub.com/op inion/highlights/is_the_russian_federation_a_threat_to_the_international_order.

Laruell, M. 2009. *In the Name of the Nation: Nationalism and Politics in Contemporary Russia*. New York: Palgrave Macmillan.

Laruell, M. 2015. 'Foreword', in M. Laruelle (ed.), *Eurasianism and the European Far Right: Reshaping the Europe–Russia Relationship*. Lanham, MD: Lexington Books, pp. xi–xv.

Laruell, M. 2015. 'Dangerous liaisons: Eurasianism, the European far right, and Putin's Russia', in M. Laruell (ed.), *Eurasianism and the European Far Right: Reshaping the Europe–Russia Relationship*. Lanham, MD: Lexington Books, pp. 1–31.

Levada Centre. 2013. 'Russian public opinion 2012–2013'. Retrieved 9 December 2015 from www.levada.ru/sites/default/files/2012_eng.pdf.

Levada Centre. 2015a. 'Rossiyanie smutnoe predstavlyayut budushchee strany'. Retrieved 8 December 2015 from www.levada.ru/23-04-2015/rossiyane-smutno-p redstavlyayut-budushchee-strany.

Levada Centre. 2015b. 'Vneshnepoliticheskie orientatsii'. Retrieved 8 December 2015 from www.levada.ru/2015/10/13/vneshnepoliticheskie-orientatsii.

Levada Centre. 2015c. 'Economy and defense'. Retrieved on 9 December 2015 from www.levada.ru/eng/economy-and-defense.

Markedonov, S. 2012. 'Putin's Eurasian aspirations'. *National Interest*, 29 May. Retrieved 7 December 2015 from http://nationalinterest.org/commentary/putin s-eurasian-aspirations-6973?page=show.

Mezhevovo, M. 2015. *Naselenie Rossii. Demograficheskie itogi 2013 goda. Kratkii doklad.* Institut Demografii NIU VShE. Retrieved 7 December 2015 from http://demreview.hse.ru/data/2015/03/02/1091038910/DemRev_1_3_2014_5-32%20.pdf.

Morozova, N. 2009. 'Geopolitics, Eurasianism and Russian foreign policy under Putin', *Geopolitics* 14(4): 667–686.

MPC. 2013. *MPC – migration profile: Russia*. June. Retrieved 8 December 2015 from www.migrationpolicycentre.eu/docs/migration_profiles/Russia.pdf.

Oushakine, S. A. 2009. *The Patriotism of Despair. Nation, War and Loss in Russia.* Ithaca, NY and London: Cornell University Press.

Putin, V. 2012. 'Rossiya: natsional'nyi vopros', *Nezavizimaya Gazeta, politika.* 23 January. Retrieved 8 December 2015 from www.ng.ru/politics/2012-01-23/1_nationa l.html?print=Y.

Remizov, M. 2012. 'Nationalism and geopolitics: A case for Russia', *Global Affairs*, 7 October. Retrieved 5 January 2016 from http://eng.globalaffairs.ru/number/Nationa lism-and-Geopolitics-A-Case-for-Russia-15686.

Ruget, V. and B. Usmanalieva. 2010. 'How much is citizenship worth? The case of Kyrgyzstani migrants in Kazakhstan and Russia'. *Citizenship Studies*, 14(4): 445–459.

Sakwa, R. 2015. 'Challenges for Eurasian integration', in P. Dutkiewicz and R. Sakwa (eds), *Eurasian Integration – The View from within.* London and New York: Routledge, pp. 12–30.

Shiraev, E. 2013. *Russian government and politics.* Basingstoke: Palgrave Macmillan.

Troitskaya, O. 2012. 'Eurasian Union and migration', Russian International Affairs Council, 28 June. Retrieved 8 December 2015 from http://russiancouncil.ru/en/inner/?id_4=554#top-content.

Vinokurov, E. and V. Pereboyev. 2015. 'Labour migration and human capital in Kyrgyzstan and Tajikistan: Impact of accession to the SES', *Eurasian Integration Yearbook 2013*. Eurasian Development Bank. Retrieved 20 December 2015 from www.eabr.org/general//upload/CII%20-%20izdania/YearBook-2013/a_n6_2013_07.pdf.

Virkkunen, J. and P. Fryer. 2015. 'Keskiaasialaiset ja Venäjän työmarkkinoiden muutos', *Idäntutkimus* 2: 49–65.

4 Beyond conjunctures of Russia's national future

Migrants and refugees in Russia's political discourse in 2013 and 2014

Jussi Lassila

Within the framework of Russia's national identity politics, this chapter examines the political usage and public discussion of migration with regard to two cases situated on the opposite sides of the change that occurred in Russia between 2013 and 2014. First we examine how the opposition's new front-man, Alexei Navalny, used the Muscovites' emphasised anti-immigration moods in his campaign during the Moscow mayoral election in 2013. Navalny's campaign resulted in an extraordinary success when against all expectations he came second in the race and nearly took the election into the second round. Navalny's ultimate breakthrough into federal-level politics coincided with the year in which Russia's anti-immigration mood reached a hitherto unseen peak. Moreover, Navalny's success was accompanied by an even more worrisome trend from the Kremlin's viewpoint: a consistent decrease in President Putin's public support. However, by March 2014, Putin's ratings had dramatically recovered and avenues for oppositional politics had been radically curtailed. The second case of the chapter focuses on this side of the change, by examining prevailing media representations of Ukrainian refugees, who superseded the role of migrants in the summer 2014 in Russia's public discussion. The chapter shows that dominant discourses of migration create a sort of continuum regardless of these dramatically changed political conjunctures. They evoke similar visions of Russia's ideal state of affairs in which an ethnicised hierarchy of labour linked to politically contextualised flows of foreigners plays the major role.

Introduction

In November 2013, the clear majority of Russians agreed with the statement, 'Russia for ethnic Russians' (*Rossiya dlya russkikh*). This statement has become one of the major indicators in monitoring ethnic relations in Russia. According to the Levada Centre – the main body measuring perceptions of this statement – the overall proportion of its sympathisers in 1998 was 43 per cent, while in late 2013 the proportion was 66 per cent ('Kak Vy ...' 2011; 'Rossiyane o ...' 2013). In light of these results, the director of the Levada Centre, Lev Gudkov (2013), pointed out that Russians are no longer ashamed

DOI: 10.4324/9781315657424-4

of supporting a statement which has been seen as the central signifier of ethnic nationalism in the multi-ethnic state. In today's Russia, following the collapse of the Soviet ideological tenet of nationless communism and holding second place in the number of immigrants in the world (United Nations 2013), the growing importance and public support of ethnic nationalism can be seen as an intersection of ideational compensation for the lack of fixed national and state identity. Similarly, ethnic nationalism points at an overall dissatisfaction with the state's policies regarding the role of ethnically non-Russians (*ne russkie*). Hence, in late 2013, that overall support for a Russia made up of ethnic Russians (66 per cent) was accompanied by a clear reluctance to support immigrants from southern republics (61 per cent; only 6 per cent sympathised with or respected them) and 71 per cent supported the slogan 'stop feeding the Caucasus' (*Khvatit kormit' Kavkaz*) ('Rossiyane o ...' 2013). What is more, in November 2013, public support for President Putin reached the lowest point so far; 'only' 61 per cent of Russians claimed to trust him (which is alarming in an authoritarian presidential system), while, for instance in September 2009, when he was prime minister, 88 per cent of Russians trusted him ('Odobrenie deyatel'nosti...' 2015).

It has been commonly confirmed since March 2014, after the annexation of the Crimea, that Putin's public support has recovered back to the 2009 level; for instance, 88 per cent of Russians trusted Putin in October 2015 ('Odobrenie deiatel'nosti...' 2015). This sudden recovery prompts the question of how the growing importance of migration in Russia's public life over the last 15 years is intertwined with the two sides of Russia's major political backbone: Putin's political legitimacy before and after the revolution in Ukraine. This revolution in early 2014 – followed by Russia's dramatic political and military interventions in Ukraine – has been the hitherto most serious political conflict in the territory of the former Soviet Union since its collapse. Besides the conflict's serious international repercussions, the revolution marked a notable change in Russia's domestic politics, in the Kremlin's political performance in particular. The intensified usage of ethnic identifications, alongside the Kremlin's venture in Ukraine, demonstrates that the realm of ethnic others and 'us' has remained an elementary part of the regime's domestic legitimation, regardless of the significant political changes that the year 2014 made apparent in comparison to 2013 (Goode and Laruelle 2014). Although it would be an overstatement to argue that migration – as a central realisation of ethnic, cultural and linguistic differences between people – could create a clear-cut variable for the Kremlin's political legitimacy, it plays a vital role in it. In this vein, my aim is to examine how the issue of 'incomers' (consciously avoiding here the loaded term 'migration' in Russia) is represented with regard to two political conjunctures, one in the latter half of 2013, and another in the summer of 2014.

For the year 2013, I chose a sample of Alexei Navalny's views concerning migration expressed during his campaign in the Moscow mayoral election, and for the year 2014, I chose a sample of articles published in the Russian mainstream media in the summer concerning Ukrainian refugees. I used the Integrum databases to select this data.[1] My standpoint is that Navalny as a major oppositional challenger of the Kremlin in 2013 represents a key facet of the political usage of migration, while the issue of Ukrainian refugees provides an important baseline for Russia's migration discourse in the domestically and internationally changed political circumstances. By comparing these two themes, my goal is to clarify linkages and associations that migration and refugees as part of Russia's transnational reality generate in Russian public understanding. Before moving to the closer examination of the selected samples, I provide an excursion into the issue of migration and its identity politics ramifications in post-Soviet Russia.

Migration and nationalisms in Putin's Russia

The major event in the gradual breakthrough of nationalist thoughts into Russia's post-Soviet politics was the formation of nationalist opposition against Yeltsin's western-oriented reformist policies followed by the Kremlin's response to this opposition over the course of the Yeltsin and Putin eras. The constitutional crisis and bloody conflict in October 1993 provided the momentum for diverse pro-Soviet and nationalist forces which allied against Yeltsin, and since the mid 1990s the cornerstone of the Kremlin's identity policies has been the so-called patriotic centrism (Laruelle 2009: 23). While this was initiated by Yeltsin, it is Putin who has greatly benefited from this idea, manipulating it to his advantage in eliminating ideological oppositions and encouraging the political reconciliation of different factions through patriotic rhetoric (ibid.). In terms of nationalism, patriotic centrism represents Russia's (and the Soviet Union's) imperial continuum of state nationalism, or politically correct imperial nationalism. The central function of this tenet aims to guarantee the people's unity in the multinational state. As such, reflected for instance in Putin's presidential campaign writing on Russia's nationalities issues in January 2012, under the pressure of the large-scale protests of that time – and in particular, with regard to the nationalist segment of the protests – Putin emphasised the importance of ethnic minorities adhering to Russian cultural norms (Putin 2012). However, by the same token, for Putin the official nationalities policy must follow the Soviet-era vision of non-ethnic citizenship, which similarly acknowledges the state's multi-ethnic composition (ibid.). Following this tenet, the citizenship of *sovetskii* ('Soviet') has been replaced by *rossiiskii* ('citizens of the Russian Federation') in defining 'the banal nationalism' of the official state.[2] In this regard, the term *russkii* as an ethnic category has remained pejorative and nationalistic. At the same time, the Soviet legacy of imperial non-ethnicity in Russia's nationalities policies has become the major source of dissatisfaction among Russian ethno-nationalists (Pain 2014). According to them, today's Russia follows the Soviet Union, where non-Russian republics and autonomies were institutionalised in line with their ethnic stereotypes (for more on this, see Hirsch 2005). By contrast, identification on the basis of ethnicity is not allowed to Russians who live in Russia (Pain 2014).

It is obviously true that the majority of Russians hardly align with this kind of nationalist interpretation in explaining the rapid growth of ethno-nationalist sentiments among Russians during the last ten years. Indeed, the connotation of the word *natsionalizm* has generally remained negative among the Russians (Dubin 2014), in addition to the ethno-nationalists' relatively marginal role as a political movement. However, when nationalism is left aside and shifted from its ideological and political realm to the framework of xenophobia, that is, of ethnic and cultural 'others', the picture changes. While in 2005 the overall proportion of those Russians who sensed ethnic tensions in the region they live was 27 per cent, in 2013 the level was 43 per cent (Dubin 2014: 8). In a similar vein, the proportion of those who felt negative emotions with regard to people coming from Caucasus, Central Asia and southern countries had grown to 61 per cent (2013) from 43 per cent (2005) (ibid.: 9). Anti-immigrant sentiments have become particularly strong in the big cities, and in 2013 migration had become the most acute problem among the Muscovites (55 per cent shared this view in comparison with 30 per cent in 2010) (ibid.: 10–11).

Antipathy towards migrants – almost exclusively perceived as people from Caucasus and Central Asia – has become the clearest indicator of ethnic nationalism, and even more importantly, an indicator of the change in the Soviet legacy of the overly pejorative associations of nationalism. Russians are increasingly reluctant to share the view of the importance of the Soviet type of multinational brotherhood or judging nationalism as a preliminary stage of fascism ('Rossiyane o …' 2013). Boris Dubin points out that the main source of the highlighted nationalism in Russia is internal; growing dissatisfaction concerning the state of affairs among the ethnic majority which presents as the 'ethnification' of societal problems (Dubin 2014: 14). Hence, migrants in Russia can be seen as victims of Russians' existing problems rather than seeing them principally as a collective threat to domestic security and order (according to this reasoning, the latter explanation is predominant for western European countries). In both cases, migration can be seen as a central platform for the ethno-culturally framed counter-mobilisation. In Russia, however, as Emil Pain (2014: 50) points out, the political power (the Kremlin) has hitherto managed to use and manipulate ethnic nationalism in preserving Soviet-type imperial nationalism as the official backbone for its own political survival and legitimacy. While imperial nationalism precludes a particular ethnic chauvinism – the governing role of ethnic Russians and the Russian language – larger avenues for the organisation of ethnic nationalist groups have been restricted; official views and policies have been able to satisfy the majority of ethno-nationalist sentiments (ibid.). This seems to be particularly true regarding the split among oppositional nationalists since the annexation of Crimea (Yudina and Al'perovich 2014). Many of those nationalists who had viewed the Kremlin critically either changed their views since the annexation, or, at least, partially calibrated them with the changed situation.[3] Moreover, prospects for spontaneous imperial-nationalist movements (for instance, around political figures such as Aleksander Dugin and Dmitry Rogozin) in challenging the regime have been minimal, since their political ideas can be easily absorbed by the Kremlin (ibid.; Laruelle 2009). In summary, the dramatic recovery of Putin's public support in line with the annexation of the Crimea, the Ukrainian crisis and the war in Donbass is tangible proof of the regime's assimilative capacity. The revolution in Ukraine and its nationalist and anti-Russian sentiments were quickly totalised as manifestations of fascism whose ultimate conqueror is Russia/the Soviet Union (the narrative of the Great Patriotic War). However, when the operation in the Crimea began, followed by fighting in Donbass, the Soviet imperial anti-fascism narrative was soon assimilated into the defence of ethnic Russians in the Crimea and in Donbass. For example, the term ethnic Russian (*russkii*) was mentioned approximately 30 times in Putin's special 'Crimea speech' on 18 March 2014, suggesting that the operation was a defence of Russia's people under hostile circumstances (Putin 2014).

Regarding the developments in Russia's domestic politics since the Ukrainian crisis, the repression shown towards the opposition does not concern the liberal, anti-war wing exclusively, but also the opposition's nationalist wing. One of the central actors and organisers of the nationalists' annual event, 'The Russian March', Alexander Belov was arrested just before the 2014 march, and in 2015 another central figure in the event, Dmitry Demushkin, was prohibited from attending the event (Dergachev and Petrov 2015). While the split among the nationalists with regard to the Ukrainian event had already dramatically decreased the number of march participants in 2014, in 2015 the split had become deeper, boosted by administrative means: the previously large-scale march had transformed into a few pint-sized demonstrations, some organised by pro-Kremlin entities (ibid.; Laine 2015). The Ukrainian crisis seemingly plays a role in the public acceptance of the view 'Russia for Russians' as well. In July 2014, acceptance of the statement 'Russia for ethnic Russians' had dropped to 54 per cent from the 66 per cent of October 2013 ('Natsionalizm...' 2014). However, when measured in different terms, there was no actual change during that period concerning the claim 'the government should restrict the flow of incomers'. In October 2013, 78 per cent of Russians supported the claim, in July 2014 the percentage was 76 per cent, while in 2002 it was 45 per cent (ibid.). However, in other words, xenophobic sentiments towards incomers over the last 12 years shows a unanimous growing trend. Let us now move to 2013, and take a closer look at the year's major political event in Russia.

Migration in Alexei Navalny's political rhetoric

Within the large-scale protests in Russia in 2011–12, the frontman and personality of the new oppositional and protest movement, its development, expansion and novel techniques became Alexei Navalny, a lawyer and blogger born in 1976. Indeed, after the regime had recovered from the December 2011 shock and managed to calm down the protests by establishing Vladimir Putin in his third presidential term, it was Navalny who distinguished himself as the most capable threat to the Kremlin's status quo. At its latest, this happened during his successful campaign during the Moscow mayoral election in August–September 2013, his exclusion from the state-controlled television channels notwithstanding. Against all expectations and opinion polls, the second place in the election with 27.24 per cent of the votes ('Rezul'taty vyborov ...' 2013) proved his skills in combining a highly creative use of the Internet with traditional oratory on the streets. In terms of Navalny's political freshness and his overall liberal agenda, his more or less explicit orientation towards ethno-civic nationalism cast an interesting twist. Navalny has been a key figure in Russia's national–democratic movement, which has challenged the traditional division of post-Soviet Russian nationalism between imperialists (either Soviet or anti-Soviet) and ethno-nationalists (comprising various xenophobic and racist movements) (Laruelle 2014: 277–8; see also Moen-Larsen 2014).

I see two major reasons why Navalny's campaign rhetoric in the Moscow mayoral election offers a vantage point on the issue of migration in Russia. First, it was the election in which the development of Russia's xenophobic sentiments reached its peak, while also being the most concrete proof of the Kremlin's vulnerability under open political competition in the most important region, Moscow. Second, Navalny was not the initiator of using anti-immigration in the campaign: that started with the Kremlin's candidate, and ultimate winner, the sitting mayor, Sergei Sobyanin (Verkhovskii 2014). Thus, in terms of polls on the election results that predicted Sobyanin's landslide victory and Navalny's marginal support – eventually ending in a situation where the second round was close between Sobyanin (51 per cent of votes) and Navalny – it is essential to examine the issue of migration in Navalny's campaign rhetoric as a central ideational component in his electoral success.

Besides constant references to highly suspicious statistics concerning crimes conducted by migrants (Podrabinek 2013), Navalny's populistic mastery also paid close attention to personal 'common fear' when faced with migrants. Here is one quote from his numerous meetings with Muscovites – the way in which Navalny took to the street also separated him from competing candidates – cited in the web journal *Bol'shoi Gorod* (Aivazian 2013):

Do you know that 40% of the young male population of Tajikistan lives in Russia? And the majority of them in Moscow. Sobyanin needs people who can be easily despoiled. Raisa Semenova, this question does not worry you only. 80% of Muscovites answer in social polls that the topic of migration worries them.

Navalny easily shifted the focus from the obvious unreliability of his statistical references to migration's emotional repercussions among Muscovites. For instance, in a meeting of voters in the Vodnoi stadion metro station, he pointed out, 'I'm not worried about numbers related to migration, I am worried about every stolen handbag from women in my region' (Naval'nyi 2013a). When viewing recordings of these campaign meetings, it is easy to see how Navalny's links migration to its 'mundane realities'; in particular, to corruption. Following his story during the meeting in the Vodnoi stadion, he mentions a pensioner, physically in good shape, who told him that he would like to work as a caretaker for the staircase where he lives, and whose official monthly salary is approximately 30,000 roubles. However, this was not possible and a Tajik caretaker continues to work there. According to Navalny, the reason for this is that the official salary of this Tajik is the same, 30,000 roubles, but this Tajikistanin actually earns 12,000, because he is ready to 'pay' the remaining 18,000 to the employing entities – authorities and companies – which provide the job (ibid.). While mediating everyday xenophobia via such emotionally resonating narratives, Navalny avoids explicit ethno-nationalist aspects, although migration is a regular topic in his campaign speeches which evoke applause in his audiences (see, for instance, Naval'nyi 2013a; 2013b; 2013c). The best testimony on Navalny's views on migration during the campaign can be found in the interview on the *Ekho Moskvy* radio station conducted by its editor-in-chief, Aleksei Venediktov which was dedicated to the topic of migration, although other issues were also touched upon (Naval'nyi 2013d). While Venediktov aims to highlight the economic importance of migrants in terms of their labour as well as their spending in Moscow after remittances to their native countries,[4] Navalny downplays this argument by contrasting the realm of migrants with the practices of a modern city:

They receive money but, forgive me, they live here, they use metro which is subsidized by the city. They don't have insurance but they use medical services for which we pay. They use education (their kids). They ... well, no matter whether we want or not want to admit, they conduct pretty many crimes [this statement is followed by a dispute with Venediktov] ... In addition, the most important thing: we cannot speak about the value of slave labour in terms of additional value simply because we speak about the value of slavery ... These people, unfortunately, live as slaves. And if they were working according to the guaranteed 8-hour day with paid days off, insurance, if taxes were paid from their salaries, then their salaries and their value of work would not differ from any Muscovite or from any other. By calling these people here to the position of slaves, dragging and settling them into houses to be demolished, into basements, apartments crowded by 30 people, we simply encourage those means of production which we had in the 19th century ... The principal employer for migrants is the city, city entities or private entities which work for the city ... whatever, we are those employers, we eventually pay this money ... We must prohibit hiring foreigners within the year in order to stimulate companies to improve the productivity of labour.

This part of the interview encapsulates all of the central components of Navalny's political usage of migration during the campaign as well as pinpointing his liberal ethno-nationalism more generally (Laruelle 2014; Moen-Larsen 2014). The main thrust of Navalny's argument is to prefer a situational logic of 'common reasoning' instead of pursuing ideologically loaded markers, for instance, nationalist or democratic ones (Lassila 2016). In other words, despite revealing his distaste for Central Asian and Caucasian migrants and stressing their cultural incompatibility with 'us', Navalny equates the situation with the corruption. While corruption figures as a nodal point of his common reasoning, all ideologically resonating orientations – from racism and nationalism up to democracy and humanism – can be absorbed into this point. Since 'we' want to live in a modern, rich megalopolis,[5] where 'we' as common taxpayers are the main driving force, migration and its cultural factors as well as the existing inhuman exploitation of slave labour simply hinder this development. In this vein, the loopholes and controversies of his argumentation, for example in highlighting the number of crimes conducted by migrants (Podrabinek 2013), is systematically bypassed by a paradigmatic populist logic of equivalence pointed out by Ernesto Laclau (2005: 120): 'an equivalential chain [between various demands of citizens] can weaken the particularism of their links but cannot do away with it altogether'. In other words, Navalny does not 'invent' corruption and migration as new political openings which would be tabooed by the political power: they are recognised as a problem by both the regime and official publicity (for more, see Hutchings and Tolz 2015: 185–91). Instead, he links these two into the logic of equivalence. In this equivalence, one problem is not highlighted at the cost of another, but the problem of migration is constructed as acutely linked with the problem of corruption, and eventually with the problem of the existing political rule (for more, see Hutchings and Tolz 2015: 185–91; Lassila 2016). Thus, despite the sitting governor Sobianin being the actual initiator of using antipathy towards migrants in his election campaign, for Sobyanin, migration is strikingly framed in line with cultural prejudices without linking it to economic issues. Here is one of Sobyanin's views at the beginning of his campaign (Sobyanin 2013):

It is better for people who do not speak Russian well, who have a completely different culture, to live in their own countries. For that reason we do not welcome their adaption in Moscow ... after working here they must go to their families, to their home in their countries ... I think Moscow is a Russian (*rossiiskii*) city and it must remain like that. It's not Chinese, Tajik and not Uzbek.

However, immediately after this anti-migrant view in line with outspoken ethno-cultural prejudices, Sobyanin continued

> [W]e are always happy with our guests, Russia is a multinational country, and all nationalities are mixed. It is very dangerous, simply extremely dangerous, particularly for our city to pick them [particular ethnic groups] up separately, to contrast ones with other cultures.

Sobyanin's sudden reference to official nationalities principles which underscore multicultural brotherhood somewhat contradicts his explicit claim of cultural incompatibility between 'us' and migrants mentioned in the same breath. Regarding the excerpt's ethno-nationalist beginning, the usage of the term *rossiiskii* ('citizen of the Russian Federation') instead of *russkii* ('ethnic Russian') – which would be more plausible in such a context – is contrived as well. Although the controversy in question does not allow us to judge that Sobyanin's anti-immigration views are simply the opportunism of the sitting mayor in the face of Muscovites' dramatically increased anti-immigrant sentiments, it anyway shows Sobyanin's dependence on official views in relation to migration; outspoken xenophobia is followed by ritualistic mentions of the multinational state. Likewise, Navalny's longstanding goal of demanding visas from citizens of Central Asia, repeatedly mentioned in his campaign (Naval'nyi 2013a, 2013b, 2013c, 2014), is not touched upon. While various tightening measures have been recently introduced to migrants from Central Asia – Sobyanin referred to them in his campaign – visas have been out of the question. This geopolitical dimension in terms of sustaining direct links and influence upon Central Asia is the main explanation for the Kremlin's reluctance to establish a visa regime for these countries (Virkkunen and Fryer 2015).

Going back to Navalny, the complexity between territorial borders and ethno-cultural features fuels his link between the fights with corruption and migration, although his constant demand for a visa regime concerns Central Asian states which do not belong to the Russian Federation. Here an important practice of corruption – and obvious facet of the Kremlin's geopolitical control over these states – is to grant Russian international passports to citizens of these states. According to Navalny, Russia granted 500,000 international passports to citizens of Kyrgyzstan in 2013 alone (Naval'nyi 2013d). Since such measures seemingly torpedo attempts to require various kinds of permit to arrive and work in Russia – for instance, quotas for foreign labour (see below) – Navalny sees the visa regime as the central means of cutting corruption and the flow of migrants. It is noteworthy that in this case Naval'nyi regularly forgets to use 'illegal' as an attribute for this particular category of migrants, which is hardly coincidental (Naval'nyi 2013d). In other words, the migrant is depicted as a facet of illegality, extended to the illegal practices of the existing authorities.

In terms of Russia's multi-ethnic composition, the ethnic dimension of migration does not follow the state borders of the Russian Federation. The same antipathy to migrants from Central Asia is targeted at inhabitants of Russia's Caucasian territories, particular those from Chechenia and Dagestan, the territories that 'should not be fed any more' ('Rossiyane o …' 2013). Whereas the demand for a visa regime for these people is a far more complicated issue than for Central Asians, explicit ethno-nationalist markers (implying a separation between Russia and its Caucasian subjects) with suspicious international comparisons are touched upon (Naval'nyi 2013d):

> Aleksei Venediktov: Senator McCain says that 'we have 20–30 million illegal immigrants'. He doesn't know either. A country with such a huge visa regime, and he doesn't know. Is this the reason why you speak about this as well? Thirty people in an apartment. One arrives, starts a family, children are born. So, it's difficult to count on figures, right?
>
> Navalny: Well, first of all, these are different things. In spite of that, USA builds the wall against Mexico and even Obama votes for the wall with Mexico but here it is said, 'please, come here'. In addition, it's necessary to understand that the people (this is important as well) who arrive from Mexico are Christians, people from a more developed country. Here a rural population from very backward Central Asian countries, principally Muslims, are arriving.

While cultural racism is eventually explicated, Navalny constantly converts it into 'practicalities of Moscow's modern way of life', implying his responsibility as a potential mayor and not forgetting his sarcastic compassion for Central Asians (Naval'nyi 2013d):

> Today we are told, 'You know, the number of Muslims has so rapidly grown in Moscow. Let's build mosques for all of them'. However, they still arrive. We cannot build mosques for all, and Muscovites are against the great number of mosques. Regardless of acknowledging their problems, while sympathizing with them, we must say, 'My friends, we cannot take here all the citizens from Uzbekistan and Tajikistan. We love and value them so much, but we introduce the visa regime and call them here in small numbers'.

For Navalny, the backwardness associated with migrants fulfils the equivalence between migrants and corruption; corrupted regimes are backward and forced to resort to labour detrimental to Russia's modernisation. This aspect becomes apparent when migrants as a group are related to Russia's closest ethnic neighbours, Belarus, and in particular, Ukraine. In an answer to Venediktov's question, 'What is the difference between Ukraine and Tajikistan?' Navalny answers as follows (the excerpt above is another part of his answer) (Naval'nyi 2013d):

First of all, as I mentioned, people who arrive from Tajikistan are youth coming from villages. 40% of existing male Tajiks in the world, under 40 years old, they live here, in Russia. They are only capable of the least qualified jobs, in addition to the completely collapsed system of education in Tajikistan. In general, there ... from Ukraine can arrive programmers, from Ukraine can arrive a person ... who can drive a tractor, complex vehicles, qualified workers on construction sites. From Uzbekistan such a person cannot arrive – nobody teaches him there.

These views behind the extraordinary electoral success of the opposition's major candidate in surprisingly open circumstances in September 2013 ended up at the dramatically different conjuncture that followed the Kremlin's annexation of Crimea and war in Eastern Ukraine in 2014. Not only had the situation for the opposition changed (Navalny was arrested in late 2013 and condemned to house arrest) but also the political space for national identifications had changed: the Slavic brother Ukraine had become enemy number one as a state. However, it prompts the question how this change was represented with regard to the phenomenon which momentarily superseded the nature of migration in Russia in the summer 2014: refugees from Ukraine.

Refugees and Ukraine

In order to illustrate the role of Ukrainian refugees in Russia's media in the summer of 2014, I conducted a search with the help of the Integrum database statistics, using the search terms 'Refugee Ukraine'[6] and 'Migrant'.[7] According to 2,730 sources[8] in the period 1 April 2014–1 April 2015, we computed the figures as set out in Figure 4.1.

The line whose peak is between 31 May and 31 October 2014 is the query 'Refugee Ukraine'. Figure 4.1 shows the unanimous visibility of Ukrainian refugees in the Russian media during summer 2014, clearly superseding the relatively stable role of migrants. Next I was interested in how the issue of labour – regularly spelled out by Navalny with regard to migrants – was linked to the topic of Ukrainian refugees. Using Integrum's popularity rating,[9] I searched the same set of sources (with additional data consisting of information on governmental organisations which was not available in Integrum's statistics) with the parameter 'Ukraine labour'.[10] Despite the dispersed results that the query yielded, among the first four items in the query's popularity rating, three discussed Ukrainian refugees in relation to labour (items from the newspapers *Kommersant'* and *Izvestiya* and the news agency *IA Regnum*). On 11 July 2014, *Izvestiya* published the article 'Oblast increases the quota for foreigners due to refugees' (Ivushkina 2014). In line with the newspaper's relatively clear pro-governmental stance, it is revealing that Ukrainians are not mentioned in the title. The issue is about the necessity to increase the quotas in the Moscow oblast that the government has decided for subjects of the Federation. Along with the Soviet-era echoes in which subjects

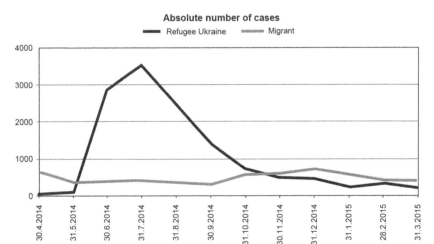

Absolute number of cases

Figure 4.1 Frequency of mentions of 'Refugee Ukraine' and 'Migrant' 1 April 2014–1 April 2015 in the selected dataset

and agents perform a kind of competition in fulfilling the state's tasks, now various regions are planning to 'ask the ministry of labour to increase quotas for their regions'. At the end of the article, after repeating various bureaucratic procedures required for changes to these quotas, an excerpt from the head of the Moscow oblast employment committee, Mikhail Korotaev, finally touches upon the ethnic underpinning of the existing restrictions on foreign labour (Ivushkina 2014):

> There are 75,000 vacancies in the oblast, of which 4,000, 8,000 include accommodation. Refugees are completely eligible to apply for these vacancies. I point out that employers prefer Ukrainians to migrants from Central Asia because the first speak Russian and include more qualified specialists.

On 9 September 2014, *Kommersant'*, whose stance towards the government is more or less ambiguous, published an article titled 'Ukrainian refugees were placed into the reserve of labour' (Kozlov 2014). It reports recent decisions made by the government concerning the substantial simplification of the procedure for employing Ukrainian citizens escaping the war, informed by the Prime Minister Medvedev:

> we must provide an opportunity to these people to not only stay in the territory of our country, but also make immediate decisions about employment ... Moreover, there are many qualified persons among them: engineers, doctors, teachers.

Both of these articles pinpoint how the sudden reality of refugees is signified; while being exclusively linked to Ukraine, they are tangibly contrasted with migrants. And, whereas migrants are linked to labour, it is 'refugee' which allows the nature of foreign labour to be specified in highly idealised terms. Perhaps the most striking item in the query was that from the information agency Regions.ru, published on 26 June 2014 and entitled 'Refugees from Ukraine are the excellent means of fulfilling our lack of labour' (Kuzin 2014). The author is a representative of the Russian Orthodox Church, protoiereus Alexander Kuzin, who did not hesitate to evoke cultural aspects, preferring them to the possible interests of employers:

> Ukrainians … are people of our belief and culture. For us this is much more preferable [solution in comparison to Tajiks] … I do not have anything against them [Tajiks, Uzbeks] but I'm just worried that we ignore the interests of our culture and of spiritual processes in society. Of course, for our employers this is not profitable since the status of refugee requires that citizen rights must be followed … citizens from Tajikistan do not attempt to receive these rights. Well, is what is profitable for employers profitable for Russia? Of course not. It leads to serious social tension which has appeared repeatedly, caused by the incompatibility of the people who arrive us from Central Asia: they don't want to live according to our traditions.

Despite Kuzin's views being expressed from a different standpoint (a representative of the Church) and under different political circumstances than those of Navalny, both of them address similar views concerning the nature of migration in Russia in the 2010s; perverted or corrupted, the interests of employers in sustaining the flow of migrants from Central Asia whose people are culturally backward compared to (and incompatible with) Russian traditions (or ideal practices of society). It is worth noting that the Russian mainstream discussion on Ukrainian labour shows a complete lack of reflection in terms of internal divisions within Ukraine, which has been the core dimension of the conflict between the countries. This lack fits the picture promoted by the official Russian propaganda since early 2014: Ukrainians are those who are with us, while those who wage war against us are more or less marginalised fascists, although on other occasions, the contemporary Ukraine is filled with massively prepared perpetrators, helped by the West to slaughter Russians (Ukrainians in Donbass). However, this imperial blindness is not only linked to the mentalities fabricated under war propaganda but can be seen in Navalny's views as well, although from reverse, pro-western standpoints. Navalny has repeatedly pointed out the similarity between Russia and Ukraine, which implies an equal blindness to those Ukrainian nationalist views which underline the full separation from Russia as a nation state. For instance, in the interview in *Ekho Moskvy* in October 2014, Navalny repeats the similarity between the countries and envisions the necessity of union between Russia and Ukraine (Naval'nyi 2014). As a mirror image to Putin's visions in which Russia's Eurasian course is the guideline for Ukraine, for Navalny, Ukraine's pro-western course should be the orientation for Russia. In the realm of migration, both of these political opposites are entangled with the idea of seeing Russia as a powerful modern state with strong ethnic preferences.

Conclusions

While the overall negativity of the word 'migrant' among many ethnic Russians is not a surprise regarding the rapid growth of xenophobic sentiments, the positive framing of Ukrainian refugees in the mainstream media should be related to the extreme anti-Ukrainian propaganda in Russia's official media since early 2014. On the one hand, the sharp contrast which emerges from the comparison between the Ukrainian state and Ukrainians fits with the Kremlin's assimilative capacity in instrumentalising nationalisms – ethnic and imperial – for its own political legitimacy. On the other hand, the link between the executive political power and the mainstream media, regardless of their close relations in Russia, should not be seen in too straightforward a manner. As Hutchings and Tolz (2015: 252) point out, we should not over-simplify the relationship between the Kremlin and the state-aligned media in terms of privileging transitive meaning, conveyed from the state to the media, over transactional meaning which arises from multi-directional interactions involving state, media, popular and other discourses. In comparing Navalny's campaign rhetoric on migration and the mainstream media views on Ukrainian refugees, we see that both views – let us generalise them here as oppositional and pro-governmental – adapt themselves into common persisting discourses concerning migration, labour and modernisation, instead of a situation in which oppositional anti-migration rhetoric would be replaced by the absence of Central Asian migrants for the sake of Slavic refugees. However, it is obvious that the state-controlled public discussion has partially managed to surpass domestic political concerns (migration being one of the most acute) with harsh anti-western and anti-Kiev propaganda, as the Integrum statistics above and the cited opinion polls indicate. Whereas the number of Ukrainian refugees in summer 2014 was a fact which could not be neglected whatever practices the state's media followed (centralised partisan or more democratic), it was a political choice to frame these refugees with regard to migrants along with existing ethnic and cultural perceptions. From the Kremlin's viewpoint, a transitive meaning would mean a straightforward idea of surpassing popular prejudices towards migrants without mentioning them, or even highlighting their importance in terms of Russia's Eurasian orientation, rather than mirroring them against Ukrainians in negative terms. In other words, public discussion on Ukrainian refugees draws transactional meaning along with existing popular discourses.

This allows us to suggest that the discussion on migration in Russia in relation to the major political junctures divided by the annexation of Crimea has not changed the basic current of this discussion. As echoed by Navalny, Ukraine has figured as a wishful counterpoint to migrants, predominantly associated with being culturally alien to Russians. As such, this overall reluctance about the everyday realities of Russia's multicultural composition and the recently emphasised Eurasian allies in Central Asia pinpoints a major challenge for the regime in sustaining the idea of a multi-ethnic empire, regardless of the various manipulations of ethnic nationalism posed by the official media discourse (Hutchings and Tolz 2015). Regarding the success that Navalny gained in the mayoral election, it can be argued that Navalny 'civilised' and 'normalised' (see Moen-Larsen 2014) the ethno-nationalist and racist underpinnings of the dominant migration discourse in depicting European and 'natural' conditions for Russia's modernisation. It is thus noteworthy that Russia's extreme anti-western propaganda related to the Ukrainian conflict – launched by a 'Western backed fascist junta in Kiev' – is generally absent from the public discourse on Ukrainian refugees. Instead, this post-Crimean refugee discourse easily conforms to the discourse advocated by Navalny before the crisis, in which migrants and Ukrainians are contrasted in terms of qualified and backward labour, justified by cultural factors. It is also noteworthy how particular expressions such as 'illegal migrant' and 'migrant', or 'refugee' and 'Ukrainian', are used interchangeably. The migration discourse, in both political junctures, shows the vagueness regarding the major division of Russia's nationalisms, imperial and ethnic (Laruelle 2009, 2014). For Navalny, the obvious emphasis lies on ethnic nationalism but his views on Ukraine illustrate the fact that that particular imperial twist is also present (Lassila 2016). Whereas the annexation of Crimea brilliantly shows how the explicit imperial operation was transformed into 'the defence of ethnic Russians', the dominant refugee discourse shows – not least due to the conflation of 'Ukrainian' and 'refugee' – how ethnic and imperial nationalisms are intertwined with a seemingly sincere willingness to help people in distress. On the one hand, this help is motivated by ethnic and cultural closeness, and, on the other, the discourse is overly blind to Ukraine's internal political divisions and its nation-state dimensions.

In terms of the discursive continuum from 2013 to 2014, Navalny's framework of the overall need for Russia's modernisation, projected onto the usage and productivity of labour, is concretised by the opportunity to replace unpleasant representatives of backwardness and crime with culturally close relatives with qualified labour skills. In other words, the economic frame allows the racist currents of the discussion to be civilised. At the same time, this dominating frame does not resonate with the issue of supply and demand, the most obvious driving force in any usage of foreign labour. Besides all of the obvious and possible deviations and inhumanity – spelled out by Navalny – Russia's migration dynamics follow the global dynamics between 'the rich north and poor south': poorly paid jobs in the labour markets of richer countries are filled by workers from poorer countries. This is exactly the situation between Russia and Central Asia. The Russian discussion somewhat suggests that the structural problem of the low productivity of work is exclusively linked to migrants, not to poor Russian institutions of labour, and that the solution would be the elimination of the backward labour in favour of qualified workers. This notion supports Dubin's view on the ethnification of Russia's general poor state of affairs as the main explanation for ethnonationalist sentiments.

Along with the growing number of refugees from Ukraine and the worsening economic situation, the vision of ethnically framed qualified workers as a remedy for the migration problem has gradually merged into a more straightforward xenophobia. For instance, in Kaliningrad, the local unemployed have been preferred to foreigners, and for those vacancies which are still available, Ukrainians have been preferred to Central Asians. In other words, ethnic hierarchies are persistent, but the nature of labour has not changed: Ukrainians can do those less well-paid jobs formerly done by Central Asians ('Kvota na...' 2014). In September 2014, the newspaper *Nezavisimaya Gazeta* pointed out that while the number of refugees from Ukraine had reached one million, Russians' attitudes to them had become more critical (Garmonenko 2014). Citing the Russian Foundation of Public Opinion's poll of September 2014, almost half of Russians wished to send refugees back to Ukraine as soon as possible, while the mood had been much warmer a couple of months earlier (ibid.).

Notes

1 Integrum is the largest collection of Russian and CIS databases, covering a wide range of topics. At the beginning of 2014, Integrum contained approximately 500 million documents related to Russia. The scope of more than 7,000 databases covers all national and regional newspapers and magazines, statistics, official publications, archives of the leading national and international information agencies, full texts of thousands of literary works, dictionaries, and more. For more information, see, www.integrumworld.com/about.html
2 According to Michael Billig's classical notion, banal nationalism includes the most common and generally accepted forms of the nationalism of a state: flags, coats of arms, sporting events, national songs, etc. (Billig 1995).
3 A good example is Konstantin Krylov, the leader of the National Democratic Party, and a leading theorist of Russia's Europe-oriented ethno-nationalist movement (see, for example, Krylov 2014).
4 As is known, the major part of the GDPs of poor Central Asian States comes from the remittances of migrants working in Russia; see for example, Michel (2014); Virkkunen and Fryer (2015).
5 The budget of Moscow – according to Navalny 1.6 trillion roubles – proves that in fiscal terms Moscow should be one of the wealthiest cities in the world (*Programma kandidata v mery Moskvy Alekseya Naval'nogo* 2013). Navalny regularly used this aspect in opening his campaign meetings (see, for instance, Naval'nyi 2013a, 2013b, 2014c).
6 In Russian '*bezhenets Ukraina*', which matches all items consisting of these words and their derivations.
7 In Russian Мигрант, which matches all items consisting of the word and its derivations.

8 I selected those sources which generally cover the media in the Russian Federation available in Integrum: central press, central news agencies, regional newspapers, regional news agencies, central Internet publications and Internet media, and four databases consisting of television and radio monitoring.
9 This popularity rating is based on Integrum's classification of the most relevant media on the basis of the selected databases (set of sources). In addition, the chosen items related to the given search words in the case of particular media (for example, the newspaper *Kommersant*) are ranked by Integrum based on the frequency of the search word(s) in the designated item as well as on outside links to the given item. For more, see Romanenko and Gerhenzon (2006).
10 The actual query was marked as Украина рабёчая сила /p3 which means that the words Украина (Ukraine) and рабёчая сила (labour) appear in the frames of a group of three adjacent sentences.

References

Aivazyan, A. 2013. 'Naval'nyi vyshel v narod', *Bol'shoi Gorod*, 30 July. Retrieved 13 November 2015 from http://bg.ru/city/navalniy_vstrecha_s_izbiratelyami-18924.

Billig, M. 1995. *Banal Nationalism*. London: Sage.

Dergachev, V. and V. Petrov. 2015. '"Russkii marsh" razdelilsya po "Novorossii"', *Gazeta.ru*, 16 October. Retrieved 25 November 2015 from www.gazeta.ru/politics/2015/10/15_a_7823465.shtml.

Dubin, B. 2014. '"Chuzhi"' natsionalizmy i "svoi" ksenofobii vcherashnikh i segodnyashnikh rossiyan', *Pro & Contra*, 1–2(62): 6–18. Retrieved 13 November 2015 from http://carnegie.ru/proEtContra/?fa=55472.

Garmonenko, D. 2014. 'Gostepriimstvo rossiyan zakanchivaetsya', *Nezavisimaya Gazeta*, 30 September.

Goode, P. and M. Laruelle. 2014. 'Putin, Crimea and the legitimacy trap', *Open-Democracy*, 13 March. Retrieved 13 November 2015 from www.opendemocracy.net/od-russia/j-paul-goode-and-marlene-laruelle/putin-crimea-and-legitimacy-trap-nationalism.

Gudkov, L. 2013. 'Rossiya – dlya russkikh? Uzhe ne stydno'. *Radio Svoboda*, 19 November. Retrieved 13 November 2015 from www.svoboda.org/content/transcript/25172654.html.

Hirsch, F. 2005. *Empire of Nations. Ethnographic Knowledge and the Making of the Soviet Union*. New York: Cornell University Press.

Hutchings, S. and V. Tolz. 2015. *Nation, Ethnicity and Race on Russian Television*. London and New York: Routledge.

Ivushkina, A. 2014. '"Oblast" uvelichit kvotu na inostrantsev radi bezhentsev'. *Izvestiya*, 11 July.

'Kak Vy otnosites' k idee "Rossiya – dlya russkikh"', 2011. *Levada-Tsentr*, November. Retrieved 13 November 2015 from www.levada.ru/old/archive/mezhetnicheskie-otnosheniya/kak-vy-otnosites-k-idee-rossiya-dlya-russkikh.

Kozlov, V. 2014. 'Ukrainskikh bezhentsev zapisali v trudovye rezervy', *Kommersant'*, 9 September.

Krylov, K. 2014. 'Russkie otvety na ukrainskie voprosy', *Agenstvo politicheskoi novosti*, 16 May. Retrieved 25 November 2015 from www.apn.ru/publications/article31594.htm.

Kuzin, A. 2014. 'Bezhentsy s Ukrainy – eto zamechatel'nyi sposob vospolnit' nashu nekhvatku rabochei cily', *Regions.ru*, 25 June. Retrieved 13 November 2015 from http://regions.ru/news/2517581.

'Kvota na trudovykh migrantov v Kaliningradskoi oblasti sokrashchena pochti vdvoe'. 2014. *Informatsionnoe agenstvo 'Rosbalt'*, 29 July. Retrieved 13 November 2015 from www.rosbalt.ru/kaliningrad/2014/07/29/1297540.html.

Laclau, E. 2005. *On Populist Reason*. London and New York: Verso.

Laine, V. 2015. 'Managing nationalism. Contemporary Russian nationalistic movements and their relationship to the government', *FIIA Working Papers* 88. Retrieved 14 November 2015 from www.fiia.fi/fi/publication/522/managed_nationalism.

Laruelle, M. 2009. 'Rethinking Russian nationalism', in M. Laruelle (ed.), *Russian Nationalism and National Reassertion of Russia*. New York: Routledge, pp. 13–48.

Laruelle, M. 2014. 'Alexei Navalny and challenges in reconciling "nationalism" and "liberalism"', *Post-Soviet Affairs*, 30(4): 276–297.

Lassila, J. 2016. 'Aleksei Naval'nyi and populist re-ordering of Putin's stability', *Europe-Asia Studies*, 68(1): 118–137.

Michel, C. 2014. 'Drop in migrant remittances a problem for Central Asian economies', *The Diplomat*, 23 December. Retrieved 13 November 2015 from http://thediplomat.com/2014/12/drop-in-migrant-remittances-a-problem-for-central-asian-economies.

Moen-Larsen, N. 2014. '"Normal nationalism": Alexei Navalny, LiveJournal and "the Other"', *East European Politics*, 30(4): 548–567.

'Natsionalizm, ksenofobiya i migratsiya'. 2014. *Levada-Tsentr*, 26 August. Retrieved 13 November 2015 from www.levada.ru/old/26-08-2014/natsionalizm-ksenofobiya-i-migratsiya.

Naval'nyi, A. 2013a. 'Polchasa c kandidatom: 4 vstrechi Naval'nogo s izbiratelyami', *Kinokadr.ru*, 16 August. Retrieved 13 November 2015 from www.youtube.com/watch?v=b6P7DzIlI1U.

Naval'nyi, A. 2013b. 'Aleksei Naval'yi na vstreche v Mitino', *Ruchipchannel*, 11 August. Retrieved 13 November 2015 from www.youtube.com/watch?v=25KqD6elPGo.

Naval'nyi, A. 2013c. 'Aleksei Naval'nyi v Troparevo-Nikulino'. *Teplyi Stan*, 16 August. Retrieved 13 November 2015 from www.youtube.com/watch?v=CyClBNMyR7M.

Naval'nyi, A. 2013d. 'Interv'yu, Migratsiya'. *Ekho Moskvy*, 23 August. Retrieved 13 November 2015 from http://echo.msk.ru/programs/beseda/1139878-echo.

Naval'nyi, A. 2014. 'Sbityi fokus', *Ekho Moskvy*, 15 October, Retrieved 13 November 2015 from http://echo.msk.ru/programs/beseda/1417522-echo/.

'Odobrenie deyatel'nosti Vladimira Putina'. 2015. *Levada-Tsentr*, November. Retrieved 13 November 2015 from www.levada.ru/indikatory/odobrenie-organov-vlasti.

Pain, E. 2014. 'Ksenofobiya i natsionalizm v epokhu rossiiskogo bezvremen'ya', *Pro & Contra*, 1–2(62): 34–53. Retrieved 13 November 2015 from http://carnegie.ru/proEt Contra/?fa=55472.

Podrabinek, A. 2013. 'Desyat' mifov o migrantakh', Institut sovremennoi Rossii, 28 October. Retrieved 13 November 2015 from www.imrussia.org/ru/society/1591-ten-myths-about-migrants.

Programma kandidata v mery Moskvy Alekseya Naval'nogo. 2013. Retrieved 13 November 2015 from http://navalny.ru/platform/Navalny_Program.pdf.

Putin, V. 2012. 'Rossiya: Natsional'nyi vopros', *Nezavisimaya Gazeta*, 23 January. Retrieved 24 November 2015 from www.ng.ru/politics/2012-01-23/1_national.html.

Putin, V. 2014. 'Obrashchenie Prezidenta Rossiiskoi Federatsii', Kremlin.ru, 18 March. Retrieved 25 November 2015 from http://kremlin.ru/events/president/news/20603.

'Rezul'taty vyborov Mera Moskvy 8 sentyabrya 2013'. 2013. Tsentral'naya izbiratel'naya komissiya Rossiiskoi Federatsii. Retrieved 13 November 2015 from www.moscow_

city.vybory.izbirkom.ru/region/region/moscow_city?action=show&root=1&tvd=27720 001368293&vrn=27720001368289&region=77&global=&sub_region=0&prver=0&pr onetvd=null&vibid=27720001368293&type=222.

Romanenko, F. and L. Gershenzon. 2006. 'IPS Integrum. Istoriya sozdaniya, opisanie, ispol'zovanie', in G. Nikiporets-Tagikawa (ed.), *Integrum: tochnye metody i gumanitarnye nauki*, Moscow: 'Letnii sad'.

'Rossiyane o migratsii i mezhnatsional'noi napryazhennosti'. 2013. *Levada-Tsentr*, 5 November. Retrieved 13 November 2015 from www.levada.ru/old/05-11-2013/ros siyane-o-migratsii-i-mezhnatsionalnoi-napryazhennosti.

Sobyanin, S. 2013. 'Migranty dolzhny uekhat' domoi', Dni.ru, 30 May. Retrieved 13 November 2015 from www.dni.ru/society/2013/5/30/253597.html.

United Nations. 2013. 'Statistics on international migration', Department of Economic and Social Affairs, Population Division. Retrieved 13 November 2015 from www.un.org/en/development/desa/population/migration/publications/wallchart/docs/ wallchart2013.pdf.

Verkhovskii, A. 2014. 'Etnopolitika federal'noi vlasti i aktivizatsiia russkogo natsionalizma'. *Pro & Contra*, 1–2(62): 19–33. Retrieved 13 November 2015 from http:// carnegie.ru/proEtContra/?fa=55472.

Virkkunen, J. and P. Fryer. 2015. 'Keskiaasialaiset ja Venäjän työmarkkinoiden muutos', *Idäntutkimus* 2: 49–65.

Yudina, N. and V. Al'perovich. 2014. 'Ukraina sputala natsionalistam karty'. *SOVA Informatsionno-analiticheskii tsentr*, 14 July. Retrieved 25 November 2015 from www.sova-center.ru/racism-xenophobia/publications/2014/07/d29887.

5 Migration and transnational informality in post-Soviet societies

Ethnographic study of po rukam ('handshake') experiences of Uzbek migrant workers in Moscow

Rustamjon Urinboyev

Introduction

The concept of 'informality' has become a trendy topic of research in the scholarly literature about post-Soviet societies. The amount of literature focusing on informal practices, institutions and networks in the post-Soviet space has grown rapidly over the last two decades, producing theoretically and empirically grounded accounts of different forms and manifestations of informality, such as clans and regional patronage networks, clientelism, blat networks, bribery, embezzlement, cronyism, kickbacks. In this connection, the review of existing research shows that the distinct focus on 'post-Soviet informality' highlights at least nine main themes: (1) economic informality (Alexeev and Pyle 2003; Wallace and Latcheva 2006); (2) blurred boundaries between informality and corruption (Werner 2000; Polese 2008; Urinboyev and Svensson 2013a); (3) informal political institutions and practices (Gel'man 2004; Hale 2011; Ledeneva 2013); (4) informality as a mixture of cultural and economic practices (Misztal 2002; Smith and Stenning 2006; Urinboyev and Svensson 2013b); (5) informality as a reflection of broader sociopolitical and sociocultural traditions (Ledeneva 1998; Collins 2006; Hayoz 2015); (6) the relationship between formal and informal economies (Round *et al.* 2008; Williams *et al.* 2013); (7) the (dis)continuity between Soviet and post-Soviet informal economies (Kurkchiyan 2000; Rodgers and Williams 2009; Aliyev 2015a); (8) informal practices of redistribution as an alternative to state-driven welfare distribution (Urinboyev 2013, 2014; Morris and Polese 2014); and (9) definitional, conceptual and terminological ambiguity surrounding the concept of informality (Williams *et al.* 2013; Aliyev 2015b; Polese 2015).

Despite the existence of a large diversity of scholarly explanations for and approaches to 'post-Soviet informality', one idea common to the aforementioned scholarship is that the bulk of studies focus on informal practices and institutions and their regulatory structures that take place within the boundaries of a single nation state (i.e. the scholarship is confined to a particular

DOI: 10.4324/9781315657424-5

nation state, not taking into account the increased transnational links between different places and people). Another factor that adds to this complexity is the growing use of information and communication technologies in the post-Soviet region, which may facilitate the daily exchange of information and reduce the importance of distance between different countries and people, possibly leading to the emergence of 'transnational informality'. Hence, with a few exceptions (Cieslewska 2013; Yalcin-Heckmann 2013; Turaeva 2014), not much has been said about how multidimensional flows of people, ideas, goods, social practices and cultural symbols between different post-Soviet countries mould the nature and geographic scope of informal practices in the region.

This chapter situates itself within these 'informality' debates by suggesting that the nature of informal practices in post-Soviet societies is changing, not only in terms of content, forms, actors and magnitude, but, more importantly, in terms of geographical scope, due to ongoing large-scale migratory processes, e.g. the massive inflow of migrant workers from Central Asia and the Caucasus to Russia. Moving beyond the methodological nationalism still prevalent in much informality research (Wimmer and Glick Schiller 2002), I argue that informal practices in post-Soviet societies are becoming increasingly transnational. Migrant workers, living their lives across the border of two (or more) nation states, become part of the fabric of everyday life and social relations in their home state, while simultaneously becoming part of the socio-economic processes in their receiving state, thereby facilitating the daily flow of ideas, social practices and cultural symbols between migrant sending and receiving societies. These processes are especially visible in the construction sector in Moscow, Russia, where the informal employment of migrant workers is widespread and carried out through so-called po rukam ('handshake-based') labour contracts, which involve multiple formal and informal actors with different kinds and locations of power: migrant workers, intermediaries, construction firms, Russian police officers, Chechen racketeers, and migrants' left-behind families and communities (e.g. village residents, local community leaders, leaders of mosques). Hence, this chapter, through an ethnographic study of po rukam experiences of Uzbek migrant workers in Moscow, aims to show how the interaction of the aforesaid actors across borders (via smartphones and the Internet) serve as an enforcement mechanism of the informal migrant labour market in Moscow. In doing so, I show how informality operates across borders, through different means and has an identifiable impact on the outcomes of many practices that Uzbek migrants (and other actors) engage with in Moscow. Thus, I use this case as a lens to pursue broader questions – that is, to offer a transnational framework for the study of informality in the post-Soviet context by drawing upon ideas and concepts developed within the informality literature, migration studies, law and society, and legal pluralism literature.

The rest of the chapter proceeds in the following manner. The next section presents the sociolegal context of the Russian migrant labour market, which is crucial in understanding the nuances of Russian migration governance and the perspective I take on informality. The chapter then provides the theoretical framework of the study by using the concepts of transnational social field, translocal village and the legal pluralism perspective. I then discuss the methodological considerations and present the results of multi-sited transnational ethnographic fieldwork conducted in January–September 2014 in Moscow, Russia and Ferghana, Uzbekistan. Finally, the chapter draws out the implications of the ethnographic material for informality debates and highlights the most important findings of the study.

Sociolegal context of the Russian migrant labour market

Russia, after the United States, is the second largest recipient of migrants worldwide. Currently, approximately 11 million foreign-born people reside in its territory (World Bank 2011). Migrants come to Russia primarily from the post-Soviet Central Asian republics, namely Uzbekistan, Tajikistan and Kyrgyzstan, where labour migration has become the preferred livelihood strategy for many due to deteriorating economic conditions. They typically stay in Russia for one to three years. Moscow and Saint Petersburg are the cities with the largest number of Central Asian migrant workers. Citizens of Uzbekistan, Tajikistan and Kyrgyzstan can visit Russia for up to 90 days without a visa. This means labour migrants from these countries can enter Russia without any visa. However, they are required to obtain residence registration (*registrasiya*) and a work permit (*patent*) within 30 days of their arrival. If migrants obtain these documents within this period, they can stay and work in Russia for up to one year without a visa. Of these documents, the work permit is harder and more costly to obtain, especially after the 2015 legislative changes that considerably increased the fees. Currently, Central Asian migrants must spend at least 22,000 roubles to obtain a work permit, as well as paying a 4,000 rouble monthly fee. In order to obtain a work permit, each migrant must purchase health insurance, provide proof of medical tests for HIV, tuberculosis, drug addiction and skin disease and pass a test on Russian language, history and law. All of these requirements must be fulfilled within a month.

Given that many Central Asian migrants have a poor command of the Russian language, are illiterate about legal procedures for labour migration and come to Russia with little or no money, it is highly unlikely that they would be able to meet all of these requirements within a month. The recent increase in the work permit fees has compelled many Central Asian migrants to work illegally, since they have to choose between working legally and sending money home. They usually end up choosing the latter option. Therefore, most of the migrants have irregular status, for example, lacking migration registration, residential registration or a work permit (see e.g. Ahmadov 2007; Marat 2009; Reeves 2013). A large proportion of these migrants work in the construction sector (Marat 2009), where there is a high demand for cheap and young foreign labour. Therefore, most of the irregular migrants are concentrated in the construction industry, as it is the only place where they are able to find work without documents.

As an antidote to these trends, the Russian authorities are constantly introducing draconian laws and developing border control infrastructure, for example by widening the grounds for issuing re-entry bans to migrants who have violated laws during their previous stay (see e.g. Maier 2014). Even for breaches of administrative regulations (e.g. minor traffic violations, unpaid mobile phone bills) Central Asian migrant workers – who often return home seasonally – are denied re-entry to Russia. On 23 September 2014, the Russian Federal Migration Service (FMS) announced that nearly one million foreigners were banned from re-entry to Russia in 2014 (Bobylov 2015).

However, these control measures have produced unintended consequences: rather than reducing the number of irregular migrants, they have created additional incentives for irregular migration. First, migration laws are just part and parcel of the 'unrule of law' in Russia (Gel'man 2004) which is characterised by the prevalence of informal rules and norms over formal institutions. There is an extensive literature that provides an abundance of evidence on the different dysfunctionalities of the Russian legal system (see e.g. Humphrey and Sneath 2004; Guillory 2013; Ledeneva 2013). Under these circumstances, one possible inference is that the more restrictive the laws are, the higher the rate of bribes that migrants give to police officers, migration officials and border guards in order to continue to work in Russia. Second, migrants are becoming increasingly aware of the fact that they might not be able to re-enter Russia if they return home seasonally. Therefore, irregular migrants are reluctant to return home, preferring to stay and work in Russia for an indefinite period of time. Accordingly, the FMS's 2015 statistics show that nearly three million foreign nationals who are now in Russia have already violated the legal terms of stay (Pochuev 2015). Most of these foreigners are citizens of Uzbekistan (40 per cent) and Tajikistan and Kyrgyzstan (20 per cent) (see e.g. Bobylov 2015).

Using the evidence from international migration literature and legal pluralism scholarship (Menski 1993; Ballard 2006; Shah 2011; Kubal 2013a) as a starting point, it seems reasonable to assume that the existence of millions of irregular migrants have some repercussions for the functioning of formal institutions in Russia, as well as leading to the emergence of informal structures and responses (i.e. a 'parallel legal order') that migrants use in order to cope with the restrictive legal environment, regulate their working life and seek redress for grievances (see e.g. Reeves 2013). It is also reasonable to assume that we need to focus on everyday transnational bonds between sending and receiving societies if we are to better understand the impact of migratory processes on informality and governance trajectories. These arguments thus raise the question of how migrants build relationships with employers in Russia, what strategies and tactics they utilise in order to cope with the risks and uncertainties of informal employment and whether it is possible to glean the patterns of a 'parallel legal order' of the migrant labour market. Another equally important question arising from this perspective is what effect everyday transnational interactions may have on the practices that migrants engage with in Russia. By ethnographically attending to the po rukam experiences of Uzbek migrant workers in Moscow, this chapter intends to address these questions and thereby draw out the implications of the ethnographical material for the informality literature.

Conceptualising 'transnational informality'

As I argued in the previous sections, the Russian legal environment in general, and the sociolegal context of Russian migrant labour market in particular is characterised by the 'unrule of law'. Under these circumstances, it can be assumed that migrants do not deal with the 'rule of law', but rather invent various tactics and strategies to adapt to the existing 'informality environment' in order to 'get things done'. This means migrants may produce various 'legal orders' that provide alternative (to state law) means for regulating their working life and seeking redress for their problems. Such a normative pluralism is referred to as 'legal pluralism' in the legal anthropological scholarship (Merry 1988; Griffiths 2003). Legal pluralism emphasises the coexistence and clash of multiple sets of rules that mould people's social behaviour: the law of the nation state, indigenous customary rules, religious decrees, moral codes and practical norms of social life (Nuijten and Anders 2007). From this point of view, state law is just one among many other normative orders in society. Accordingly, in a place such as Russia, where nearly three million migrants are concentrated in the informal economy, the study of informality should be sensitive to 'legal baggage' that migrants carry to their host country. The 'legal baggage' may contain different values, different attitudes to state law and different patterns of behaviour towards state law and its institutions (Kurkchiyan 2011; Kubal 2013b), which mean that the host country's legal environment may become even more legally plural with the arrival of new legal cultures. Hence, the legal pluralism perspective is instructive in recognising both formal and informal practices and structures stemming from host country's sociolegal context as well as from migrants' 'legal baggage' that they bring to their host country.

However, the legal pluralism perspective has conceptual limitations, as it is confined to the social processes taking place within the boundaries of a particular nation state. Wimmer and Glick Schiller (2002) argue that we need to move away from methodological nationalism and thereby broaden our analytical lens, as migrants are often embedded in multilayered, multisided transnational social fields, involving both those who move and those who stay behind. From this perspective, the concept of the 'transnational social field' (Levitt and Schiller 2004) provides useful tools when trying to conceptualise the potential array of political, economic and social relations linking those who move and those who stay behind. Levitt and Schiller (2004: 1009) define the transnational social field as 'a set of multiple interlocking networks of social relationships through which ideas, practices, and resources are unequally exchanged, organised and transformed … National social fields are those that stay within national boundaries while transnational social fields connect actors through direct and indirect relations across borders'. Hence, individuals within transnational social fields, through their everyday activities and relationships, come into contact with the regulatory powers and institutions of more than one state that determine their access and action and organise and legitimise gender, race and social status. Their daily rhythms and activities are shaped not only by more than one state simultaneously but also by social institutions, norms and pressures, such as norms of neighbourhood communities, networks of reciprocity and exchange, social sanctions (gossips, ostracism), that exist within many states and across their borders (ibid.).

There is another scientific field of importance to this study that investigates how the village-defined moral economy (e.g. traditional modes of trust, obligation, shame and neighbourliness) is extended across borders. The most pertinent literature that comes to mind in this respect is Velayutham and Wise's (2005) notion of a 'translocal village'. Building on Appadurai's work on translocalism (1995), Velayutham and Wise develop the notion of the 'translocal village' to describe a particular form of moral community based around village-scale, place-oriented familial and neighbourly ties that have subsequently expanded across extended space. This concept allows us to visualise the everydayness of material, family, social and symbolic networks and exchanges that connect two different localities (that is, Uzbekistan's Shabboda village to Moscow in this chapter). Hence, the reproduction of the translocal village takes place through the extension of affective regimes of guilt, shame, neighbourliness and obligation. In this connection, this concept has a strong relevance to this chapter as it helps to explain the direct links between a particular village (and its governance structures) and Uzbek migrants' everyday life and practices in Moscow.

Thus, equipped with the concepts of transnational social fields, the translocal village and the legal pluralism perspective, it could be inferred that the study of informal practices and structures cannot be confined to the political and geographical boundaries of a particular nation state and that we also need to focus on the intersection between the practices, exchanges and experiences of those who have migrated and those who have stayed in place. Using this framework allows for a more systematic study of the transnational informal practices that have not been sufficiently addressed by traditional informality scholarship.

Methodological considerations

This chapter is based on eight periods of multi-sited transnational ethnographic fieldwork in January–September 2014 in Moscow, Russia and Fergana, Uzbekistan, as part of a project on migration and legal cultures in post-Soviet societies. The field sites were chosen because Moscow is the city with the largest number of Uzbek migrants, whereas Ferghana is one of the main migrant-sending regions in Uzbekistan because of its population density and high unemployment rate. I had the advantage of knowing the Uzbek and Russian languages. Due to my village background and Uzbek ethnicity, I was well connected to the Uzbek migrant worker community in Moscow. This enabled me to participate in migrants' daily life and thereby become a typical migrant worker.

During these eight field trips, a rich stock of ethnographic material was collected, mainly through observations and informal interviews. For the purpose of this chapter, the ethnographic material was collected in two different settings: Moscow province and Fergana region.

First, I conducted an ethnographic study at a construction site in Solnechnogorsk town, Moscow province, where Uzbek migrant workers live and work. Being in the 'field', I closely followed the everyday life and experiences of Uzbek migrant workers, observing their relationship with migrant middlemen and Russian employers (e.g. Russian middleman, construction firms). These observations gave me first-hand information on (a) how migrants, migrant middleman and Russian employers negotiate and agree on the terms and conditions of informal employment, (b) the strategies and tactics that migrants use to get paid for their work, and (c) the role of 'street actors and laws' (i.e. Chechen racketeers) in mediating financial disputes between migrants and migrant middleman.

Second, simultaneously, keeping up with the pace of developments in the Uzbek migrants' lives in Moscow, I conducted ethnographic fieldwork in the Fergana region, in the village I call Shabboda, where migrants and middleman hail from. My aim was to explore the processes of everyday material, emotional, social, and symbolic exchanges between Shabboda village and Moscow and how these transnational interactions impact the outcomes of practices that Uzbek migrants (and other actors) engage with in Moscow. During the field research, I regularly visited migrants' left-behind families and carried out observations and informal interviews with village residents at 'migration talk hotspots' such as the *guzar* (village meeting space), *choyxona* (teahouse), *gaps* (regular get-togethers) and life-cycle events (e.g. weddings, funerals) where the bulk of village information exchange regarding remittances and migration takes place.

During the field research, I strove for spontaneity and sudden discoveries and therefore went to field sites 'blank', without any pre-designed fieldwork strategy or theoretical understanding. Moreover, I treated migrants as experts on the migration situation in Russia, thereby refraining from bringing in my own perspective. My position in relation to my informants was fluid, sliding between 'insider' and 'outsider' status. I was an 'insider' when relations between migrants, their left-behind families, middleman and Russian employers were smooth, but I became an 'outsider' when conflict arose among the parties. In such circumstances, I approached each actor privately and maintained the confidentiality of information. The informants were asked for their consent to participate in the study. Due to the sensitivity of the data, I have changed the names and whereabouts of all informants and omitted any information that could be dangerous to the relevant individuals.

Uzbek migrants' po rukam experiences in Moscow

In search of empirical clues, on 23 January 2014, I travelled to Moscow, Russia for ethnographic field research. The afternoon flight from Copenhagen to Moscow on Aeroflot took just under three hours. I arrived at Moscow Sheremetyevo airport in the evening. After going through customs and passport control, I walked towards the airport forecourt, where Misha, an Uzbek migrant worker, was waiting for me in his car. As Misha and I hail from the same district in Fergana, Uzbekistan, I was excited to meet my *zemlyak* (fellow countryman) for both personal and academic reasons. Misha welcomed me with a smile; we shook hands and hugged each other, as we had not seen each other for seven years. Afterwards, I put my belongings in the boot, got into the car and we quickly headed to the north-east of Moscow city where my hotel was located.

Sheremetyevo airport is not so far from Moscow city centre; it takes 25–30 minutes to drive to the centre outside the rush hour. But as I arrived in the evening when traffic congestion on the Moscow Ring Road is at its highest, our trip lasted more than two hours. Nonetheless, the traffic jam was a good opportunity for us to hold some catch-up conversation about what had happened since the last time we met. I briefly told Misha about my migration research and asked him if he could help me collect data about Uzbek migrant workers' everyday life and experiences in Moscow. Misha seemed interested in my work and promised that he could put me in touch with migrant workers. Misha is one of the pioneer migrants who brought many of his co-villagers and acquaintances (circa 200 migrants) to Moscow. He arrived in Moscow in 2002 when labour migration was still a new phenomenon in Uzbekistan. He currently works as a posrednik (middleman) in the construction sector, acting as an intermediary between migrant workers and Russian construction firms. The last time I had met Misha, in Moscow in August 2007, he was working as a taxi driver, earning $US500–600 per month. This was where Misha made Russian acquaintances and built up extensive networks that later paved the way for him to become a posrednik in the construction sector – the highest rung on the career ladder that many migrant workers strive to reach. He apparently was very fond of his work and believed that his role as a posrednik was pivotal in the migrant labour market.

I was truly intrigued by Misha's success story and subsequently became interested to know more about his work. I particularly wondered what role and functions the posrednik fulfilled in the migrant labour market, how a posrednik builds relationships with migrant workers and Russian employers and whether there was some form of written (formal) contract that regulates the terms and conditions of working relationships between different parties. When I asked him these questions, he explained that he usually concludes po rukam ('handshake') style agreements with migrant workers, Russian posredniks and construction firms. He also said that his work has nothing to do with the law and bureaucracy; rather he relies on *ko'cha qonunlari* (laws of the street) and *erkakchilik* (literally 'manliness') rules to get things done. Although I had some pre-understanding of the migrant labour market situation in Moscow, the terms and slang Misha used were new to me. Seeing my puzzled face, he quickly noticed my poor knowledge of street life and provided the following account of how things work in the construction industry, particularly focusing on his posrednik role and how he concludes po rukam agreements with migrant workers, Russian posredniks and construction firms:

> The construction industry and the way it works resemble a pyramid. It is wide near the bottom and narrows gradually as it reaches the top. This means you find *zakazchiks* [clients], *genpodryadchiks* [general contractors] and *subpodryadchiks* [sub-contractors] at the top of a construction pyramid and a huge army of migrant workers at the bottom. Migrant workers do all the work but those who are at the pinnacle take almost all the money and leave very little for migrants. We, posredniks, are located in the middle of the pyramid and hence our role is the most delicate and problematic one. Most migrant workers hate us, believing that all posredniks deceive and exploit them; but strangely enough, if any chance arises, all migrants want to be a posrednik.
>
> Let me explain more in detail how this pyramid is built. At the top of the pyramid we have the *zakazchik*, an organisation that receives state funding for the implementation of various construction projects. The *zakazchik* usually concludes an agreement with a *genpodryadchik* for the implementation of construction, installation and design projects. According to the agreement, the *genpodryadchik* is fully responsible for the implementation of construction–installation and design work. However, the *genpodryadchik* is not directly involved in the construction work, as they mainly act as a coordinator and intermediary agent, using several *subpodryadchiks* as assistants for implementing construction work. A *subpodryadchik* is a construction firm [hereafter 'firma'] that is supposed to perform construction, installation and design work by finding and employing skilled builders.
>
> Actually this is where all of the fairy tales about the law end and the real po rukam style work begins. Typically, the firma tries to implement construction projects as cheaply as possible. If the firma employs Russian citizens, it has to pay decent salaries, employment tax and social security contributions. But the cost of the labour force becomes very high if it opts for this option. Therefore, the firma prefers migrant workers to Russian citizens since migrants don't require any papers [work permit and employment contracts] and work much harder and longer even if they get

paid a lot less than Russian citizens. But the *firma* never contacts migrants directly, trying to avoid possible legal problems in case migrants are caught during an *FMS oblava* [raid conducted by the Russian Federal Migration Service]. Instead, the firma usually works via its representative. The representative's main task is to find a posrednik, usually a Russian citizen [hereafter 'Russian posrednik'] who can link the firma with migrant workers. The agreement between the firma representative and the Russian posrednik is reached by shaking hands [po rukam], which means that the firma doesn't have any legally binding relationship with the Russian posrednik.

In turn, the Russian posrednik is expected to find well-skilled migrant construction workers who can perform the tasks in accordance with the standards set by the government. Of course, it is difficult for the Russian posrednik to build workable and trustworthy relationships with migrants given that most migrants' command of the Russian language is poor. Moreover, the Russian posrednik cannot properly coordinate the work process and ensure that the migrants he enters into a relationship with are well skilled in construction work. Therefore, Russian posrednik contacts an Uzbek or Tajik posrednik [hereafter 'migrant posrednik'] with whom he has previously worked. The agreement between the Russian and migrant posredniks is concluded by shaking hands. Many construction projects in Moscow are implemented po rukam style. Legally speaking, nobody is formally employed to perform construction work, but interestingly enough, many construction projects in Moscow are being completed every month, thereby giving the impression that high-rise buildings are growing like trees, without any human involvement.

I am one of those migrant posredniks who enters into po rukam working relationships with Russian posredniks, Generally, as a migrant posrednik, I can fulfil three functions depending on the nature of the *zakaz* (job offers): posrednik, *brigadir* and *prorab*. I may act as a posrednik and provide firmas with skilled migrant workers. In this case I am not involved in any construction work and my main responsibility is to secure a salary for migrant workers. For my posrednik service, I get a dolya (share), which means every migrant gives 10–15 per cent of his salary to me. Sometimes I work as a *prorab*, leading and supervising large group of migrants in construction projects. In such cases, I don't do any physical work and my main task is to control the quality of work. I can also be a *brigadir* if I form a construction team consisting of 10–15 migrants. Unlike the posrednik and *prorab*, the *brigadir* leads the brigada and does physical work like all other migrants in the brigada. The only advantage is that the *brigadir* gets a higher salary than the others due to his leadership role and rich experience in construction work.

Very few posredniks are able to combine all these three functions. I am a universal posrednik. Due to my rich life experience I am not afraid of taking risks and therefore can work in all these three capacities. In order to be a universal posrednik, one must speak Russian fluently, know 'street life', have a lot of Russian acquaintances, build a reliable brigada and be highly skilled in construction work. I arrived in Russia 12 years ago and worked at different places and interacted with both good and bad people. I have extensive connections within the construction sector [e.g. construction firms and Russian posredniks], so they contact me with various *zakaz*. I connect migrant workers with Russian employers, negotiate the terms and conditions of the construction work and serve as a guarantor of the contract to all parties involved.

I have a trustworthy working relationship with a Russian posrednik, who contacts me with many *zakaz,* asking me to form a brigada for the implementation of various construction and installation works. We discuss and agree on the financial terms and conditions of the construction work by assessing its type, duration and magnitude. The Russian posrednik takes responsibility for the salaries and timely provision of materials and equipment needed for construction work. My main role is to find well-skilled migrant construction workers, take full responsibility for the quality of the construction work and address migrants' daily concerns [e.g. accommodation, food] and legal problems [e.g. police problems]. It is not so easy to find well-skilled and reliable migrant construction workers. I have to make sure that the migrants don't steal construction materials and perform their tasks in accordance with state standards. I try to find migrants whom I know and trust, and who follow my instructions. If I approach migrants that do not share a common village or district origin with me, it is unlikely that they would agree to work with me. There have been many *lohatron* ['fraud'] cases in Moscow where posredniks have cheated on migrants and didn't pay their salaries. Therefore I build my construction brigada by inviting my village acquaintances and *mahalla* [local community] friends and neighbours to work for me. It is easier that way instead of having to establish relationships with a new lot of people. My co-villagers don't ask me to provide a written contract. My *erkakcha gap* [literally 'man's word'] is enough for them. Given that many migrants are paperless, po rukam style work is the best option as it allows migrants to work without any documents.

As you see, being a migrant posrednik means taking on lots of obligations. But my work also has advantages. For instance, I don't have to do physical work and my main role is to lead and supervise the brigada so that they do everything properly. I don't take that much money for my service because almost all members of my brigada are my co-villagers and *mahalla* acquaintances. I just take 15 per cent dolya for my work.

This spontaneous conversation with Misha was an excellent introduction to migrants' everyday life in Moscow, which enabled me to obtain my first insights into how Uzbek migrants cope and gain access to the labour market in the restrictive Russian legal environment. In referring to po rukam, Misha was actually talking about the highly informal nature of migrant labour market in Moscow. This was the first time I learned about the informal contract between migrant workers, middleman and Russian construction firms where migrants could get access to the labour market without any work permits and Russian language skills. Hence, po rukam style construction work seemed like a sophisticated and highly efficient system that benefits all the parties involved. However, Misha's story was not fully complete, as he did not talk about the cases where one of the parties (the migrant, Russian posrednik or construction firm) fails to comply with the po rukam contract. Given the highly informal nature of the migrant labour market in Moscow, I wondered how the po rukam contract works in practice and whether there are any regulatory structures in place that can resolve disputes when one of the parties does not fulfil their contractual obligations.

I think Misha's story unconsciously refined many of my initial assumptions about the migrant labour market and generated specific research questions that became the focus of my fieldwork. Even though I had spent just a few hours in Moscow, it felt like I had already immersed myself in the field. In this regard, my interest in po rukam experiences of migrant construction workers was quite a spontaneous process. Misha, having noticed my interest in his work, invited me to visit his workplace in Solnechnogorsk (Moscow province) so that I could acquaint myself with his construction team (hereafter 'brigada'). This invitation was a wonderful opportunity for me to see and experience migrant workers' everyday life, so I accepted it with a great enthusiasm. Before leaving me at the hotel, Misha said that he would pick me up from my hotel tomorrow at 8 a.m. I thanked him and we agreed to meet the next day.

As planned, on the next day, Misha picked me up from my hotel and we headed to Solnechnogorsk. For Misha, it was just a typical working day, but this trip was a very special experience for me. We arrived at the construction site at about 10 a.m., at which time all of the brigada members were working on the 17th floor in spite of the freezing cold weather (the outdoor temperature was −25 degrees Celsius). As the brigada was busy working I tried to do some observation on the construction site and gathered information about brigada members and their living and working conditions. Misha's brigada consists of 12 migrant workers and their main job is to install new windows in mid- and high-rise buildings. On average, the brigada works 10–12 hours per day, without taking any days off. They are allowed to take a day off only in exceptional circumstances, for example if there is a lack of materials (e.g. silicone caulking, nails) needed to complete the window installation. Misha purchases the necessary food items (bread, vegetables, rice, pasta, cooking oil, etc.) and the brigada make meals for themselves. This means every day one migrant, on a rotating basis, is assigned to prepare lunch and dinner for everyone. There is no clear boundary between work and non-work activities in the brigada's everyday life. The same construction site serves as both workplace and accommodation. The brigada's accommodation is located on the fourth floor and consists of two rooms: one narrow, cramped room full of rudimentary bunk beds, with old mattresses, blankets and old clothes used as pillows, and one slightly bigger room for handwashing, cooking and eating facilities that fails to meet even basic hygiene standards. The indoor temperature is around 20 degrees due to the presence of two electric heaters. The brigada has access to an outdoor toilet, but there is no bathroom facility available for their use.

The brigada returned to their room at about 1 p.m. to have lunch. Almost all brigada members have smartphones with access to the Internet. They regularly used Odnoklassniki (a popular social media site in the post-Soviet space) in order to check the latest news, view photos of girls and send instant messages to their left-behind families and friends. Some migrants made phone calls to their family, telling them that they were fine and would send money home as soon as they got their salary. Mansur, today's 'chef on duty' prepared *osh* (a festive Uzbek rice), so all members of the brigada looked satisfied and happy. The *osh* was served in a large bowl and shared by everyone sitting at the table. While eating *osh* they mainly discussed how to avoid errors in installing windows and perform tasks in accordance with state standards. As brigada leader, Misha gave instructions, distributing tasks and telling them to be more industrious. The brigada members attentively and obediently listened to his instructions and orders, treating him as a boss. Some migrants who smoke asked Misha to bring Winston (cigarettes) the following day, while others requested him to top up their mobile phones. One of the migrants asked Misha to send money to his family, as his father needed money for urgent medical treatment. Although Misha had not yet received payment from Stas (the Russian posrednik), he tried to fulfil the requests of his brigada using his personal savings. Misha also tried to meet the bathing needs of the brigada. He said that today he would take three brigada members to his apartment in Moscow city so that they could take a shower and get some rest. As an observer, I felt that Misha was acting not only as a posrednik but also exhibiting paternalistic leadership by treating his brigada in a fatherly manner and providing for their needs on a rotating basis. The roles and relationship between Misha and his brigada seemed well organised and balanced, giving me the impression that a po rukam style contract indeed works.

As I visited the construction site on a daily basis, I was able to develop a close relationship with all members of the brigada. As the brigada members and I hail from the same district, almost all of them knew or had heard about me, which led to my being accepted as *svoi* ('our own') – an 'insider' with whom both work and non-work issues could be shared and discussed. In turn, I also tried to show open-mindedness and briefly told them about my research, introducing myself as a migration researcher writing about Uzbek migrant workers in Russia. Accordingly, my first field trip (23–29 January 2014) helped me establish a close relationship with the migrant communities and enhanced my understanding of Uzbek migrants' everyday working life and experiences in Moscow.

Another research aim that spontaneously emerged in the course of my field research was to explore the processes of everyday material, emotional, social, and symbolic exchanges between Misha's brigada and their left-behind families and communities. My assumption was that technological developments would produce simultaneity of events and instantaneous interactions between migrant sending and receiving societies, possibly leading to the emergence of transnational ties and networks. As all brigada members used smartphones and social media, I inferred that there must be a daily exchange of information between the brigada and their sending community. I was particularly interested to investigate whether it is possible to glean the patterns of transnationalism in the case of Misha's brigada and their left-behind families and communities, and if so, how these transnational interactions impact the outcomes of practices that Misha and his brigada (and other actors) engage with in Moscow.

Armed with these research questions, I travelled to the Fergana region, Uzbekistan for two weeks of fieldwork during 31 January–15 February 2014. Shabboda, where the families of Misha and his brigada live, is a village in the Fergana region, consisting of 28 *mahalla*, and has a population of more than 18,000 people. The income-generating activities of the village residents are made up of multiple sources, ranging from cucumber and grape production, remittances, raising livestock for sale as beef and informal trade, to construction work, daily manual labour (*mardikorchilik*), fruit-picking jobs and brokerage. However, remittances sent from Russia constitute the main source of income for many households. Likewise, migration is a widespread livelihood strategy, simply a 'norm' for young and able-bodied men in Shabboda village. We mainly see elderly people, women and children on the streets of the village during the 'migration season'. Wherever I went and whomever I talked with, the central topic of conversation was migration and remittances. Most village residents had sons or close relatives working in Russian cities, predominantly in Moscow. Accordingly, they seemed well informed about the living and working conditions of migrants in Russia. This was largely due to technological developments that had reduced the importance of distance and created an everyday information exchange between Shabboda village and Moscow. Shabboda, in this sense, was a truly 'translocal village', as everyday material, family and social exchanges directly connected it to Moscow.

Misha and his brigada's Moscow adventures were the centre of 'village talk'. Given that Misha provided many village residents with jobs in Moscow, his family members enjoyed high social status and prestige in the village. Therefore, when invited to weddings, Misha's father was always offered a 'best table' and served more quickly than others. Misha was especially praised by the parents of his brigada for employing and taking care of their sons. However, not all villagers shared this view. Some of the residents I encountered said that Misha's posrednik work was not compatible with the principles of Islam as he took dolya from migrants' salaries without doing any physical work. Some even believed that Misha 'eats a lot' and covertly steals from his co-villagers. Despite these negative views, most village residents I encountered expressed positive views about Misha.

After a two-month break, I returned to Moscow for follow-up fieldwork during 5–15 April 2014. Like the last time, I visited Misha's brigada in Solnechnogorsk on a regular basis. But this time things were different. Although the brigada had already completed half of the window installation work, they had not been paid for their work since January. I also learned that two migrants had already quit the brigada due to payment delays and that other members were also considering leaving. On the whole, the brigada's daily conversation primarily revolved around the questions of why they were experiencing payment problems and what measures they could take in order to get paid for their work. At the same time, they were under strong pressure to send money home, because their left-behind families were dependent on remittances to meet their basic needs. Misha's situation was especially delicate because he had actually failed to secure the migrants' salaries. But he insisted that he was also a *musofir* (alien) in Russia just like everyone else, and blamed Stas and the firma representative for the payment problems. The brigada seemed to feel empathy towards Misha and did not hold him responsible for the payment delays.

Despite being present on the construction site on a daily basis, Stas kept avoiding any possible contact with brigada members, completely refusing to discuss financial issues with them. He often stated that he had made an agreement with Misha, not with the brigada, so he discussed all matters only with him. This situation eventually led to hostility and frustration, as brigada members felt ignored and voiceless even though they did all the hard work. As a result, the brigada questioned Stas's honesty and discussed several options for how to retaliate if they did not receive the promised salary. Several migrants suggested that they should either break all of the installed windows or steal construction materials. Others suggested that they should do physical or material harm to Stas, for instance by burning his car or punishing him physically. However, given his personal responsibility for the brigada's actions, Misha asked the brigada to be more patient and refrain from taking any collective measures; otherwise, their salary and safety would be at stake. In Misha's view, the only realistic solution would be to continue to work with Stas, given the fact that the brigada members were working without any legal work permits. Even if they worked legally and filed a complaint with the Russian Federal Migration Service or court, the migrants' chances of success was near zero, since Stas and the firma could easily win the case by paying a bribe to the state officials. Misha believed that migrants are nobody in Russia and thereby warned the brigada that they might easily end up in prison if they caused material or physical damage to Stas. Fearing the consequences of their plans, the brigada obeyed Misha and decided not to take any retaliation measures against Stas. However, the brigada were reluctant to do any further work, demanding that Stas paid at least one-third of their salary. As a brigada leader, Misha had to keep things going and convinced the brigada that he would secure their salary by the end of April if they completed the window installation work. The brigada continued to work in April, believing that Misha would keep his word.

Thus, the situation in the brigada was developing in completely different ways from what I observed during my first fieldwork. Feelings of helplessness and anger were clearly visible in the brigada's daily conversation. Despite the payment delays, most brigada members seemed to trust and accept Misha's leadership. However, two brigada members did not trust Misha and decided to quit the brigada. These events signalled that something serious was under way or taking place in the brigada that I was probably unaware of due to my 'outsider' status. In this regard, I looked to the left-behind families and communities of the brigada as an alternative source of information.

To further understand the situation, I travelled to Fergana for more field research between 27 April and 21 May 2014. After arriving in Shabboda village, I visited Misha's and the brigada's families in order to find out what was actually happening in the brigada's life. The first thing I noticed was that the brigada's Moscow disputes and problems were gradually moving to the village. Family members were well informed about the latest developments in Moscow. From my conversations, I found that Misha had failed to live up to his promises and could not secure the brigada's salary by the end of April. These developments eventually led to the brigada splitting and subsequently, a dispute arose between Misha and the brigada over money. At the same time, the brigada's family members started to put pressure on Misha's family and demanded that either Misha or his parents must take responsibility for their sons' salaries. However, Misha's parents refused to take any responsibility, arguing that the dispute should be discussed and resolved in Moscow, where it was taking place, not in the village. In mid May, I learned that Misha had made a new promise that he would get money from the Russians by the end of June, and thereafter all of the brigada members would get paid for their work. Their family members decided to wait one more month, hoping that Misha would keep his word this time. Subsequently, dispute halted and remained muted in the village. Most people I met at the village's 'migration talk' sites, e.g. the *guzar* (village meeting space), *choyxona* (teahouse) and weddings, were still unaware of these developments.

When I returned to Moscow in the summer of 2014 (29 July–6 August 2014), I learned that the brigada had totally split and the migrants were working in different places. Most of them had found new jobs at a construction site in Balashikha city (Moscow province), while others were working at the bazaar or meat warehouse. Misha no longer had employees and was working alone, doing *haltura* (daily window installation work) for individual (private) persons. Misha and the brigada members were in open confrontation, as Misha had again failed to fulfil his promise. Since the brigada worked informally, they were aware of the fact that they could not resort to legal measures to address their grievances. However, not wanting to lose their money, the brigada instead approached a group of Chechen protection racketeers, asking them to recover their money from Misha and, offering 20 per cent of the total sum of the money as a payment for their protection service. I have discovered that Chechen racketeers were known as the *qozi* ('judges') among Central Asian migrants, providing an alternative (to the state) justice and dispute settlement through threats and violence. However, the brigada's appeal to the racketeers was futile, as Misha had stronger connections at the OMON, the Special Purpose Mobility Unit of the Russian Police. When I asked Misha about the details of the incident, he passionately talked about his triumph over the Chechens:

> I tried to explain to the brigada why payment was delayed, but they didn't want to understand me. Things are simply beyond my control. Even though we are all co-villagers, they didn't show any mercy and shamelessly used Chechen racketeers against me. I was willing to pay them but after what they did to me they wouldn't get anything from me. This incident happened in mid July. They called me demanding that I must pay their salary immediately. I told the brigada that I would give them money as soon as I get payment from Stas. Afterwards, the tone of the conversation suddenly changed and they started to threaten me saying that they would give me to the Chechen racketeers. Many migrants get terrified when they hear the word Chechen, because Chechens are violent and rule street life in Moscow. So the brigada thought that I would be also scared to death and surrender immediately.
>
> Seemingly, the brigada underestimated me. I have been living in Moscow since 2002, so I have also lots of powerful connections on the street. I told the brigada that they can give me to any Chechen racketeer. At the same time, I informed them that if they used racketeers against me, we, all sides, must abide by the 'laws of the street'. According to the street laws, if the brigada decide to use Chechen racketeers as *qozi* [judge], they must fully waive their claims against me, because they are transferring the case to the racketeers. In other words, they quit the game automatically. In that case, I owe money to the Chechen racketeers, not to the brigada. This means the brigada demands money from the Chechens, as they take full responsibility for recovering the money from me. If the Chechens don't succeed, the brigada lose all the money and I no longer owe anything to the brigada. Hence, I told the brigada that they must be men and abide by the street rules if they use racketeers. They accepted these conditions and we agreed that our relationship ended here.
>
> A few days later, the Chechen racketeers contacted me by phone. We agreed to meet for a *razborka* [violent showdown] in Moscow's Bibirevo district on 17 July 2014 at around 10 p.m. During the phone conversation they told me that I owed them 800,000 Russian roubles and that I must bring this amount to the *razborka*; otherwise, they warned me that my life would be in danger. But I answered them that they wouldn't get even a single rouble from me and that they could do with me whatever they

want. I knew that the *razborka* would be violent as I refused to pay. Therefore, I contacted my friends who work at the OMON, requesting them to protect me during the *razborka*. They are always eager to protect me, because I thank them with *ko'ki* [Uzbek metaphor for US dollars].

As agreed, I arrived at the meeting point at 10 p.m., of course, together with my five Russian friends. Not wanting to be identified as police officers, my friends didn't wear their uniform, so they all looked like typical street guys. As I expected, the Chechens were 25 minutes late. At around 10.30 p.m., seven Chechens arrived. However, after seeing that I was accompanied by five tall Russians, they didn't dare to approach me. Without saying a single word, they quickly returned to their car and drove away in an unknown direction. Since then, I have never seen or heard them.

Misha looked psychologically strong and criticised the brigada members for their unfair and greedy behaviour. Referring to the street laws, he believed that he was no longer obliged to pay the brigada. Thus, for Misha, this was the end of the dispute.

During this fieldwork, I invited all 12 brigada members for dinner at an Uzbek cafe in order to see 'the other side of the coin'. From my conversation with them, I learned that they were still determined to continue 'the battle'. While acknowledging Misha's victory 'on the street', they still insisted that Misha must pay the brigada's salary, regardless of the circumstances. In particular, Baha openly expressed his views and said:

> Of course, we lost the game according to the laws of the street. But this doesn't absolve Misha from responsibilities. His actions are not compatible with religious norms. According to Islam, it is harom [sinful] to steal someone's money. It is also harom to take dolya from someone's salary. We worked hard even during the cold winter months and fulfilled our work duties, while Misha gave us orders and did not do any physical work. We agreed that he would take at least 15 per cent dolya from our salaries, so his main task was to guarantee that we receive money on time. So if he can't get money from Stas or the firma, this is his personal problem, not ours. We shook hands with him, not with the Russians. We don't care whether he pays our salary from his own pocket or gets it from the Russians. He is constantly blaming the Russians, but we don't want to hear anything about his private deals with the Russians. The only thing we care is our po rukam agreement with Misha.

Bek, the youngest member of the brigada, argued that almost all Russian people are honest and never cheat migrants (*O'ris aldamaydi*). He believed that Misha was just using Stas as an excuse to steal their money. On the other hand, Nodir, another migrant, was of the opinion that Misha and Stas were accomplices and were 'staging the show together' to fool the brigada. While observing their conversation, I noticed that they were considering various options to recover their money from him. When I asked what measures they were most likely to take, they replied that they were going to spread gossip about Misha in the village, hoping that it would force him and his family to pay their salary.

Accordingly, shortly after the Moscow field research, I travelled to Fergana (7 August–2 September 2014) in order to follow the latest developments in the village. From my observations there it became apparent that the dispute was again moving to Shabboda village. Brigada members were constantly calling their families in the village, asking them to put more pressure on Misha's family by spreading gossip at *guzar, choyxona* and weddings where people gather and conduct the bulk of village information exchange. When I visited these social spaces, I observed that most village residents already possessed information about how 'Misha exploited and "ate" his fellow villagers' money'. Most residents were of the opinion that Misha was supposed to secure the brigada's salary irrespective of the circumstances, since the brigada trusted him and worked hard during the cold winter. They argued that a person must never assume this role if he cannot keep his word. Some villagers even accused Misha of human trafficking and exploitation, which is a criminal act according to Uzbek legislation. Moreover, the villagers held Misha responsible for the brigada's legal problems, since the migrants did not have money to get work permits due to the payment delays and therefore were banned from re-entering Russia for five years. The villagers also referred to religious norms to interpret Misha's actions, saying that it was not acceptable to take dolya from someone's salary in Islam. In this way, Misha was seen as a bad Muslim who earns money through harom means.

The relationship between the families of Misha and the brigada was especially problematic. The brigada's families regularly visited Misha's house and made scandal on the street, telling all the neighbours about the money conflict. They also spread gossip at wedding ceremonies where the majority of villagers gather. Moreover, the *oqsoqol* (community leader) and *imom* (leader of the mosque) interfered and warned Misha's parents that the details of the dispute would be made public during the Friday prayers at mosque if Misha refused to pay his fellow villagers' salaries. The brigada's families were also considering using legal measures as a last resort if the situation persisted:

> We are currently spreading gossip about Misha in the village. We hope this strategy will give some result. If Misha's parents continue to ignore us, we will contact Uzbek law enforcement bodies, for example, *uchast-kovoy* [local police], *prokuratura* [public prosecutor] or SNB [National Security Service]. But we are not rushing to take that measure. Misha is our neighbour and we don't want to ruin his life. So we want to give him one more chance before officially reporting him to the law enforcement bodies.

Misha's family was thus under huge village pressure. Most villagers began to look at them as bad Muslims who do not hesitate to eat harom food. From my observations I noticed that life was no longer endurable for Misha's family, as they had to face daily hints and sarcastic remarks on the village streets. Misha's father's situation was particularly bad. Because of the widespread gossip and rumours about his son, he could no longer attend village *guzar* and weddings where most people socialise. When I asked Misha's father how he was going to solve this problem, he replied that he would call Misha these days and ask him to pay his debts immediately. Thus, the village pressure was slowly changing the course of developments.

Immediately after Fergana fieldwork, I headed to Moscow (2–30 September 2014) to find out whether village events were having any impact on Misha and the brigada's actions in Moscow. As I expected, Misha was well informed about the latest village news. He was very frustrated and angry at the brigada, but at the same he was pragmatic and knew that he needed to do something to settle the dispute once and for all, otherwise his family would continue to suffer from village pressure. When I asked him how he was going to settle it, he said that he had already borrowed money from his friends and that he would pay the brigada's salary within a few days. After a few days, I invited all of the brigada members for lunch at an Uzbek cafe located in Moscow's Babushkinskaya district. From our conversation, I learned that Misha had indeed paid them, so all of them looked satisfied. Hence, the extension of village-level affective regimes of guilt, shame and gossips across borders proved to be an enforcement mechanism that determined the outcome of a dispute. Although Misha was able to stand against the Chechen racketeers, village pressure eventually turned out to be his 'Achilles heel' that forced him to pay the brigada's salaries from his own pocket.

Discussion and concluding remarks

The dispute that arose between Misha and his brigada reveals something about the nature of the migrant labour market in Moscow, which, to a large extent is informal but has well-functioning regulatory mechanisms. As shown in the previous section, there are a myriad of structures, both formal and informal, that negotiate and regulate the 'rules of the game' in the migrant labour market across borders (e.g. construction firms, Russian and migrant middlemen, Chechen racketeers, Russian police officers, migrants' left-behind families, village residents, *imom* and *oqsoqol*, and (symbolically) Uzbek law enforcement bodies). Hence, the Russian migrant labour market is governed by plural legal orders that interact across borders simultaneously.

The ethnographic data contributes additional empirical evidence to the informality literature, particularly that concerned with the post-Soviet context, that the lack of formal rules does not necessarily mean that there are no rules. Hence, informality grows and establishes itself as a governance tool in areas where the state cannot or does not want to rule, thereby leaving room for citizens' initiatives (Polese *et al*. 2014; Davies and Polese 2015). My data also confirms the findings of Williams and Round (2011) that 'the informal' never exists in a vacuum but in a constant, reiterative relationship with 'the formal'. In this sense, it can be stated that the informality I observed in the Russian migrant labour market does not qualitatively differ from the mainstream accounts of the shadow or second economy that we find in the scholarly literature about post-Soviet societies (see e.g. Ledeneva 1998; Humphrey 2002; Williams and Round 2011; Morris and Polese 2013, 2015). However, my research differs in one aspect from the previous research by adding the 'transnational' perspective to the study of informality. As argued in the previous sections, most accounts of 'post-Soviet informality' tend to confine the unit of analysis to social processes taking place within the boundaries of a particular nation state. However, an investigation of the Uzbek migrant workers' po rukam experiences takes us beyond conventional understandings of informality into the subject of 'transnational informality' and the plural legal orders that operate beyond nation states.

I have argued that the informal practices in post-Soviet societies are becoming transnational in light of migratory processes and therefore we need to move away from methodological nationalism and broaden our analytical lens to include everyday transnational bonds when analysing informal processes. As my findings indicate, due to the inability or unwillingness of the Russian authorities to regulate the migrant labour market, another parallel legal order has emerged as a governance tool. In other words, when informal structures within the boundaries of a particular nation state cannot provide functional regulation, this vacuum may be filled by informal structures located in another country. Hence, the case study of Uzbek migrant workers' po rukam experiences demonstrates the existence of 'transnational informality' that serves as a regulatory mechanism of informal labour in Moscow's construction sector. Hence, drawing on the concepts of transnational social fields, the translocal village and legal pluralism, this study suggests that there is a need to rethink the concept of informality so that it is no longer automatically equated with the boundaries of a single nation state.

Note on transliteration

Throughout the chapter, Russian and Uzbek words are spelled according the standard literary form. They are used based on the following two criteria: (1) whether a Russian/Uzbek word or phenomenon is central to the study; (2) if an English translation does not fully capture the meaning of the Russian/Uzbek word or phenomenon. Russian and Uzbek words are presented in italics. The principal exceptions are po rukam, posrednik, brigada, firma, harom and dolya, since these words are frequently used or have a central place in the chapter.

Acknowledgements and funding

I would like to acknowledge the University of Helsinki's Aleksanteri Institute, the Finnish Centre for Russian and East European Studies, for hosting me as a visiting researcher, which led to the completion of this chapter.

This research is funded by the Swedish Research Council (Vetenskapsrådet) under the International Postdoc Programme.

References

Ahmadov, E. 2007. 'Fighting illegal labour migration in Uzbekistan', *Central Asia-Caucasus Institute*. Retrieved 30 July 2013 from http://old.cacianalyst.org/?q=node/4681.

Alexeev, M. and W. Pyle. 2003. 'A Note on measuring the unofficial economy in the former Soviet republics', *Economics of Transition*, 11(1): 153–175.

Aliyev, H. 2015a. 'Institutional transformation and informality in Azerbaijan and Georgia', in J. Morris and A. Polese (eds), *Informal Economies in Post-Socialist Spaces*. London: Palgrave Macmillan, pp. 51–69.

Aliyev, H. 2015b. 'Post-Soviet informality: Towards theory-building', *International Journal of Sociology and Social Policy*, 35(3/4): 182–198.

Appadurai, A. 1995. 'The production of locality', in R. Fardon (ed.) *Counterworks: Managing the Diversity of Knowledge*. London: Routledge, pp. 204–225.

Ballard, R. 2006. 'Ethnic diversity and the delivery of justice: The challenge of plurality', in P. Shah and W. Menski (eds), *Migrations, Diasporas and Legal Systems in Europe*. London: Routledge-Cavendish, pp. 29–56.

Bobylov, S. 2015. 'Glava FMS: Pochti 1 mln Inostrantsev Zakryt V"ezd v Rossiyu', TACC. Retrieved 22 September 2015 from http://tass.ru/obschestvo/1460698.

Cieslewska, A. 2013. 'From shuttle trader to businesswomen: The informal bazaar economy in Kyrgyzstan', in J. Morris and A. Polese (eds), *The Informal Post-Socialist Economy: Embedded Practices and Livelihoods*. London and New York: Routledge, pp. 121–134.

Collins, K. 2006. *Clan Politics and Regime Transition in Central Asia*. Cambridge: Cambridge University Press.

Davies, T. and A. Polese. 2015. 'Informality and survival in Ukraine's nuclear landscape: Living with the risks of Chernobyl', *Journal of Eurasian Studies*, 6(1): 34–45.

Gel'man, V. 2004. 'The unrule of law in the making: The politics of informal institution building in Russia', *Europe-Asia Studies*, 56(7): 1021–1040.

Griffiths, J. 2003. 'The social working of legal rules', *The Journal of Legal Pluralism and Unofficial Law*, 35(48): 1–84.

Guillory, S. 2013. 'Corruption, not migrants, is Russia's problem', *The Nation*, 20 August. Retrieved 15 January 2016 from www.thenation.com/article/corruption-not-migrants-russias-problem.

Hale, H. E. 2011. 'Formal constitutions in informal politics: Institutions and democratization in post-Soviet Eurasia', *World Politics*, 63(04): 581–617.

Hayoz, N. 2015. 'Cultures of informality and networks of power in post-Soviet non-democracies', in R. Beunen, K. V. Assche and M. Duineveld (eds), *Evolutionary Governance Theory*. Cham: Springer, pp. 73–85.

Humphrey, C. 2002. *The Unmaking of Soviet Life: Everyday Economies after Socialism*. Ithaca, NY: Cornell University Press.

Humphrey, C. and D. Sneath. 2004. 'Shanghaied by the bureaucracy: Bribery and post-Soviet officialdom in Russia and Mongolia', in I. Pardo (ed.), *Between Morality and the Law: Corruption, Anthropology, and Comparative Society*. Aldershot: Ashgate, pp. 85–99.

Kubal, A. 2013a. *Socio-Legal Integration: Polish Post-2004 EU Enlargement Migrants in the United Kingdom*. Aldershot: Ashgate.

Kubal, A. 2013b. 'Migrants' relationship with law in the host country: Exploring the role of legal culture', *Journal of Intercultural Studies*, 34(1): 55–72.

Kurkchiyan, M. 2000. 'The transformation of second economy into the informal economy', in A. Ledeneva and M. Kurkchiyan (eds), *Economic Crime in Russia*. London: Kluwer Law International, pp. 83–97.

Kurkchiyan, M. 2011. 'Perceptions of law and social order: A cross-national comparison of collective legal consciousness', *Wisconsin International Law Journal*, 29(1): 366–392.

Ledeneva, A. 1998. *Russia's Economy of Favors: 'Blat', Networking and Informal Exchange*. Cambridge: Cambridge University Press.

Ledeneva, A. 2013. *Can Russia Modernise? Sistema, Power Networks and Informal Governance*. Cambridge: Cambridge University Press.

Levitt, P. and N. G. Schiller. 2004. 'Conceptualizing simultaneity: A transnational social field perspective on society', *International Migration Review*, 38(3): 1002–1039.

Maier, A. 2014. *Tajik Migrants with Re-entry Bans to the Russian Federation*. Dushanbe, Tajikistan: International Organization for Migration, No. ENG0285.

Marat, E. 2009. *Labor Migration in Central Asia: Implications of the Global Economic Crisis*. Stockholm: Silk Road Studies Programme, Institute for Security and Development Policy.

Menski, W. F. 1993. 'Asians in Britain and the question of adaptation to a new legal order: Asian laws in Britain?' in M. Israel and N. Wagle (eds), *Ethnicity, Identity, Migration: The South Asian Context*. Toronto: University of Toronto Press, pp. 238–268.

Merry, S. E. 1988. 'Legal pluralism', *Law and Society Review*, 22(5): 869–896.

Misztal, B. 2002. *Informality: Social Theory and Contemporary Practice*. London: Routledge.

Morris, J. and A. Polese. 2013. *The Informal Post-Socialist Economy: Embedded Practices and Livelihoods*. London and New York: Routledge.

Morris, J. and A. Polese. 2014. 'Informal health and education sector payments in Russian and Ukrainian cities: Structuring welfare from below', *European Urban and Regional Studies*.

Morris, J. and A. Polese. 2015. *Informal Economies in Post-Socialist Spaces: Practices, Institutions and Networks*. New York: Palgrave Macmillan.

Nuijten, M. and G. Anders. 2007. *Corruption and the Secret of Law: A Legal Anthropological Perspective*. Farnham: Ashgate.

Pochuev, M. 2015. 'Law imposing 10-year entry ban on violators of sojourn procedures comes into force', *TASS*. Retrieved 22 September 2015 from: http://tass.ru/en/russia/770591.

Polese, A. 2008. '"If I receive it, it is a gift; if I demand it, then it is a bribe": On the local meaning of economic transactions in post-Soviet Ukraine', *Anthropology in Action*, 15(3): 47–60.

Polese, A. 2015. 'Informality crusades: Why informal practices are stigmatized, fought and allowed in different contexts according to an apparently ununderstadable logic', *Caucasus Social Science Review*, 2(1): 1–26.

Polese, A., J. Morris, B. Kovács and I. Harboe. 2014. '"Welfare states" and social policies in Eastern Europe and the former USSR: Where informality fits in?', *Journal of Contemporary European Studies*, 22(2): 184–198.

Reeves, M. 2013. 'Clean fake: Authenticating documents and persons in migrant Moscow', *American Ethnologist*, 40(3): 508–524.

Rodgers, P. and C. C. Williams. 2009. 'The informal economy in the Former Soviet Union and in Central and Eastern Europe', *International Journal of Sociology*, 39 (2): 3–11.

Round, J., C. C. Williams and P. Rodgers. 2008. 'Everyday tactics and spaces of power: The role of informal economies in post-Soviet Ukraine', *Social and Cultural Geography*, 9(2): 171–185.

Shah, P. 2011. 'When South Asians marry trans-jurisdictionally: Some reflections on immigration cases by an "expert"', in L. Holden (ed.), *Cultural Expertise and Litigation. Patterns, Conflicts, Narratives*. Abingdon: Routledge, pp. 35–52.

Smith, A. and A. Stenning. 2006. 'Beyond household economies: Articulations and spaces of economic practice in postsocialism', *Progress in Human Geography*, 30(2): 190–213.

Turaeva, R. 2014. 'Mobile entrepreneurs in post-Soviet Central Asia', *Communist and Post-Communist Studies*, 47(1): 105–114.

Urinboyev, R. 2013. *Living Law and Political Stability in Post-Soviet Central Asia. A Case Study of the Ferghana Valley in Uzbekistan*. Lund: Media-Tryck.

Urinboyev, R. 2014. 'Is there an Islamic public administration legacy in post-Soviet Central Asia? An ethnographic study of everyday Mahalla life in rural Ferghana, Uzbekistan', *Administrative Culture*, 15(2): 35–57.

Urinboyev, R. and M. Svensson. 2013a. 'Living law, legal pluralism, and corruption in post-Soviet Uzbekistan', *Journal of Legal Pluralism and Unofficial Law*, 45(3): 372–390.

Urinboyev, R. and M. Svensson. 2013b. 'Corruption in a culture of money: Understanding social norms in post-Soviet Uzbekistan', in M. Baier (ed.) *Social and Legal Norms*. Farnham: Ashgate, pp. 267–284.

Velayutham, S. and A. Wise. 2005. 'Moral economies of a translocal village: Obligation and shame among South Indian transnational migrants', *Global Networks*, 5(1): 27–47.

Wallace, C. and R. Latcheva. 2006. 'Economic transformation outside the law: Corruption, trust in public institutions and the informal economy in transition countries of Central and Eastern Europe', *Europe-Asia Studies*, 58(1): 81–102.

Werner, C. A. 2000. 'Gifts, bribes, and development in post-Soviet Kazakstan', *Human Organization*, 59(1): 11–22.

Williams, C. C. and J. Round. 2011. 'Beyond competing theories of the hidden economy', *Journal of Economic Studies*, 38(2): 171–185.

Williams, C. C., J. Round and P. Rodgers. 2013. *The Role of Informal Economies in the Post-Soviet World: The End of Transition?* Abingdon: Routledge.

Wimmer, A. and N. Glick Schiller. 2002. 'Methodological nationalism and beyond: Nation-state building, migration and the social sciences', *Global Networks*, 2(4): 301–334.

World Bank. 2011. *Migration and Remittances Factbook*. Washington, DC: World Bank.

Yalcin-Heckmann, L. 2013. 'Informal economy writ large and small: From Azerbaijani herb traders to Moscow shop owners', in J. Morris and A. Polese (eds), *The Informal Post-Socialist Economy: Embedded Practices and Livelihoods*. London and New York: Routledge, pp. 165–185.

6 Between exploitation and expulsion

Labour migration, shadow economy and organised crime

Yuliya Zabyelina

Introduction

Research on migration from less developed to developing countries, so-called South–South migration (SSM), as opposed to South–North migration (SNM) or migration from developing to developed countries, emerged in the literature in the early 2000s, immediately attracting considerable scholarly and policy attention. SSM is larger than SNM (Hujo and Piper 2010; World Bank 2011) and bears several unique features. First, SSM allows for a relatively high mobility of migrants across national borders due to weak border control regimes and poor governance structures in developing countries. SSM is also poorly documented and is often described as irregular migration (Hujo and Piper 2010). Second, SSM is generally less skilled (De Lombaerde *et al.* 2014). Third, whereas South–North migrants may eventually apply for residency, attain citizenship and receive vocational training or advanced education, South–South migrants rarely have access to such privileges and are more likely either to stay temporarily and return home upon termination of their contract or seek employment in the shadow economy. The presence of a shadow economy is another characteristic feature of SSM. It is often the outcome of an incoherent economic policy, low societal integration of migrants, corruption and widespread hostility towards migrants.

The Russian Federation, together with India and South Africa, are the largest receiving countries of SSM (Dilip and Shaw 2007). In fact, Russia is the world's second most frequent destination country for migration after the United States, with 12.3 million migrants present in the country as of 2010 (World Bank 2011). Because of visa-free agreements between the Russian Federation and most post-Soviet states, citizens of countries such as Ukraine, Uzbekistan, Tajikistan and Moldova can enter Russia without restrictions. Importantly, the governments of some Central Asian republics, for example Tajikistan and Kyrgyzstan, have in fact encouraged their citizens to seek work in Russia or elsewhere – a move intended to alleviate political and social tensions at home. In Tajikistan, as some scholars have suggested, the 'social responsibility of the state was basically transferred to labour migrants' (Di Bartolomeo *et al.* 2014: 21).

DOI: 10.4324/9781315657424-6

The majority of migrants from Central Asia are temporary labour migrants, *gastarbeiter*, [1] who generally come to Russia legally under the visa-free regime. Those who are not able to obtain work authorisation, however, often stay in the country illegally. Therefore, a distinctive feature of Russia's economic system is a large and continuous presence of a shadow economy predicated upon cheap and legally unprotected labour. Although employment in the shadow economy may be a short-term solution for labour migrants, in the long term, their participation in the shadow economy on such a massive scale may be fraught with serious negative consequences: labour migrants who work without any legal protection or social guarantees often fall prey to manipulative middlemen, exploitative employers, bribe-seeking public officials and abusive criminal organisations.

The goal of this chapter is to study the marginalisation and exploitation of irregular migrants under the conditions of a shadow economy. Based on a review of existing literature, analysis of official data, court files and news media (in Russian and English), the chapter offers a qualitative analysis of the nexus between Russia's shadow economy and irregular migration, with a focus on criminal conspiracies, such as forced labour, corruption and drug trafficking.

The chapter is divided into four parts. The first part describes the development of migration policy in the Russian Federation and its impact on the formation of a shadow economy largely predicated on foreign labour. The second part examines the coping strategies of irregular migrants and discusses the role of ethnic communities that provide basic public services unavailable to irregular migrants from formal institutions. The third part focuses on the ways in which the shadow economy has produced a diversified set of jobs, forcing irregular migrants into low-paid, insecure and exploitative arrangements. The last part offers an overview of how public officials, law enforcement and migration officers, and members of criminal organisations have victimised irregular migrants, and how irregular migrants get involved in drug trafficking.

Although this analysis is not exhaustive, it helps to support the overarching argument of the chapter that migrant labour in a shadow economy in Russia has led to the formation of a criminogenic environment conducive to the expansion and sophistication of criminal activities, but worst of all, to the structured exploitation of irregular migrants. The embeddedness of the migrant workforce in the shadow economy in Russia has therefore amplified the magnitude of the victimisation of labour immigrants, who are often unable to report crimes committed against them because of widespread corruption and fear of deportation.

Migration policy and the shadow economy

The origins of the current migration policy in the Russian Federation go back to the early 1990s when the Federation Migration Service (FMS) was created in 1992 with the task of managing the arrival of refugees and return of ethnic

Russians from other post-Soviet countries. Despite the adoption of several migration control laws, e.g. the laws On Refugees (1993) and On Forced Migrants (1995), and the Concept of the State Migration Policy of the Russian Federation (1996), very limited control over the influx of labour migrants was established, largely due to institutional failures, lack of funding and expertise in migration management and large-scale corruption (Nozhenko 2010).

After Vladimir Putin took presidential office, after a two-year abolishment the FMS was re-established in 2004. Although the agency lost its independent status and was integrated into the Ministry of Internal Affairs (MVD), it was mandated to manage citizen registration and enforce migration policy. During this period, migration became increasingly 'securitised', whereby tight immigration control gradually became the dominant theme in migration management. Over the next several years, immigration remained a security issue, while immigrants were increasingly perceived by the general public as potential criminals. The mandate of the FMS was expanded beyond the tasks of implementing the state policy on migration and included law enforcement functions of the control and supervision of migration. For example, Law No. 115-FZ On the Legal Status of Foreign Citizens on the Territory of the Russian Federation, adopted in 2002, introduced bureaucratic barriers that complicated the registration process for irregular migrants. A quota system for foreign workers led to a growth in corruption and the expansion of irregular employment (Nozhenko 2010). Consequently, the red tape, along with corruption, put more pressure on irregular migrants and forced them into the shadow economy. According to Russian experts, in 2009 the proportion of irregular labour migrants increased to 61 per cent compared to 53 per cent in 2008 (Mukomel' 2011: 45). In addition, in 2006, the Russian president signed the decree On the Measures to Aiding Voluntary Return of Compatriots Living abroad to the Russian Federation, aimed to encourage the voluntary repatriation of ethnic Russians by granting them citizenship and employment. This law considerably reduced the chances of labour migrants of other ethnicities finding formal employment.

In the late 2000s, the Russian government made several attempts to liberalise foreign labour migration but did not receive much public support because of the popular dislike of non-Slavic migrants and a surge in ethnic violence (Judah 2013; Schenk 2010). The most recent such attempt, the Concept of the Russian Federation State Policy on Migration 2012–25, focuses on skilled labour and aims to stimulate the resettlement of low-qualified immigrants back to their countries of origin or elsewhere. It establishes new categories of labour immigrants – e.g. managers, farmers, students, entrepreneurs and persons with significant achievements in science or art – and introduces harsher penalties for violating the rules of entry and stay in the Russian Federation. In addition to fluency in Russian and familiarity with Russian history, it also introduces mandatory requirements for labour migrants, such as possession of medical certificates and patents.[2]

The high costs of patents and the difficulty of complying with educational and linguistic requirements will preclude irregular migrants from leaving the shadow economy (Myhre 2014). Moreover, should the Russian government decide to curtail the shadow economy and deport irregular migrants, especially from Central Asian republics, to the backdrop of a sharp currency devaluation in 2015 as well as western sanctions and low oil prices, this decision may not only impact Russia's economic development but also jeopardise national security. According to some sources, more stringent requirements for migrant workers and tightening immigration controls have caused not so much the outflow of migrants back to their home countries but their recruitment by terrorist organisations ('Russia's big fear ...' 2015). The majority of Tajiks fighting for ISIS in Syria, for instance, have allegedly been recruited while working as labour migrants in Moscow (Turovsky 2015).

Is informal 'normal'? The role of migrant communities in the shadow economy

Scholars who have studied public perceptions of irregular migration in Russia have emphasised the prevalence of xenophobic and pejorative attitudes towards migration (Dolotkeldieva 2013; Schenk 2010). The negative image of migrants is often reinforced by biased portrayals by the mass media that have contributed to animosity, fear and distrust. Due to cultural, linguistic and religious differences between immigrants and the host country population, many labour migrants arriving in Russia keep a low profile and avoid interactions with state institutions. The underdevelopment of a formal migrant infrastructure – 'public and non-public service institutions which ensure that migrants are legal, informed, and safe, at different stages of migration' – also contributes to the alienation of irregular migrants, because their social integration becomes their own responsibility (Iontsev and Ivakhnyuk 2013: 8).

Moscow's urban mosaic, for instance, has morphed into a series of self-segregated, low-income, ethnic (mainly non-Slavic) migrant enclaves that form a distinctive but low-profile social order. These irregular migrant communities thus secure for themselves access to basic public goods, such as employment, healthcare, housing, education and individual security. As a result, ethnic enclaves develop a sophisticated parallel infrastructure (i.e. markets, ethnic cuisine cafes, snack bars, travel offices, entertainment facilities, clinics). According to Sokolov (2013), this enables irregular migrants to live, earn an income and establish a certain level of adaptation in the host environment. This infrastructure also cushions the shock of resettlement to a new country, secures uninterrupted residence and steady access to jobs and facilitates the protracted establishment of a large irregular population as well as the continuity of new arrivals. Relying on this informal migration infrastructure, irregular migrants are able to devise specific survival strategies and develop intra-group solidarity, organise recruitment and build up a system for the supply and distribution of the community's resources.

Job placement for migrant workforce is often arranged via this informal migrant infrastructure: migrants do not usually deal directly with the employer but have an intermediary: '[s]ometimes workers are passed between several intermediaries before "reaching" the employer ... There is no regulation to determine the legitimacy of the employer, and his/her name is seldom mentioned' (Tyuryukanova 2005: 44). Ryazantsev (2014: 53) suggests that 'the quota system for documents allowing foreigners to work in Russia for migrants and employers is non-transparent and time-consuming, and this creates a shadow labour market ... and quota-trading through middlemen'. In this way, a unique feature of migration in the Russian Federation is the presence of an underground industry run by private managers of migration. They provide migration and employment services, ranging from the preparation of documents needed for an extended legal stay to registrations, work and residence permits and passports.

Migrant enclaves have a fixed spatial location adjacent to public areas that are partially or fully beyond official oversight. These unregulated public spaces vary in size from small designated areas serving as a meeting point for migrants (e.g. metro stations, cafes) to large permanent bazaars. For instance, for several years after the break-up of the Soviet Union, the Cherkizovsky wholesale market was Europe's largest outdoor bazaar, occupying nearly 300 hectares in the Izmaylovo district of Moscow, near the Cherkizovskaya metro station. Informal employment and 'under the table', 'off the books' and 'cash-exclusive' practices were common and typical of Cherkizovsky. In its heyday, Cherkizovsky was known as 'a city within a city' because of its underground labyrinths which provided employment to over 50,000 immigrants who worked in illegal workshops (Zabyelina 2012).

Cherkizovsky, however, could not have survived for so long without the 'protection' of the law enforcement agencies or the state agencies responsible for issuing migration-related documents. From its inception, a tacit agreement of non-interference between the law enforcement and Cherkizovsky's wholesale traders, supported by a mutually reinforcing kickback scheme, made any attempts to shut down the market unsuccessful. The substantial revenues generated by the market and its contribution to the Russian economy may also explain the authorities' unwillingness to close it. After three attempts since 1999, Cherkizovsky was officially shut down only in June 2009, over numerous sanitary violations and illegal activities[3] (Zabyelina 2012).

Surprisingly, many illegal migrants appear to be content with the status quo achieved from informal migrant infrastructures, despite their vulnerability to exploitative schemes. The embeddedness of labour migration in the shadow economy promotes a business model that depends on a constant circulation of foreign labourers who are underpaid, insecure and ready to tolerate the unfair conditions. The shadow economy thus plays an important but equally ambiguous role in Russia: on the one hand, it provides jobs to irregular migrants and helps them survive economic hardship; on the other, it facilitates a fundamentally asymmetrical power relationship between foreign labourers and their employers.

Irregular migrants and trafficking economies

Labour exploitation

Despite the visa-free migratory regime for visitors from most post-Soviet countries, labour migrants are often unable to obtain legal employment. Because immigrants can only stay in the country for 90 days and are required to obtain employment authorisation paperwork in Russia,[4] irregular migrants seek employment in the shadow economy, where exploitative labour conditions are common (e.g. withholding of documents, non-payment for services provided, physical and psychological abuse, extremely poor living conditions).

One of the earliest systematic studies on labour exploitation of immigrants in Russia was conducted by the International Labour Organization Special Action Programme to Combat Forced Labour, launched in 2003. This study found that elements of forced labour could be observed for 10 to 30 per cent of migrants (Tyuryukanova 2005). '[O]nly 9% of labour migrants in Russia were never confronted with any form of coercion like debt bondage, involuntary work, limited freedom of movement, and so on' (Tiurukanova 2006: 55). Experts have noted that 'almost all victims of forced labour do not believe in the authorities' ability to assist them and show little interest in bringing their exploiters to justice' (Tiurukanova 2006: 55).

Having interviewed 146 migrants who had previously worked or were still working in the construction industry in 49 cities or towns in Russia, Human Rights Watch (HRW) revealed the exploitation and abuse of labour migrants by employers, employment agencies and other intermediaries, whereby they are forced to 'work excessively long hours, threatened and physically abused them, and provided substandard on-site living conditions and unsafe working conditions' ('Are you ...?' 2009: 1). HRW also raised concerns about abuse linked to the preparations for the 2014 Olympic Games in Sochi, citing migrant workers' complaints' about employers failing to provide contracts or promised wages, as well as cases of police detention on false charges of those who tried to report victimisation ('World Report ...' 2014).

Ryazantsev's (2014) study (carried out for the Task Force against Trafficking in Human Beings of the Council of the Baltic Sea States and the Ministry of Foreign Affairs of the Russian Federation) also reported cases of labour exploitation and violation of labour employment rights in Russia. Specifically, it discussed the most common abusive practices such as reliance on oral agreements, unregulated duration of shifts and working hours, confiscation of employee's documents and as a 'dual' record-keeping system used not only for tax evasion but also to pay lower wages to migrant workers.

Revenues generated by forced labour attract a range of stakeholders, including corrupt law enforcement and FSM officers. The complicity of public officials in labour exploitation is one of the reasons why addressing this crime is difficult. According to Russian sources ('V Astrakhanskoi …' 2008), there have been criminal cases involving Russian officials allegedly facilitating victims' recruitment for forced labour (often via kidnapping), providing protection to exploiters and helping them avoid penalties for engaging illegal workers. In one such case, it was established by a city court of Akhtubinsk, Astrakhan Oblast, that Magomed Vasaitov ran an organised criminal group whose members were convicted and sentenced under CCRF Art. 127: Illegal Deprivation of a Person's Liberty, which is not Related to his Abduction, CCRF Art. 33: Complicity in a Crime and CCRF Art. 286: Exceeding Official Power. One of the group members, Sergei Kakalia, a local policeman, and his collaborator inspection officer at the railway station, Marsa Musagaliyev, seized the passports and migration cards of ten Tajik and Uzbek citizens, took them into police custody and demanded money for the return of their passports. When the detainees refused to pay, the conspirators sold the victims to Vasaitov's men, who delivered them to local farms to work as agricultural labourers (ibid.).

Initially, labour exploitation was primarily domestic, whereby lucre-seeking entrepreneurs took advantage of immigrants, especially newly arrived ones, who hardly spoke any Russian and were not familiar with Russia's laws. In recent years, however, there has been a gradual shift towards the internationalisation of trafficking. This trend has become more pronounced with the tightening of migration policy and stricter deportation rules. For example, one of the largest cases of human smuggling and forced labour involved an international organised crime syndicate that arranged the trafficking of foreign citizens, who were forced to work in 'ghost' sweatshops – factories that did not officially exist but employ migrant labourers without registration. In July 2013, two businessmen and their domestic and foreign accomplices, an official of the FMS and two suburban Moscow police officers, were arrested. They were accused under CCRF Art. 127.2 of organising the illegal entry of foreign citizens, primarily nationals of Vietnam, to Russia and forcing them to labour at an illegal garment factory in Moscow. Twenty underground workshops hosted 800 Vietnamese illegal immigrants who produced counterfeit clothing of various brands (US Department of State 2014; 'V Moskve …' 2014). A dormitory for illegal workers was located on the premises of a sports complex, Izmailovo, located in the immediate proximity of the infamous Cherkizovsky market.

The police are often involved in illegal practices through not only accepting bribes from migrants but actively seeking them with threats. Tyuryukanova (2005: 59) points out that '[m]igrants employed in the informal sector, are effectively defenceless in the case of racketeering, in which the police itself often plays a role'. Abusive practices particularly victimise members of ethnic minorities. According to a 2003 statement by Svetlana Gannushkina, a human rights defender of the NGOs Memorial and Grazhdanskoe Sodeistvie and a contender for the 2010 Nobel Peace Prize, prepared for the Office of the

High Commissioner on Human Rights, the main agents of the persecution of migrants are various units of the MVD that use false accusations and fabricated criminal evidence, e.g. police planting drugs, ammunition or explosives, against immigrants (Danish Immigration Service 2015). Unfair treatment by the police directed towards the Chechen communities in Russia, for instance, was common in the aftermath of the Russian military campaign in Chechnya and terrorist attacks in Moscow attributed to Chechen terrorist organisations. In the aftermath of the explosion in a Moscow theatre in 2002 by a group of armed Chechens it was very difficult for Chechens to receive temporary registration in Moscow, despite the fact that many of those who sought it were internally displaced persons entitled to benefits in accordance with this status (Light 2010). Since the late 2000s, however, malfeasance by the police against migrant workers from Central Asia has gained prominence. In 2012, there was a series of arrests of members of the transport police from the Moscow Domodedovo and Vnukovo airports. The investigation alleged that airport officials engaged in the systematic extortion of unofficial payments for the right to leave the airport from citizens of Uzbekistan and Tajikistan (Vzglyadov 2012).

With regards to police malfeasance, Light (2010) suggests that the Moscow city authorities tolerate extra-legal means of coercion because the latter can be instrumental to the city's actual ability to control migration. Although such practices may boost the authorities' capacity to react to migrant flows timely and effectively, such abusive police practices keep the migrant workforce in a state of constant fear and insecurity, promote the social exclusion of migrants and create important barriers for them to access essential social services. Such an approach may also increase social tensions, lead to the alienation of migrant groups and intensify their distrust of state institutions and the police in particular.

Drug trafficking

Confronted with labour exploitation in a shadow economy and with limited opportunities for legal employment and protection, irregular migrants become more vulnerable to recruitment by drug trafficking groups, which paradoxically not only poses a threat but also serves as a means of survival. Little is known about the ways in which criminal organisations intersect with irregular migrants. This section examines the under-studied intersection of labour migration from Central Asia to Russia and drug trafficking activities.

The Russian Federation is a major consumer market for illicit opiates, mainly heroin, flowing northwards from Afghanistan via Central Asia (UNODC 2014: 27). Russia's susceptibility to the drug trade increased with the opening of its borders in the 1990s, the collapse of economies in neighbouring countries and the rise of regional conflicts such as the civil war in Tajikistan (1992–1997). Central Asian governments' inability to stimulate economic development and provide sufficient public goods, as well as their geographical proximity to Afghanistan, created several powerful push factors for an impoverished rural population to seek income from drug trafficking activities (Marat 2006; Paoli *et al.* 2007). In 2009, up to 90 tons of Afghan heroin were trafficked into Central Asian republics with 75–80 tons destined for the Russian Federation (UNODC 2011: 44). Despite some decline in opiate trafficking in the following years (UNODC 2014), the so-called Northern Route running mainly through Tajikistan and Kyrgyzstan still remains the main heroin trafficking gateway to Russia, Kazakhstan and Eastern Europe.

High commercial traffic along the Northern Route serves as an impediment to the efficiency of law enforcement in disrupting drug trafficking flows. In particular, the abolition of customs along with the introduction of simplified procedures for shipments and cross-border trade established by the Eurasian Customs Union (EACU) agreement between Russia, Belarus and Kazakhstan signed in 2010 has not resolved drug trafficking-related problems for Russia, but has created a strong need for more law enforcement cooperation among EACU countries, especially Russia and Kazakhstan (Glazkova 2014).

In addition to the high commercial load and the endurance of the visa-free regime (Glazkova 2014) the Northern Route is also profitable for traffickers because of the high intensity of cross-border movements of people, mainly labour migrants. A study by the International Organization of Migration (IOM 2006: 42) specified that '[i]n the core of the organizational structure of smuggling of migrants through Central Asia lies a network formed by people making profit on other people's eagerness to find jobs and better life beyond the boundaries of their home countries. Sometimes such networks develop links with organised criminal groups and serve to also support drug smuggling and trafficking in persons'. Shuttling between their home country and Russia, where many of them work on seasonal constructs, labour migrants are attractive targets for drug trafficking organisations that have exploited impoverishment and economic decay in Central Asia to recruit drug mules – couriers transporting drugs. While many labour migrants refuse to act on those criminal opportunities, the poorest and most vulnerable are often forced to take the risks, as they find themselves caught up in financial strain and facing pressure from ethnic and clan ties (Golunov *et al.* 2008: 63).

Until recently, men have dominated drug trafficking from Central Asia. MVD officials (MVD 2008) have, however, stressed that government crackdowns on male visitors and labour migrants from Central Asian republics have increased involvement in drug trafficking by women, who attracted very little law enforcement attention in the past. As law enforcement officials encountered a series of drug seizures from female drug couriers in the late 2000s, they became more alert to the possibility of the involvement of women in this crime ('Legendarnaya …' 2008). This trend is not exclusive to Russia, but reflects the global dynamics of drug trafficking such as the situation that has become prominent in Mexico, where women have acquired leadership positions in drug trafficking cartels (Carey 2014).

Beyond recruiting women, drug traffickers also reduce the risk of apprehension by recruiting drug couriers willing to carry narcotics in their body cavities, usually the gastrointestinal tract. Small quantities of narcotics are packed into latex products (e.g. the fingers of latex gloves, condoms) that drug couriers swallow and later retrieve from their excrement upon arrival. This group of drug couriers is known in the Russian law enforcement jargon as *verbliudy* (Russian 'camels'). Identifying them via a routine customs check is very difficult. If the airport does not have high-sensitivity X-Ray equipment, drug couriers may only be detected when a drug package ruptures and they have to be examined by medical staff. In 90 per cent of cases of damage to at least one package, the outcome is lethal ('Legendarnaya ...' 2008).

Smuggling drugs from Central Asia in body cavities has been prominent since the mid 2000s. Moscow Domodedovo airport has particularly attracted a large influx of drug mules from Tajikistan: from 2009 to 2013, 392 criminal cases were filed with an average of around seven criminal cases per month or one to two arrests per week (Sotnikova 2013). According to the Head of Department of the Anti-Drug Customs Unit at Domodedovo Airport, heroin smuggled by drug mules has a higher quality and enhanced purity. It is more concentrated than heroin offered by street dealers: 0.5 kg of this concentrated heroin makes 3–5 kg of ready-to-use substance.

Although labour migrants recruited by traffickers are on the lowest rung in a drug trafficking organisation, they are indispensable for distributing the illegal product on the street, because informal markets are a common conduit for drug retailing. For example, the drug trade was a pervasive problem at the already discussed Cherkizovsky market. Its large size, underground pavilions, the presence of private security units hired by informal entrepreneurs and the overall environment of chaos and lawlessness made the detainment of drug trafficking networks challenging for the FSKN (Zabyelina 2012). Evidence also suggests that the shadow economy and underground migrant infrastructure allow drug traffickers to effectively conceal their activities within migrant communities. Addressing a more recent trend in drug trafficking, FSKN's Head, Viktor Ivanov, pointed out that when the wholesale trade in vegetables and fruits had been completely monopolised by the migrant community, this industry became prone to criminal interference, as narcotic drugs were repeatedly found in loads of fruits and vegetables and stored at warehouses (Glazkova 2014).

Although questions about the extent to which labour migrants are involved in drug trafficking remain unanswered, the FMS states that, '[i]llegal migration and illegal labor by migrants have a negative impact on various aspects of society and state. They pose a threat to national security of the country and contribute to growing shadow economy and corruption, and increase social tensions. Illegal migrants are recruited by ethnic gangs specialised in drug trafficking' and other criminal activities ('Doklad o ...' 2013). Poor migration control has been often seen as the main factor hampering the fight against drug trafficking in Russia. Therefore, the FMS was mandated by the

Russian government to engage in the realisation of Combating Drug Trafficking projects, in collaboration with the FSKN, Ministry of Economic Development, Ministry of Health and other agencies. The FMS became responsible for managing a fingerprint identification system and database. The biometric databank is expected not only to facilitate the identification and registration of foreign citizens but also to ensure the suppression of illegal production and trafficking through more efficient control over migration ('Doklad o …' 2012).

In contrast to the official position, scholars (e.g. Golunov *et al.* 2008) have warned about unreported intra-group victimisation and the possibility that irregular immigrants are forced into drug trafficking and that the pattern is similar to human trafficking: the debt incurred by the migrant is so great that they cannot resist demands from their debtor to engage in illicit activity. Marat (2006: 105) writes, 'the drug trade provides incentives for the illegal trafficking in people. Young men and women from impoverished areas are forced to smuggle and retail heroin and opiates into Russia and the Baltic states'. Thus, it may be erroneous to associate the drug trade with labour migrants who are fearful of mandatory deportation and detention, ineligibility for lawful residency, loss of asylum or inability to get it, temporary or permanent bars to citizenship and stiff federal sentences from attempts at unauthorised re-entry. The little existing information on labour migrants precludes any conclusive interpretation of the nexus between the migrant workforce and drug trafficking.

Conclusion

Migration in Russia is closely intertwined with the shadow economy. On the one hand, it generates immense and fast revenues, thus making any decisive political action against informal economic practices very unlikely. It provides irregular migrants with employment without work authorisation and makes it possible for them to receive assistance from and socialise in migrant communities. These communities are hidden from the public gaze because of an often prevalent public dislike for migrants and even direct persecution by radical organisations. Irregular migrants who fall out of informal communities often have to pay protection money to powerful persons (middlemen, public officials, criminal gangs, etc.) in order to find employment and avoid arrest and deportation. On the other hand, transactions in the shadow economy undermine the Russian government's ability to effectively control migratory flows, secure the full modernisation of labour in compliance with international standards, collect taxes and respond to corruption and drug trafficking. Informal employment makes the risks of the exploitation and abuse of labour migrants more pronounced and distances them from the institutions and organisations where they could seek assistance and legal protection. Such a situation fertilises the ground for the recruitment of deprived individuals by organised crime groups and terrorist organisations.

To resolve this impasse, policymakers need to recognise that the shadow economy is fundamentally linked to the welfare of many poor individuals who rely on it for a living. Policymakers who shape the migration and labour markets in Russia must therefore take into account the implications of migrant workforce exploitation and the development of larger security and criminal justice threats, such as drug trafficking.

Although amendments to Law No. 115-FZ On the Legal Status of Foreign Nationals in the Russian Federation include several provisions that tighten employers' responsibility for violations of labour legislation and legislation on labour protection, progress has to be made in promoting efforts to support victims. It is essential that state and non-state strategies be developed towards irregular migrants' legalisation and social inclusion, and assistance and compensation to victims of abuse and trafficking-like practices. The Russian government should also develop stringent guidelines for law enforcement and public officials to ensure protection guarantees for victims of human trafficking so that they are not subjected to secondary victimisation while in the custody of the police or when detained in deportation centres.

Finally, the authorities should work on earning migrant communities' trust and support. Interventions should also be made at the social micro-level aimed at generating positive attitudes towards immigrants. The authorities should focus on raising public oversight over crimes committed against immigrants and encourage the reporting of these crimes to the relevant state agencies.

Notes

1 Although 'labour migrant' is the official term used to refer to guest workers in the Russian Federation, it is common in Russian sociopolitical discourse to use the German word *Gastarbeiter* (Russian: *gastarbaitery*).
2 This rule applies to visa-free foreigners who enter Russia to work for legal entities and individual entrepreneurs. The monthly price for a patent in 2014 was 4,000 roubles.
3 Large labour rights violations in Cherkizovsky in relation to Vietnamese citizens were recorded before the market's closure. In December 2008, an underground factory producing textile goods, where more than 800 illegal migrants from Vietnam worked and lived, was shut down.
4 Before January 2014, when an amendment of Art. 5 of Law No. 115-FZ On the Legal Status of Foreign Nationals in the Russian Federation entered into force, setting out the new rules for foreign citizens who do not require a visa to enter Russia. Before this change, migrants who were authorised to stay in the Russian Federation for 90 days and habitually travelled to the nearest border in order to re-enter Russia for another 90 days, could no longer exceed a stay of 90 days without additional paperwork, such as a patent, an authorisation, a residence or work permit, etc. The amended law clearly specifies that the duration of temporary stay in the Russian Federation of a foreign citizen, who is not required to hold a visa, may not exceed 90 days in total per 180 days, except for cases stipulated by this Federal Law. Those who violate this provision are denied entry to the Russian Federation for three years.

References

'Are you happy to cheat us? Exploitation of migrant construction workers in Russia'. 2009. Human Rights Watch. Retrieved 9 November 2015 from www.hrw.org/sites/default/files/reports/russia0209web_0.pdf.

Bommes, M. and G. Sciortino. 2011. 'In lieu of a conclusion: Steps towards a conceptual framework for the study of irregular migration', in M. Bommes and G. Sciortino (eds), *Foggy Social Structures: Irregular Migration, European Labour Markets and the Welfare State*. Amsterdam: Amsterdam University Press, pp. 213–229.

Campana, P. and F. Varese. 2015. 'Exploitation in human trafficking and smuggling', *European Journal of Criminal Policy Research*, online. DOI 10.1007/s10610-015-9286-6.

Carey, E. 2014. *Women Drug Traffickers: Mules, Bosses, and Organized Crime*. Albuquerque: University of New Mexico Press.

Chawrylo, K. 2012. *A New Concept of Migration Policy in Russia*. Warsaw: Centre for Eastern Studies. Retrieved 16 November 2015 from www.osw.waw.pl/en/publikacje/a nalyses/2012-06-20/a-new-concept-migration-policy-russia.

Cvajner, M. and G. Sciortino. 2010. 'Theorizing irregular migration: The control of spatial mobility in differentiated societies', *European Journal of Social Theory* 13(3): 389–404.

Danish Immigration Service. 2015. 'Security and human rights in Chechnya and the situation of Chechens in the Russian Federation – residence registration, racism and false accusations'. Retrieved 13 December 2015 from www.nyidanmark.dk/NR/rdonlyres/662FD8CA-B89C-438C-B532-591500571951/0/ChechnyaFactfindingreport26012015FI NALinklforside.pdf.

Decker, S. H. and M. T. Chapman. 2008. *Drug Smugglers on Drug Smuggling: Lessons from the Inside*. Philadelphia, PA: Temple University Press.

De Lombaerde, P., Guo, F. and H. P. Neto. 2014. 'Introduction to the Special Collection', *International Migration Review* 48(1): 103–112.

Di Bartolomeo, A., S. Makaryan and A. Weinar. 2014. *Regional Migration Report: Russia and Central Asia*. Florence: European University Institute.

Dilip. R. and W. Shaw. 2007. *South–South Migration and Remittances*. Washington, DC: International Bank for Reconstruction and Development. Retrieved 4 December 2015 from http://siteresources.worldbank.org/INTPROSPECTS/Resources/334934-1110315015165/SouthSouthMigrationandRemittances.pdf.

'Doklad o rezul'tatakh i osnovnykh napravleniyakh deyatel'nosti Federal'noi migratsionnoi sluzhby na 2012 god i planovyi period 2013 i 2015 godov' (Report on the achievements of the main activities of the Federal Migration Service in 2012 and the planning period of 2013 and 2015). 2012. Federal'naya Migratsionnaya Sluzhba. Retrieved 13 December 2015 from http://92.fms.gov.ru/about/statistics/pla ns/details/59631/2.

'Doklad o rezul'tatakh i osnovnykh napravleniyakh deyatel'nosti Federal'noi migratsionnoi sluzhby na 2013 god i planovyi period 2014 i 2016 godov' (Report on the achievements of the main activities of the Federal Migration Service in 2013 and the planning period of 2014 and 2016). 2013. *Federal'naya Migratsionnaya Sluzhba*. Retrieved 13 December 2015 from www.fms.gov.ru/document/5832.

Dolotkeldieva, A. 2013. 'Kyrgyz migrants in Moscow: Public policies, migratory strategies, and associative networks', in M. Laruelle (ed.), *Migration and Social Upheaval as the Face of Globalization in Central Asia*. Boston: BRILL, pp. 187–211.

Gallagher, A. T. 2009. 'Human rights and human trafficking: Quagmire or firm ground? A response to James Hathaway', *Virginian Journal of International Law*, 50(1): 789–848.

Glazkova, L. 2014. 'Interv'yu V. P. Ivanova zhurnalu "Rossiiskaya Federatsiya segodnya' (V.P. Ivanov's Interview in *Russian Federation Today* (in Russian). *FSKN* 15 January. Retrieved 10 November 2015 from http://fsknmsk.ru/official/ivanov/intervyu-v.p.-iva nova-zhurnalu-%C2%ABrossijskaya-federacziya-segodnya%C2%BB.html.

Golunov, S., V. Stashin, S. Kozhirova, G. Olekh and L. Reshetnikova. 2008. 'Drug trafficking along the Russian-Kazakh Border', in R. Orttung and A. Latta (eds), *Russia's Battle with Crime, Corruption and Terrorism*. New York: Routledge, pp. 52–76.

Hujo, K. and N. Piper. 2010. *South–South Migration: Implications for Social Policy and Development*. New York: Palgrave Macmillan.

IOM. 2006. *Baseline Research on Smuggling of Migrants in, from, and through Central Asia*. IOM Technical Cooperation Centre for Europe and Central Asia. Vienna: IOM International Organization for Migration.

Iontsev, V. and I. Ivakhnyuk. 2013. *Migrant Integration Models in Modern Russia*, CARIM-East Research Report 2013/13. Robert Schuman Centre for Advanced Studies, European University Institute.

Judah, B. 2013. 'Russia's Migration Crisis', *Survival* 55(6): 123–131.

Karydis, V. 1998. 'Criminality or criminalization of migrants in Greece? An attempt at synthesis', in V. Ruggiero, N. South and I. Taylor (eds), *The New European Criminology: Crime and Social Order in Europe*. London: Routledge, pp. 350–368.

Laruelle, M. 2013. 'Kazakhstan: Central Asia's new migration crossroads', in M. Laruelle (ed.), *Migration and Social Upheaval as the Face of Globalization in Central Asia*. Boston, MA: BRILL, pp. 87–108.

'Legendarnaya sluzhba otmetit yubilei' [The legendary agency celebrates anniversary]. 2008. Ministry of Internal Affairs of the Russian Federation, 2 October. Retrieved 15 December 2015 from https://mvd.ru/news/item/191455.

Liebert, S. 2009. *Irregular Migration from the Former Soviet Union to the United States*. New York: Routledge.

Light, M. 2010. 'Policing migration in Soviet and post-Soviet Moscow', *Post-Soviet Affairs*, 26(4): 275–313.

Marat, E. 2006. 'Impact of drug trade and organized crime on state functioning in Kyrgyzstan and Tajikistan', *China and Eurasia Forum Quarterly* 4(1): 93–111.

Mukomel', V.I. 2011. 'Integration of migrants: Challenges, policies, social practices' [in Russian], *Mir Rossii* 20(1): 34–50.

Myhre, M. H. 2014. *Labour Migration from Central Asia to Russia: State Management of Migration*. NOBR Report, Norwegian Institute for Urban and Regional Research. Retrieved 9 December 2015 from www.nibr.no/filer/2014-5.pdf.

Nozhenko, M. 2010. *Russian Federation: Country Profile #20*. Focus Migration. Hamburg Institute of International Economics (HWWI). Retrieved 3 December 2015 from http://focus-migration.hwwi.de/Russian-Federation.6337.0.html?&L=1.

'Official Statistics for 2015'. 2015. Federal Migration Service of Russia. Retrieved 6 December 2015 from www.fms.gov.ru/about/statistics/data/details/174173.

Paoli, L., I. Rabkov, V. Greenfield and P. Reuter. 2007. 'Tajikistan: The rise of a narco-state', *Journal of Drug Issues* 37(4): 951–980.

'Russia's big fear: Migrant workers become ISIS militants'. 2015. Russia Direct. Retrieved on 7 December 2015 from www.russia-direct.org/analysis/russias-big-fear-migrant-workers-become-isis-militants.

Ryazantsev, S. 2014. *Trafficking in Human Beings for Labour Exploitation and Irregular Labour Migration in the Russian Federation: Forms, Trends and Countermeasures.* Moscow/Stockholm: Council of the Baltic Sea States Secretariat. Retrieved 1 December 2015 from www.cbss.org/wp-content/uploads/2012/11/russian_eng_REPORT_PDF.pdf.

Salt, J. 2000. 'Trafficking and human smuggling: A European perspective', *International Migration* 38(3): 31–56.

Schenk, C. 2010. 'Open borders, closed minds: Russia's changing migration policies: Liberalization or xenophobia?' *Demokratizatsiya* 18(2): 101–121.

Sokolov, D. 2013. 'Criminological analysis of organization of illegal migration', PhD dissertation. Moscow: Academy of the Prosecutor General's Office of the Russian Federation.

Sotnikova, A. 2013. 'Interv'yu s nachal'nikom otdela po bor'be s kontrabandoi narkotikov Domodedovskoi tamozhni' [interview with Yuriy Cherkashin, Head of Anti-Drug Trafficking Customs Unit at Domodedovo Airport]. RBK, 27 August. Retrieved 11 December 2015 from www.rbc.ru/viewpoint/27/08/2013/871887.shtml.

Tiurukanova, E. V. 2006. *Human Trafficking in the Russian Federation: Inventory and Analysis of the Current Situation and Responses.* Moscow: United Nations. Retrieved 7 December 2015 from www.unicef.org/ceecis/Unicef_EnglishBook%281%29.pdf.

Turovsky, D. 2015. 'How Isis is recruiting migrant workers in Moscow to join the fighting in Syria', *The Guardian*, 5 May. Retrieved on 7 December 2015 from www.theguardian.com/world/2015/may/05/isis-russia-syria-islamic-extremism.

Tyuryukanova, E. V. 2005. *Forced Labour in the Russian Federation Today: Irregular Migration and Trafficking in Human Beings.* Geneva: International Labour Office. Retrieved 7 December 2015 from www.ilo.org/wcmsp5/groups/public/—ed_norm/—declaration/documents/publication/wcms_081997.pdf.

Tyuryukanova, E. V. 2008. 'Illegal, trafficked, enslaved? Irregular migration and trafficking in persons in Russia', in M. D. Ulusoy (ed.) *Political Violence, Organized Crimes, Terrorism, and Youth.* Amsterdam: IOS Press, pp. 104–133.

UNODC. 2010. *The Globalization of Crime*: A *Transnational Organized Crime Threat Assessment.* Vienna: United Nations Office on Drugs and Crime.

UNODC. 2011. *The Global Afghan Opium Trade: A Threat Assessment.* Vienna: United Nations Office on Drugs and Crime.

UNODC. 2014. *World Drug Report 2014.* Vienna: United Nations Office on Drugs and Crime.

US Department of State. 2014. *Trafficking in Persons Report 2014.* Washington, DC: United States Department of State. Retrieved 13 December 2015 from www.state.gov/documents/organization/226848.pdf.

'V Moskve uchastnikam prestupnogo soobshestva, obvinyaemym v ispol'zovanii rabskogo truda, vynesen obvinitel'nyi prigovor' [Members of an Organised Crime Group Sentenced for Forced Labour]. 2014. Ministry of Internal Affairs of the Russian Federation, 24 April. Retrieved 15 December 2015 from https://mvd.ru/news/item/3374208.

'V Astrakhanskoi oblasti osuzhdeny militsionery, torgovavshie lyud'mi' [Astrakhan policemen sentenced for human trafficking]. 2008. *Vesti* 1 August. Retrieved 12 December 2015 from www.vesti.ru/doc.html?id=198260&cid=17.

Vzglyadov, A. 2012. 'Pravookhraniteli vymogali v aeroportakh den'gi u uletayuschikh na rodinu gastarbaiterov' [Airport law enforcement officers extorted money from departing migrant workers]. *Kommersant*, 29 August. Retrieved 14 December 2015 from www.kommersant.ru/doc/2010343.

World Bank. 2011. *Migration and Remittances Factbook 2011*. Second Edition. Washington, DC: International Bank for Reconstruction and Development. Retrieved 5 December 2015 from http://siteresources.worldbank.org/INTLAC/Resources/Factbook2011-Ebook.pdf.

'World Report 2014: Russia'. Human Rights Watch. Retrieved 13 December 2015 from www.hrw.org/world-report/2014/country-chapters/russia.

Zabyelina, Y. 2012. 'Costs and benefits of informal economy: Shuttle trade and crime at Cherkizovsky Market', *Global Crime*, 13(2): 95–108.

7 Religion and the integration of migrants

Kaarina Aitamurto

Introduction

The discussion about the integration of migrants in Russia began relatively late, and it was only a few years ago that the first steps in creating concrete policies were implemented. In public discussions, as well as in policy documents, the emphasis is usually on the cultural integration of migrants, while their economic, social and political engagement is omitted. In conclusion, social problems, including the fact that many migrants are compelled to function in the domain of the shadow economy, are explained in terms of their cultural illiteracy rather than structural reasons (Shnirel'man 2008). The construction of cultural otherness is more often made in the framework of religiosity, Islam in particular. This tendency is not unique to Russia; a similar religionisation of migrants and the migration issue had already taken place earlier in western Europe.

  This chapter analyses Russian debates on the role of religion in the integration of Muslim migrants in Russia within the political elite, the media and Muslim organisations. In addition to cultural discourse, another feature of the presentations of Islamic identity of migrants as a potential social problem is linked to the securitisation of the migration issue. The threat of radical Islam, spreading among the migrants and spread by them, is exaggerated in the media. Because of this fear, the promotion of 'traditional Islam' by official Islamic organisations is preferred over informal networks of Muslims. However, due to the scarcity of resources, as well as occasional inadequate abilities, the official Islamic organisations are not always able to meet these demands. Suspicions concerning grass-roots, unofficial networks of Muslims correspond to the common tendency in the discussions on integration to see migrants as objects, not as active agents.

Islamic religiosity and migrants in post-Soviet Russia

Because of the scale of illegal migration, it is difficult to estimate the number of Muslims as a proportion of the migrants in Russia, but according to the statistics of the Federal Migration Service (FMS, Federal'naya

DOI: 10.4324/9781315657424-7

Migratsionnaya Sluzhba), in 2011, a little over 40 per cent of migrants were Muslims (Starostin 2012). However, not all of them consider themselves as religious or are religiously observant (Zaionchkovskaya *et al.* 2009: 33; Vendina 2009: 131). In addition to personal differences, national cultures vary and, for example, Tajiks are usually more religious than migrants from Kyrgyzstan. The social context of their home countries and their migration history influences the religious activity of communities. For example, Tajiks were the first large migrant group to emigrate from Central Asia and due to their longer-standing presence in Russia, as well as the commonness of their religious education, Tajiks have attained a stronger position in Russian mosques as imams than other migrant minorities (Makarov and Starostin 2014). Although there is no reliable statistical data from Russia, some American studies demonstrate that religiosity is often a more enduring component in migrant minorities than, for example, language or culture. In addition, the ability of churches or mosques to maintain the feeling of connectedness to one's roots is another reason why many migrants become more religious in their new home countries than they were at home (Senses Ozyurt 2013: 1620–1). A small qualitative survey conducted by Guzel Yusupova (2013) among Muslim migrants in St Petersburg and Moscow suggests that the increase of religiosity is more common among people with less education and in a more disadvantaged position. Yusupova notices that, for them, both the emotional and practical support of the religious community is especially vital.

The Muslim minorities in such big cities as Moscow and St Petersburg are extremely heterogeneous in terms of religious tradition, ethnicity and socio-economic position, and therefore it is not surprising that the community is divided into various groupings. For example, in St Petersburg there are ethnically coloured prayer rooms for different ethnicities, such as Ingushetians, Dagestanians, Azerbaijanis and Tajiks. At the same time, a small prayer room at the very centre of the city in Apraksin Dvor gathers people of many ethnicities. In my private discussions with Russian scholars of migration and Muslims, two contradicting views occur. One the one hand, migrants are noticed to form small informal communities and organise prayer rooms on the basis of ethnicity. On the other hand, other scholars point out that in the uncertain environment of Russian megapolises, such ethnic groups as Kyrgyzs and Uzbeks, who traditionally have conflicting relationships, may find common ground in their religious identity. According to Aleksei Malashenko, while earlier migrants to Russia identify themselves as Tajiks or Uzbeks, religious identification has become more common recently. Religious identity is seen as a unifying element in the face of Russian nationalism and, in this sense, even a 'means for survival' ('Aleksei Malashenko: Islam … ' 2013).

Particularly in a country like Russia with a poor state-sponsored system of support for migrants, the mosque is a natural place for many Muslims to seek company and support in an alien environment. Therefore, it is not surprising that Russian mosques and Muslim organisations have been almost compelled to begin to consider undertaking social work with migrants. Initially – and to a large part even today – this work was done on a voluntary basis with very little resources. Despite the statements by the political elite on the role of the Muslim community in integrating migrants, the state still provides relatively few resources for this work. The growing number of migrants within mosque-goers decreases the average income of all mosque-goers. Consequently, even maintaining the premises can be a great financial burden for the Muslim community, leaving few resources for social work. Organised support for migrants includes legal and social counselling as well as Russian language and Islam classes and children's clubs, to name just a few. Here as well, the quantity of potential clients proposes challenges. A representative of an Islamic cultural centre in St Petersburg explained that due to the number of migrants, they cannot advertise their Russian language courses, and that these courses are primarily intended to train people who then can teach the skills they have acquired in their own communities. Some migrant communities may also prioritise need in their areas of origin. For example, a Dagestanian Islamic centre in St Petersburg has been involved in such charity projects as gathering exercise books for children in Dagestan, despite the fact that many of the people attending this centre have meagre incomes.

Given that support for migrants is predominately carried out as local initiatives, there is great variance both in the volume of such work and in its methods. While some mosques are very active, in others the work can be rather insignificant. For example, in my interviews with some Russian imams in Moscow and St Petersburg, the only example of charity and social work they mentioned was the open food service during the festival of Kurban Bayram. A recent survey in Samara reveals that while a substantial proportion of local Muslim migrants go to mosque more or less regularly, they consider the Muslim organisations' social work with migrants to be ineffectual (Uryupin 2013).

However, although not all Muslim organisations have the resources or competencies to offer efficient and relevant support for migrants, mosques as a meeting point can provide networks and information for them as well as emotional comfort. European and North American studies, building on Putnam's (2000) theory of engagement in various associations as a source of social capital, have shown that for migrants, mosques are often places where civic skills are disseminated and learned (Senses Ozyurt 2013). Russian scholars disagree as to whether Islamic religiosity helps or hinders the integration of migrants in contemporary Russian society. While some point out the benefits of the religious community for newcomers in, for example, establishing networks, finding moral support and learning about the surrounding society, others claim that religiosity isolates migrants from the rest of society (Dmitrev *et al*. 2013). The critical views are usually based on the fear that Islamic networks turn into cultural ghettos instead of helping the integration of migrants into the society. Nevertheless, the criticism can also be suggested to reflect a distrust of non-official and thus uncontrollable actors. A frequent concern among scholars and commentators on migration issues is the propaganda of radical Islam among disadvantaged migrants (Dmitrev *et al*. 2013: 76).

'Integration' of migrants as a policy objective

The discussion about the need to have an efficient integration policy for migrants emerged in Russia later than, for example, in western Europe. Although Russian scholarly literature has addressed such issues as interethnic relationships or the adaptation of migrants, the study of integration policies mostly originates from the beginning of the 2000s. As early as the beginning of the 1990s, the Federal Migration Programmes were mentioning the 'adaptation and integration of migrants', but very few practical measures were implemented to attain this goal (Mukomel 2013: 5). A turning point was President Putin's speech in 2012, in which he noted that the integration of migrants had been largely ignored in the migration policy. The same argument could be found in the Concept of National Migration Policy for the Russian Federation until 2025, published later that year (Iontsev and Ivakhnyuk 2013: 6; Kontseptsiya 2012). Although the FMS has introduced some initiatives, such as migrant integration centres (Krainova 2012), it seems that the policies are not very widespread or effective.

The understanding of the term 'integration' varies greatly, not only between different countries, but also between societal actors (e.g. Kortmann 2015: 58 −60), and its definition is always a political act. In recent years, the expression the 'integration and adaptation' (*integratsiya and adaptsiya*) of migrants has established itself in Russian political and policy jargon, as, for example, in the FMS's project to introduce a law on the 'integration and adaptation of migrants', which has not materialised (on the project, see Besnyak 2014).

The dual formulation can be suggested to be designed to avoid the accusations which the term 'adaptation' may invite as a one-sided demand to migrants to abandon their own culture. However, in the Russian discussion, the word adaptation (*adaptsiya*) is understood in other ways as well. An eminent scholar of ethnic relations in the Soviet Union and Russian Federation, Leokadiya Drobizheva (2010), defines adaptation as a two-way process between the host society and migrants, who preserve their cultural identity while also adapting to the host society.

In European countries such as Germany and the Netherlands, Muslim and migrant organisations criticise the word 'adaptation' as indicating a demand to assimilate into the majority. In the definition of the concept of integration by these leaders, such words as recognition and accept repeat and are considered to be more crucial aspects of successful integration than, for example, even learning the language of the host society (Kortmann 2015). Russian Muslim organisations have conducted relatively little discussion about the terminology concerning integration policies. Typically, instead of challenging and opening up the terms for analysis, the Muslim leaders have adopted the terms as such, and in this way, participated in the negotiations on their understanding.

In October 2013, in the 225-year celebrations of the founding of the first muftiate in Ufa, President Putin gave a speech which evoked much discussion among Muslim leaders. The most quoted parts of this speech were Putin's call to 'socialisation' (*sotsializatsiya*) of the Russian umma as a 'development of the traditional Muslim way of life, thinking and viewpoints in concordance with contemporary social reality' and the notion of the significance of the Muslim organisations' contribution to the 'social adaptation' of migrants ('Nachalo vstrechi … ' 2013). In the leading Muslim organisations, the speech was interpreted as praise for their work and a promise of deepening cooperation and support for their work with migrants, even though some Muslim activists, mainly from outside the biggest muftiates, expressed their scepticism towards the state's willingness to distribute any significant resources to Muslims for this work (Guseinova and Abdullaeva 2013). However, the Fund to Support Islamic Culture, Education and Science even announced the publication of the text, referred to as the 'Ufa these', in Russian, English, Arabic, Turkish and Persian ('Ufimskie tezisi' 2014). In the following years, the term 'socialisation' appeared in the title of several high-profile Islamic events, such as the IX Islamic Forum, which in 2013 was organised under the title 'Socialisation of umma in the strategic development of civil society' and the conference 'Russian Muslims: Socialisation, Enlightenment and Tradition', held in Kazan in January 2015. Surprisingly, hardly any attention was paid to the indication of the word 'socialisation' as implying that Russian Muslims are in some way separate from Russian society and needing to be included in it. Perhaps informed by political tact and tactics, Muslim leaders chose to understand the word either in the meaning of 'contributing to society' or of being generalised to include all Russians. In his speech in the Federal Public Chamber, the First Deputy Chairman of the Union of Muftis of Russia, Damir Mukhetdinov, stated: 'The theme of the socialization of Russian citizens in general, and the Muslim community in particular, becomes more important every day' ('Sotsializatsiya rossiiskogo islama … ' 2013).

Even in scholarly literature on the integration of migrants, especially in the debates on the 'success' or 'failure' of certain cases, it may be occasionally forgotten how fluid and situational the concept of integration is. Moreover, integration comprises several, not necessarily correlating aspects. For example, in her study of the integration of first- and second-generation Muslim women into American society, Saba Senses Ozyurt (2013) notices that participation in institutionalised Islamic activity simultaneously strengthens civic and political engagement and lessens acculturation. Thereby, integration can also be selective.

In western Europe, an integral or even key aspect of the successful integration of migrants is their participation in the labour market (Kortmann 2015: 1060). In Russia, this issue is hardly ever addressed: because of the illegal status of a substantial proportion of migrants as well as the weakness of social security, migrants are automatically assumed to be engaged in wage labour. The Concept of National Migration Policy until 2025 (Kontseptsiya

2012) does mention the social, economic and civic integration of migrants, as well as the importance of improving their legal status and decreasing xenophobia as central factors in successful integration. However, such topics as engagement in civic or political activism or trust in local authorities and democracy are seldom discussed as indicators of successful integration in the media, political debates or even some academic publications. In contrast, adaptation to culture figures at the centre of discussions about the integration of migrants (Achkasov and Rozanova 2013: 24–5).

The texts of various programmes and the speeches of the leading politicians divulge that they tend to understand the integration of migrants predominantly as an aspect of cultural education and not, for example, as a challenge of social work, which would make migrants feel like respected members of the society. Language or cultural education is presented as a remedy for such social problems as criminality. For example, the joint programme of the FMS and the Russian Orthodox Church (ROC), 'Enlightenment: Linguistic and Cultural Adaptation of Migrants' was commented on by the Patriarch Kirill in the following way: 'Another reason [for the project] is linked to criminality, including the formation of criminal gangs on an ethnic basis, because the lack of understanding of local culture, local language, local traditions and habits often provokes everyday conflicts' ('RPTs budet … ' 2013).

Even the Muslim leaders comply with this rhetoric when they aim to gain support for their work in the integration of migrants by stressing the Russian language and culture classes instead of, for example, talking about the legal aid organised by several Muslim organisations, occasionally connected to local mosques. Nevertheless, there are also Muslim voices that rebuke the ascent of these courses for revealing ignorance about the real challenges of migrants or even a certain cynicism. Mukhammad Basyr Gasanov, the leader of the Islamic charity foundation Amana, points out that a crucial factor in an effective integration policy would be to liberate migrants from 'slave work contracts', which often do not even allow them one free day a week to be able to take these courses (Guseinova and Abdullaeva 2013). Political scholar, Abdulla Mukhametov (2015b), points out that instead of cultural differences between migrants and Russians, the reason for many social problems rather lies in discrimination against migrants, which leads to their alienation from society.

The expression 'integration and adaptation of migrants' is frequently continued with references to Russian society and values. However, speech about 'national values' in the integration of migrants has been problematised by several scholars as an artificial construction and hierarchic evaluation. Particularly in modern societies, people subscribe to numerous competing values and world-views, therefore the ideal of adapting migrants into one defined value frame seems unrealistic at best and authoritarian at worst. Often the named 'national' values, such as 'justice', 'democracy', 'tolerance' and 'freedom', represent an idealised vision of a given nation. Mentioning them as something to which the migrants should adapt suggests that these ideals do not belong to the values of the migrants and their home countries (Moosavi 2014: 659). The idealised vision of 'national values' also aids in shifting the blame for social problems onto the culture of the migrants from the social structure of the receiving country. For example, when Russian commentators propose that education on Russian culture can prevent criminal activity, they implicitly suggest that corruption, for instance, does not belong to the structures of Russian society, but is rooted in the migrants' 'culture'.

A revealing example of the definition of 'our values', as well as of the outcomes of the scarcity of the discussion about migration is the scandal around a brochure, *A Labour Migrant's Handbook*, published by an NGO from St Petersburg, Look into the Future, with 'informational support' from the administration of the St Petersburg and Leningrad oblast of the FSM in 2011 (*Spravochnik …* 2011). The brochure, which was printed in Russian, Uzbek, Kyrgyz and Tajik, depicted Central Asian migrants as construction tools, such as a paintbrush and a putty knife, in contrast to Russian figures, such as a doctor, an officer and a museum guide, portrayed as attractive human beings. It was precisely this contrast which led the government of Tajikistan, as well as numerous NGOs, representing both these ethnicities and human rights organisations, to condemn the brochure and led to its being withdrawn as well as to the authorities denying any connection to the project ('Brochure Depicts Migrants as Tools' 2012). However, an analysis of the brochure also reveals other hierarchical evaluations about migrants and the native inhabitants of St Petersburg. Of 45 pages, 16 were devoted to information about HIV, implying that this to be the main health problem among migrants and creating a link between migrants and the HIV epidemic. The 'useful advice' of the brochure reveals further underlying assumptions about migrants. The text explains that in St Petersburg 'it is customary' to 'take care of one's personal hygiene' and to wear 'clean clothes'. The advice on what 'one should not do', include 'wearing always and everywhere national costume, because that attracts much attention, which is not always necessary' or to 'always wearing a track-suit, especially with classic shoes (track-suits are used for practicing sport)' (*Spravochnik …* 2011). In addition to suggesting that the distinctive appearance of migrants, such as national costumes, is problematical, the advice draws a picture of potentially unclean, poorly dressed migrants, in contrast to the clean, well-dressed and well-behaved native citizens of Russia.

Religionisation of migrants

Several European scholars have talked about the religionisation of the 'migrant issue' during recent decades in Europe. Whereas in the 1980s, racist discourse about migrants referred to such groups as Pakistanis, Somalis or Turks, in the 2000s these are addressed more often as 'Muslims'. Religionising discourses tend to present Muslims as a unified group and to explain the actions and specifies of Muslims as deriving from their religious identity. This development can be traced to the rise of cultural racism, developed by the French Nouvelle Droite in the 1960s as a response to the popularity of the leftish ideology. Instead of openly racist claims about the inferiority of certain 'races' or ethnicities, cultural racism is able to disguise its offensive and discriminating claims under the auspice of 'cultural criticism'. The intertwined processes of the religionisation of Muslim migrants and the rise of Islamophobia draw a Huntingtonian 'clash of civilisations', which allows Islamic and Christian world-views to be described as irreconcilable entities and presenting this as the cause of the alleged incapability and unwillingness of Muslim migrants to integrate into Christian societies (Kaya 2012: 401; Marranci 2011: 821–2).

In Russian public discussions about 'migrants', internal migrants from Caucasus are often included in this category whereas in debates on 'problems with migrants', such nationalities as Belarusians or Ukrainians seldom figure, despite the substantial size of these groups. The fuzziness and the extension of the category of 'migrant' in the discussion on the problems of migration, including criminality and the shadow economy, divulges the 'religionisation' and racist underpinnings of many debates about the 'migration issue'.

Traditional religiosity seen as promoting the integration of migrants

In western academic and social discussions about the integration of Muslim migrants, their (assumed) conservative attitudes towards, for example, sexual minorities or sexual liberation have often been understood as a problem (Joppke 2014: 1321). In Russia, conservatism and subscription to 'traditional values' is rather seen as the main contribution that Islamic religiosity can give to the integration of migrants. The root of the problems concerning the integration of migrants is explained in their alienation from the tradition of their forefathers. For example, in her book on young migrants in Russia, Voropaeva (2011: 63) writes, 'as a result of the unique "democratisation" in Russia, traditional values and norms (such as active work, brotherhood, collectivism, morality) were lost. Which lead to an imbalance between the incorrectly understood freedom and the responsibility of an individual'. As a remedy, Voropaeva calls for strengthening the collectivism in societal units such as families, instead of individualism. Although the author says very little about the role of religious leaders in reviving 'traditional values', her diagnosis of the problem is very similar to that of the (conservative) religious leaders, who frequently blame individualism and excessive freedom of choice.

In comparing the political rhetoric and media, the benefits of 'traditional religious values' is more often omitted or questioned in the latter. In the media, religious observance is frequently presented as an alien and inappropriate mode of behaviour in the urban Russian space. Moreover, the 'traditional values' of Muslims are seen as a threat to secular society, even though words such as 'secular' would not necessarily be used. For example, in the media debates about the construction of new mosques, the 'traditional

Islam' of such ethnicities as Tatars is presented as a private religious practice distinct from the Islamic religiosity of migrants, who are accused of crowding the mosques as a means to 'demonstrate their presence' (Aitamurto 2016).

The idea of the 'traditional values' of Islam is in accordance with the rise of neo-conservatism during Putin's third presidency. However, this neo-conservative rhetoric begs the question as to how deeply ordinary Russian people are willing to commit themselves to these 'traditional values'. For example, in Russian public debates, 'traditional religious values' are presented as defending the sanctity of the family. However, it is questionable whether contemporary Russians are willing to, for example, deny such things as divorce or abortion. Migrant families may have more conservative gender roles, for example, but it is arguable whether this is seen as a merit or as a social problem within the Russian audience.

In his article, 'National issue', Putin (2012) encourages cooperation between the state and 'the traditional religions of Russia', not only in education, but also in social work. Indeed, in the 2010s, the ROC infiltrated many areas of social policy, such as family counselling, rehabilitation of drug addicts and ex-prisoners. Unlike the charity work of the minority religions, the ROC has received funding from the state to fulfil these tasks. The federal project of the 'social and cultural adaptation and integration of foreign citizens in the Russian Federation' also mentions cooperation with 'religious organisations' (Proyekt zakona … 2014). By 2014, the FMS had made 42 local agreements with Muslim organisations and 80 with Orthodox Christian organisations on cooperation on migrant integration. On the federal level, the FMS signed a significant agreement with the ROC on organising Russian language and tradition courses for migrants.[1]

Two main lines can be noticed in the policies to accommodate Muslim (and other) religious minorities in non-Muslim areas. In the United States, freedom of religion is based on an 'individual rights path', whereas most European countries have adopted a 'corporate recognition path' (Joppke 2014: 1325–6). In this model, the state seeks to cooperate with religious institutions. The problem with this approach is that the state has to select its partners, and this choice is always subjective. Typically, European states have aimed at cooperate with 'moderate' Muslim organisations and thereby weaken the radical forms of Islam. However, such politics may lead to discrimination against some Muslim organisations even if they are not engaged in violent radicalism as such. Such a distinction is also made by Putin, who mentions that policies should aim to strengthen 'official' Islamic organisations in contrast to 'non-formal' (*neformal'nye*) leaders, who, according to him, often subscribe to 'extremist' ideas (Nachalo vstrechi … 2013).

The Russian state has adopted a rather strict line concerning Islamic organisations. Several organisations, such as Hizb-ut Tahrir or the followers of Said Nursi, are banned as extremist in Russia, unlike in Europe. On a local level, officials often refuse to give registration to Islamic organisations that do not belong to the local muftiate, and the prayer rooms of such organisations are routinely raided. In public discussions, any criticism of the officials by Muslims is easily condemned as radicalism or unpatriotic activity. Consequently, the leading muftiates have adopted a very compliant rhetoric concerning the state, even concerning such controversial issues as Russia's support of Bashar al-Assad or the violations of the rights of Russian Muslims in closing prayer rooms, conducting raids on them or banning religious literature. The Islamic leaders regularly express their loyalty to the Russian state and present this loyalty as one of the core values of 'traditional Russian Islam' (Aitamurto 2015). However, this uncritical praise may occasionally seem hypocritical and self-serving in the eyes of ordinary believers and thus undermine the credibility of the muftiates.

As mentioned before, Russian Muslims have very diverging ethnic and cultural traditions. The rapid increase in migration has not only changed the composition of the Muslim minority in many Russian areas, but has also caused internal conflict. In such large cities as Moscow and St Petersburg, Tatars have traditionally formed the majority of local ummas, and are conceived as a well-integrated, well-educated and respected minority in these cities. Not surprisingly, the arrival of waves of migrants from a completely different cultural tradition of Central Asia and Caucasus, many of whom are working in non-prestige professions with illegal status have not always been welcomed by the older Muslim community. Moreover, the rise of Islamophobia as an aspect of xenophobia may have further fuelled the old Muslim minority to see the newcomers as a problem (Verkhovskii 2007: 127). A revealing example of such sentiments is the article 'Quality in quantity. Russian Muslims facing the challenges of demography and migration', published on the Islamic website, Ansar.ru (Mukhametov 2015a). The article quotes a scholar of Islam and the Chair of the Carnegie Moscow Centre's Religion, Society, and Security Programme, Aleksei Malashenko: 'If in the 1980s, among the majority of the people in our country, a Muslim was associated with a cunning, but all-in-all a close "Tatar-neighbour", in the 1990s, it [the association] is already an extremely hostile and hardly understandable "Caucasian fighter"'. The article continues: 'For some it may seem strange, but Russian Muslims are not always unanimous supporters of migration: because of it the number of their co-believers rises in quantity but not in quality'. The socio-economic gap between the well-integrated Muslim religious elite and the majority of new Muslim migrants certainly sets challenges to their communication. There is a danger that the official Muslim organisations will turn into similar representatives of their minority as the majority of the National Cultural Associations (NCAs), which in Russian big cities claim to represent their ethnic community, but are alienated from the majority of the less-advantaged members of these groups. Indeed, the role of most NCAs is quite insignificant in helping new migrants from their own ethnic group (Dmitrev *et al.* 2013: 80).

Even in the well-meant statements of the Russian Muslim leaders, migrants are often treated as objects; people who need education not only about

Russian culture, but also about 'traditional Russian Islam'. For example, the Chairman of the Council of Muftis in Russia, Ravil' Gainutdin, emphasises the need for moral education among migrants: 'It is of vital importance that Muslim migrants go through the process of adaptation in due course, get acquainted with the cultures and traditions of the nations of Russia, and first of all of the [ethnic] Russian people, that they learn the Russian language, get the spiritual–moral education without which it is impossible to adjust to a life in an unfamiliar country' (quoted in Starostin 2011). In another interview, Gainutdin ponders the role of mosques in the integration of migrants: 'It is of vital importance to form among the labour migrants, both internally and externally, the right models of behaviour, even more so because with people also ideas, occasionally destructive and dangerous, migrate' (Info Islam 2013).

However, the concept of 'traditional Islam' into which migrants should be adapted is also criticised by Muslim thinkers, who point out the artificial nature of the concept in the face of the multiplicity of traditions in Islam and the freedom of individual religious search (*ijtihad*) in the religious tradition of Islam (Mukhametov 2015b). There are also examples of integrating Muslim migrants into religious activity as equal partners. The muftiate of the Nizhny Novgorod was among the first to take an active stance in the integration of migrants. Instead of conceiving them as a potential source of social problems and radical Islam, the muftiate has employed migrants as imams, are able to reach local migrant communities (Starostin 2011).

Securitisation of Muslim migrants

In Russian discussions, nationalising Islamic religiosity is seen as a guarantee that the migrants will hold their primary loyalty to the state over their religion. Implicitly, this discussion presents Islam as a potentially dangerous religion, and thereby lays an extra burden on Muslims to prove their loyalty to the state, unlike non-Muslim migrant groups, for example, Byelorussians or Moldavians in Russia. The policy objective of domesticating the religion of Muslim migrants can be found in other European countries as well, and it is intimately linked with the securitisation of Islam and the discussion about migrants (e.g. Humphrey 2009). Securitising discourses, which began to figure in discussions about migration in the 1980s, place migration in the framework of national security, whether in terms of terrorist violence, social welfare or the purity of culture or race, instead of, for example, social politics (Alexseev 2006: 6–7). Ayhan Kaya argues that this framing draws the attention away from social and structural problems, thereby functioning as a form of governmentality. Moreover, he claims that by presenting migrants as a source of possible threats and a consequent construction of 'us' versus the 'dangerous others', the securitisation of migrants is tantamount to their stigmatisation (Kaya 2012: 403–4).

Vladimir Malakhov (2014: 1071–2), divides Russian public discussions concerning migration into four basic approaches: liberal pragmatism, humanitarian perspective, conservative–statist views and cultural fundament-alism. Whereas the last of these promotes ethnic and religious uniformity and the refusal of non-Slavic migrants, securitisation is one of the core features of the conservative–statist stance, which is represented by such high-ranking officials as Konstantin Zatulin, the first deputy chairman of the committee of the State Duma for the CIS and relations with Russian nationals abroad.

As in Putin's 'Theses of Ufa', the main challenge of the integration of Muslim migrants is indeed often presented to be the prevention of religious radicalisation. This framing defines the problem to be the activity of religious zealots among migrants, and the remedy the propagation of 'moderate reli-giosity'. In this way, the frame of 'religious radicalisation' draws attention away from such societal problems as ethnic discrimination or the societal structures which compel migrants into the domain of the grey economy as a cause of criminality. Some Muslim activists and scholars claim that the threat of radicalisation and terrorist inclinations among Muslim migrants is exaggerated in public debates, and that occasionally this is done for political purposes (Drobizheva 2010; Malashenko 2007: 36).

Islamic religiosity seen as an obstacle to integration

In today's globalised world, Islamophobic arguments and rhetoric are quickly borrowed across language barriers. One example is the concept of the 'Isla-misation' of Christian countries, which is widely used in contemporary Russia, for example, in a broadcast of the popular TV show *Poedinok* by Vladimir Solovev on 24 October 2013, hosting the head of the Liberal Democratic Party of Russia, Vladimir Zhirinovskii.[2] In the show, the men agreed that 'Islamisation' is the main problem in contemporary Russia and that this process is executed by migrants, who come to Russia and 'exploit' the Russian freedom of religion to practise Islam.

The popular leader of the opposition, Alexei Navalny (2015) writes about the security threat posed by Muslim migrants on his blog: '90% of the immi-grants in Russia are young Muslim men from the countryside, which is the very area in which terrorists enlist people. The sources of migration are Uzbeki-stan and Tajikistan, countries, to say it openly, in which the borders are very transparent and close to the hearths of aggressive Islam'. Navalny's clearly unfounded numbers[3] of migrants from these countries enforce his alarmist claim about the widespread nature of Islamic radicalism and terrorism within these people. In conclusion, Navalny argues that even economic depression is a better option than an increase of Muslim migrants: 'The only thing that can save us – if one may use such a word here – are a low level of living and economic problems. These make Russia a much less attractive destination for migration, not state politics'.

Typically, the Russian media is careful to distinguish 'traditional Russian Islam' and Islam as a religion both from Islamic terrorism and what is con-ceived as the either aggressive or illiterate Islam of many migrants (Aitamurto

2016). However, the distinction can also be intentionally evaporated, as in the discussion about the 'Islamisation' of Russia, which lumps all Muslims in Russia together. Despite the conformist rhetoric of the biggest muftiates, even these can fall into the category of suspects. There are journalists and public figures who question the competence of the official Muslim organisations in integrating migrants. Aleksei Grishin (2015), the former Chief Adviser to the Administration of the President of the Russian Federation in the Council for Cooperation with Religious Organisations, attacked one of the biggest Muslim organisations of Russia, the Council of Muftis of Russia, for being too lenient with radical Islam in his article, 'Why are the "lambs" trusted in the care of "wolves" in us?'. Grishin practically equates migrants with extremism, using the number of migrants in certain muftiates as proof of their radicalism, and ends this analysis with the policy suggestion to 'limit the activity of Muslim organisations in work with migrants' until 'order' is secured within these muftiates (Grishin 2015).[4] These kinds of attacks explain why in public, the official Islamic organisations prefer to be very cautious in criticising violations of the rights of Muslim migrants.

Conclusions

In Russia, engagement in civic or political activism or trust in local authorities and democracy are seldom discussed as indicators of successful integration. In contrast, adaptation to culture figures as the core issue in discussions about the integration of migrants. The frequency of the term 'adaptation' in the integration debates reveals that migrants are expected to adapt to Russian society, whereas very little reflection is made on the way Russian society could better accommodate migrants and cultural diversity. In this way, minorities are not necessarily perceived as active agents, able to contribute to Russian society and culture. The same understanding of migrants as objects can be seen even in the rhetoric of some Muslim leaders, who stress the need to educate migrants, who in this way are implied to be religiously illiterate. Revealingly, commentators talk more often about the problem of ill-willing propagators of radical Islam among migrants than about the reasons why such ideas might find support within or be developed by Muslim migrants in dire conditions.

The Russian authorities legitimise xenophobic claims by translating them into a socially acceptable form of 'protecting the interests of the indigenous inhabitants' or 'maintaining the social peace' (Popov and Kuznetsov 2008: 235). The credibility of such rhetoric is bolstered by the academic, political and social tendency to present interethnic relationships in the framework of conflict, or *konfliktologiya*. Ethnicity is assumed to be inseparably linked to culture, which is depicted as a given. This primordial understanding of identity highlights the incompatibility of cultures and presents conflict as the consequence of their encounters. In the media, and even in scholarly studies, one may encounter claims that there is a scientifically proved percentage of migrants, above which conflicts and social problems will inevitably grow up (Popov and Kuznetsov 2008: 228; Shnirelman 2008).

Racist features can easily be found in Russian public discussions about the problems related to migration and too often the discrimination is done not in openly racist terms, but in the form of cultural criticism towards Islam. Whereas the compatriots' programme seeks to invite to Russia foreign citizens with Russian heritage, Muslims are often explicitly or implicitly excluded from the category of 'Russians'. Revealingly, in the debates about migrants in Russian cities such as Moscow and St Petersburg, the category of these 'troublesome others' regularly extends to include internal migrants from Dagestan and Chechenia, and even all Muslims in Russia.

Unfounded exaggeration of the threat of radical Islam and the problems caused by the cultural and religious differences between migrants and native citizens is preventing rather than aiding solving social problems (see also Zaionchkovskaya *et al.* 2009: 43, 46–7). The growing Islamophobia creates an extra burden for Muslims to show their loyalty to the Russian state and society. Yet further burdens are imposed by the demands that migrants should adapt to Russian values or 'ways of life', which is occasionally presented in an idealised way as a high morality which, it seems safe to say, is not necessarily followed by many ethnic Russians either. Islamophobia and migrantophobia, the construction of the dangerous 'other', are forms of governmentality. In addition to blurring the analysis of societal problems, the 'discourses of danger' 'distance migrant communities from incorporating themselves into the political, social, economic and cultural spheres of life of majority society in a way that prompts them to invest in their ethno-cultural and religious identities' (Kaya 2012: 404).

Even though the Russian state has been more generous in granting funding for the ROC for social work with migrants, it has also recognised the potential of Muslim organisations to solve social problems connected to migration. Several imams, mosques and Muslim organisations carry out social work with migrants by providing emotional and material support. For many migrants, mosques provide places to form networks which help them to navigate and integrate into the new environment. However, the ethnic, cultural and socio-economic differences between the official imams and the Muslim migrants also pose challenges to this work. Moreover, the leaders of Islamic organisations may hesitate to openly address discrimination against migrants and the Islamophobia of the authorities for fear that this would be labelled as extremism or unpatriotic.

The twofold aim in promoting 'traditional Islam' among migrants is to encourage civic behaviour and prevent religious radicalisation. However, due to the relative scarcity of these resources, the informal networks and communities loosely connected to mosques and prayer rooms seem to be more important for migrants. The concerns that these promote cultural ghettoisation are justified if the migrants have to rely only on these to get information about the surrounding society and their rights. The main danger is that such networks are used by people in an advantaged position to gain control of the less-advantaged migrants. However, suspicions about the informal Islamic networks in the integration of newcomers to the surrounding society can also be unwarranted and be based more on prejudice against Islam. An alternative view is to see these networks as a part of civil society, which can supplement official structures.

The stereotype of Muslims as a static and a sealed community is one feature of Islamophobic rhetoric (Moosavi 2014: 656). This feature can certainly be noted in President Putin's call to 'socialise Muslims' into Russian society. However, it should be noted that here Putin's rhetoric does not necessarily differ from that of leading European politicians: a similar feature of 'othering' Muslims was noticed by Moosavi in his analysis of the statements made by ministers in Tony Blair's UK Labour government. In their speeches, these ministers, although trying in many ways to avoid the open labelling of all Muslims, presented them as a monolithic group which posed problems for British society with their 'otherness' and therefore placed onto Muslims the burden of the responsibility to 'integrate', which in that context rather seemed like a demand to assimilate (Moosavi 2014: 669).

Notes

1 Information about the project can be found on its website 'Proshveshchenie', retrieved 10 November from http://help-migrant.ru
2 The TV show can be found on countless websites. See www.youtube.com/watch?v= 1GQKooLwsNU, retrieved 11 November 2015.
3 For well-grounded criticism of Navalny's numbers and of his arguments in general, see Abashin (2015).
4 Aleksei Grishin is similar to another well-known societal figure, Roman Silant'ev, in that they both have held high administrative positions and are regularly presented in media as experts on Islam, but in the Muslim media and on the Internet are widely accused of Islamophobia. Both of them are especially critical of the CMR, which has adopted a more independent stance toward the ROC than its main rival, the Central Spiritual Board of Russia, and has brought up the discrimination against Muslims more actively.

References

Abashin, S. 2015. 'Natsional'nyi nadzor'. Grani.ru, 20 November 2015. Retrieved 20 November 2015 from http://mirror573.graniru.info/Society/Xenophobia/m.246061.html.

Achkasov, V. A. and M. S. Rozanova. 2013. 'Migrant's adaptation and integration into urban multicultural society: A case study of St Petersburg', *Journal of Multicultural Society*, 4(1): 1–31.

Aitamurto, K. 2015. 'The approved and the disapproved Islam in Russia', in G. Simons and D. Westerlund (eds) *Religion, Politics and Nation-Building in Post-Communist Countries*. Farnham: Ashgate, pp. 99–116.

Aitamurto, K. 2016. 'Protected and controlled. Islam and "desecularisation from above" in Russia', *Europe-Asia Studies*, 68(1): 182–202.

'Aleksei Malashenko: Islam dlya migrantov – sredstvo vyzhivaniya'. 2013Regnum.ru, 1 February 2013. Retrieved 10 November 2015 from http://regnum.ru/news/1620375. html.

Alexseev, M. A. 2006. *Immigration Phobia and the Security Dilemma. Russia, Europe, and the United States.* Cambridge: Cambridge University Press.

Besnyak, T. 2014. 'Migrant integriruetsya, kogda u nego budet vysokaya motivatsiya', Azerros 10 September. Retrieved 23 November 2015 from http://azerros.ru/ma intheme/20076-migrant-smozhet-integrirovatsya-pri-ego-vysokoy-motivacii.html.

'Brochure depicts migrants as tools'. 2012. *Moscow Times*, 24 October. Retrieved 7 December 2015 from www.themoscowtimes.com/news/article/brochure-depicts-m igrants-as-tools/470381.html.

Dmitrev, A. V., V. Yu. Ledenva and E. A. Nazarova. 2013. *Migratsiya v Moskve. Modeli i perspektivy.* Moscow: Al'fa.

Drobizheva, L. M. 2010. 'Politika mezhetnicheskoi integratsii i adaptii migrantov v moskovskom sotsiume', *Moskovskii Dom Natsional'nostei.* Retrieved 25 November 2015 from www.mdn.ru/cntnt/blocksleft/menu_left/nacionalny/publikacii2/stati/lm_ drobizh.html.

Grishin, A. 2015. 'Aleksei Grishin: Pochemu u nas "ovets" doveryayut pasti "volk-ami"?' Islamio.ru 6 May. Retrieved 10 November 2015 from http://islamio.ru/news/ society/aleksey_grishin_pochemu_u_nas_ovets_doveryayut_pasti_volkam_.

Guseinova, P. and T. Abdullaeva. 2013. 'Prezident Rossii Vladimir Putin prizval musul'man zanyat'sya adaptsieu migrantov', IslamvKuzbasse, 24 October. Retrieved 7 November 2015 from www.kuzbassislam.ru/news-56760.html.

Humphrey, M. 2009. 'Securitisation and domestication of diaspora Muslims and Islam: Turkish immigrants in Germany and Australia', *International Journal on Multicultural Societies* 11(2): 136–154.

Info Islam. 2013. '"Ravil" Gainutdin o migrantakh, mechetakh, khidzhabakh i problemakh ummy'. 20 March. Retrieved 20 November 2015 from www.info-islam.ru/publ/inter vju/ravil_gajnutdin_o_migrantakh_mechetjakh_khidzhabakh_i_problemakh_ummy/ 4-1-0-21948.

Iontsev, V. and I. Ivakhnyuk. 2013. *Modeli integratsii migrantov v sovremennoi Rossii. CARIM-East RR 2013/12.* Florence: European University Institute.

Joppke, C. 2014. 'Europe and Islam: Alarmists, victims, and integration by law', *West European Politics*, 37(6): 1314–1335.

Kaya, A. 2012. 'Backlash of multiculturalist and republicanist policies of integration in the age of securitization', *Philosophy and Social Criticism*, 38(4–5): 399–411.

Kremlin.ru 2013. 'Nachalo vstrechi s muftiyami dukhovnykh upravlenii musul'man Rossii'. *Kremlin.ru*, 22 October. Retrieved 5 November 2015 from www.kremlin.ru/ events/president/transcripts/19474.

'Kontseptsiya gosudarstvennoi migratsionnoi politiki Rossiiskoi Federatsii', *Prezident Rossii*, 13 June 2013. Retrieved 1 December 2015 from http://kremlin.ru/events/p resident/news/15635.

Kortmann, M. 2015. 'Asking those concerned: How Muslim migrant organisations define integration. A German–Dutch comparison', *Migration & Integration*, 16: 1057–1080.

Krainova, N. 2012. '"Adaptation Center" to help migrants integrate', *Moscow Times*, 13 November. Retrieved 1 December 2015 from www.themoscowtimes.com/news/a rticle/adaptation-center-to-help-migrants-integrate/471352.html.

Makarov, A. and A. Starostin. 2014. 'Migratsionnye protsessy na Evraziiskom prostranstve 1989–2014 gg. (obzor osnovnykh tendentsii)', *Islam v Sovremennom Mire* 4(36).

Malakhov, V. S. 2014. 'Russia as a new immigration country: Policy response and public debate', *Europe-Asia Studies*, 66(7): 1062–1079.

Malashenko, A. 2007. *Islam dlya Rossii*. Moscow: Rosspen.

Marranci, G. 2011. 'Integration, minorities and the rhetoric of civilization: the case of British Pakistani Muslims in the UK and Malay Muslims in Singapore', *Ethnic and Racial Studies*, 34(5): 814–832.

Moosavi, L. 2014. 'Orientalism at home: Islamophobia in the representations of Islam and Muslims by the New Labour Government', *Ethnicities*, 15(5): 652–674.

Mukhametov, A. R. 2015a. 'Kolichestvo v kachestvo. Musul'mane Rossii peredvyzovami demografii i migratsii', Ansar.ru 13 April 2016. Retrieved 10 November 2015 from www.ansar.ru/analytics/kolichestvo-v-kachestvo-musulmane-rossii-peredvyzovami-demografii-i-migracii.

Mukhametov, A. R. 2015b. 'Adaptsiya and otchuzhdenie? Formirovanie grazhdanskoi identichnosti rossiiskikh musul'man', Islamrf.ru, 13 May. Retrieved 11 November 2015 from www.islamrf.ru/news/amal/analytics/36498.

Mukhetdinov, D. 2013. *Rossiya + Umma = nuzhny li my drug drugu?* Moscow: Medina.

Mukomel, V. 2013. *Integration of Migrants: Russian Federation*. Florence: European University Institute.

'Nachalo vstrechi s muftiyami dukhovnykh upravlenii musul'man Rossii'. Kremlin.ru, 22 October 2013. Retrieved 5 November 2015 from www.kremlin.ru/events/president/transcripts/19474.

Naval'nyi, A. 2015. 'Gde prokhodit "orgiya tolerantnosti"?' Navalny.com 16 November. Retrieved 17 November 2015 from https://navalny.com/p/4547.

Popov, A. and I. Kuznetsov. 2008. 'Ethnic discrimination and the discourse of "indigenization": The regional regime, "indigenous majority" and ethnic minorities in Krasnodar Krai in Russia', *Nationalities Papers*, 36(2): 223–252.

'Proyekt zakona "O sotsial'noi i kulturnoi adaptsii i integratsii inostrannykh grazhdan"', *Federal'naya migratsionnaya sluzhba*, 28 February 2014. Retrieved 9 November 2015 from www.fms.gov.ru/documentation/865/details/81610.

Putin, V. 2012. 'Rossiya: natsional'nyi vopros', *Nezavisimaya Gazeta*, 23 January.

Putnam, R. 2000. *Bowling Alone: The Collapse and Revival of American Community*. New York: Simon & Shuster.

'RPTs budet uchit' migrantov russkomu yazyku i russkoi kul'ture'. 2013. Gumilevcenter.ru 22 April 2013. Retrieved 10 November 2015 from www.gumilev-center.ru/rpc-budet-uchit-migrantov-russkomu-yazyku-i-russkojj-kulture.

Senses Ozyurt, S. 2013. 'The selective integration of Muslim immigrant women in the United States: Explaining Islam's paradoxical impact', *Journal of Ethnic and Migration Studies*, 39(10): 1617–1637.

Shnirelman, V. 2008. 'Migrantofobiya i kul'turnyi rasizm', *Ab Imperio*, 2: 287–324.

'Sotsializatsiya rossiiskogo islama: prakticheskie aspekty realizatsii. Vystuplenie D. Mukhetdinova v Obshchestvennoi palate'. 2013. Dumrf.ru 4 December 2013. Retrieved 10 November 2015 from http://dumrf.ru/upravlenie/speeches/7865.

Starostin, A. 2011. 'Politika DUM Rossii po sotsiokul'turnoi adaptsii migrantov', Islam.ru, 26 December 2011. Retrieved 10 November 2015 from www.islam.ru/content/analitics/politika_dum_rosii_po_sociokulturnoy_adaptacii_migrantov.

Starostin, A. 2012. '"Islamskii faktoor " v migratsionnykh protsessakh Rossii', *Islam v Rossii*, 10 April 2012. Retrieved 15 November 2015 from http://ru-islam.livejournal. com/662656.html.

Spravochnik dlya trudovogo migrant. 2011. St Petersburg: Vzglyad na Budushchee.

'"Ufimskie tezisy": Novaya sotsializatsiya islama v Rossii – zadacha, oboznachenna Prezidentom Putinym'. 2014. *Islamskaya kul'tura* 1: 8–12.

Uryupin, K. V. 2013. 'Vzaimodeistvie musul'manskikh religioznykh organizatsii s trudovymi migrantami is Zakavkaziya I Srednei Azii (na primere Samarskoi oblasti)', *Sovremennye problem nauki I obrazovaniya* 1.

Vendina, O. I. 2009. 'Kul'turnoe raznobrazie I "pobpchnie" effekty kul'turnoi politike v Moskve', in Zh. Zaionochkovskaya et al. (eds), *Immigranty v Moskve*. Moscow: Tri Kvadrata, pp. 45–147.

Verkhovskii, A. M. 2007. 'Publichnye otnosheniya pravoslavnyh I musul'manskih organizatsii na federal'nom urovne', in A. V. Malashenko (ed.), *Islam v Rossii. Vzglyad iz regionov*. Moscow: Aspekt Press, pp. 123–153.

Voropaeva, A. V. 2011. *Molodye migrant v sotsiokul'turnom prostranstve Rossii.* Moscow: Al'fa.

Yusupova, G. 2013. *The Influence of Islam on Social Networks of Low-Skilled Migrants from Central Asia to Russia, MPC AS 2013/01.* Florence: European University Institute.

Zaionchkovskaya, Zh., N. Mkrtchyan and E. Tyuryukanova. 2009. 'Rossiya pered vyzovami immigratsii', in Zh. A. Zaionchkovskaya and G. S. Vitkovskaya (eds) *Postsovetskie transformatsii: otrazhenie v migratsii*. Moscow: Tsentr migratsionnykh issledovanii. Institut narodnokhazyaistvennogo proghrozirovaniya RAN, pp. 9–62.

8 Implications of migration for the development of Russian social policy

Linda J. Cook

Introduction[1]

The end of the Cold War was a 'watershed event' in the history of global migration, ending political constraints that had kept migration levels low until 1990 and increasing global economic integration. Movement of both documented and undocumented migrants has been on the rise worldwide, and Russia has become a major receiving state, drawing the second largest labour migrant population in the world after the United States. Over the past two decades more than six million have migrated to Russia legally and illegally, most to work in Moscow and other major cities. While these labour migrants come from many countries the single largest group arrives from Central Asian states, with Tajikistan a major contributor. Approximately 10 per cent of Tajikistan's population of 7–8 million – more than 30 per cent of working-age men and a smaller number of women – totalling an estimated 1.3 million people, reportedly lived and worked in Russia during 2012–13. From 2000, Russia's economy has depended on them for unskilled and semi-skilled work in construction and services. For its part Tajikistan has relied on migrants' remittances for one-third to one-half of its GDP, making it one of the most remittance-dependent states in the world. In sum, migration has become an institutionalised part of the political economies of both Russia's highly stratified 'global cities' and the Eurasian periphery. Russia's 2008–9 recession and especially the current economic downturn have greatly decreased demand for migrants' labour, leading to return of many to Tajikistan and a resulting decline in remittances (Abdurazakova 2011: 5; Buckley 2008; Heleniak 2008; Ganguli 2009; Hertzer 2009; Migranty 2007; Trudovaia 2010; Yudina 2005).

My research contributes to the understanding of this political economy a study of Tajik labour migrants in Moscow from 2000–15, focusing on their access to healthcare and other basic social services. I ask whether the Russian government's policies give migrants access to public health services and medical insurance in Moscow, and what alternatives and practices migrants find if needed services are inaccessible in the formal sector. I consider what social rights are guaranteed by Russia's commitments to international conventions, and whether migrants' labour status as legal/registered or illegal/unregistered matters in determining rights and access. Field work in Moscow and Dushanbe, Tajikistan provides evidence about experiences with different kinds of health issues, i.e. accidents, infectious and non-infectious diseases, pregnancy and childbirth, and where migrants turn for help in cases of urgent health needs or emergencies. My study also contributes to a growing literature on NGOs that asks whether they are substituting for states to fill gaps in public provision (Cammett and McLean 2011; Kulmala 2011; Tsai 2011). I ask how many NGOs work with migrants in Moscow, what kinds of services or advocacy they provide, and whether they fill unmet social needs.

The chapter is based on documentary research as well as more than 20 interviews the author conducted in Moscow and Dushanbe from 2012–15 with representatives of Moscow-based NGOs that work with migrants, Dushanbe-based international organisations including UNDP (United Nations Development Project); WHO (World Health Organization); IOM (International Organization for Migration); US AID (Agency for International Development), as well as government health officials and academic experts.[2] The study also draws on three focus groups conducted in Tajikistan during summer, 2013: in Dushanbe, in Qurghonteppa City, Khatlon Region, with migrants who returned infected with TB, and in the Nuroboddistrict, Rasht Valley, with returned women migrants.

To preview the conclusions, my research confirms that a large population of Tajik and other Central Asian labour migrants has lived precariously in Moscow with few legal or social rights. The Russian government generally complies with its international commitments to provide emergency medical care for all migrants and education for children; beyond these, most migrants have little access to public services. A small network of IOs, NGOs and human rights lawyers provides help and advocacy but has very limited capacity. Most Tajik migrants work, live and meet basic needs in conditions of social exclusion and legal invisibility that drive shadow economies in labour and social sectors. Growth of large marginalised populations and shadow economies undermine human security and welfare provision in Russia. At the same time, migrants' lack of job rights or claims to social compensation makes them a disposable labour force that can facilitate labour market adjustment and welfare retrenchment in the current downturn.

The chapter proceeds as follows: the next section briefly explains the economic and political factors that have driven migration, as well as the rules and practices that have kept the labour and lives of most Tajik migrants 'in the shadows'. The third section, the core of the chapter, reviews international and domestic policy frameworks governing migrants' *de jure* social rights, and presents evidence on their *de facto* access to healthcare and social services in Moscow. It also discusses NGOs and formal and informal private social providers. The chapter concludes with a discussion of risks and realities for migrants and implications for Russia's welfare state.

Push-and-pull forces driving migration

Migration from Tajikistan to Russia has proceeded in a five stages constituting 'waves' and 'reverse waves': the first wave came, in the 1990s, the immediate post-Soviet period and the 1992–7 civil war in Tajikistan: a small, largely skilled Russian-speaking group, prominently including health and education professionals, migrated to Russia, representing both 'brain drain' from Tajikistan and 'brain waste' as many migrants experienced downward occupational mobility, working below their educational qualifications or outside their professional specialties. By 2000, more than 25% of the total tertiary-educated population of Tajikistan was in migration, damaging services for Tajikistan's population (Heleniak 2012: Figure 2).

The second wave, between 2000 and 2008, came during a period of rapid economic growth in Russia and 'take-off' of migration: Central Asian migrants entered the Russian labour market *en masse*, increasing their share of all migrants from 6 per cent to about 50 per cent (Cook and Johnson 2013). They were less skilled than the first wave, ranged in age from school-leavers to middle-aged; most were competent in the Russian language; most stayed through the 2008–9 recession. The following third wave between 2005–2010 included migrants who were mostly18–29 year olds with secondary education and poor Russian language skills, representing a 'brawn drain' from Tajikistan. Many left Russia during the 2008–9 recession.

The fourth wave, between 2010 and 2013, took place during a time of economic recovery. Migrants who left during the 2008–9 recession returned with additional newcomers. Returnees were generally older, better educated and more experienced than the third wave, while the new migrants were generally school-leavers with poor Russian language skills. The fifth reverse wave, since 2013, has consisted of outflows caused by the economic crisis and declining job openings.

Most migrants are men, married but migrating without their families. Those with formal labour contracts are more likely to bring families. As numbers of male migrants increased more women, both mothers with children and young women without families, joined the migration. More than 90 per cent work in Russia, about half in Moscow, mainly in construction, trade, housing and cleaning services, agriculture and maintenance (FIDH 2011: 9; Hemmings 2010).

Large-scale out-migration ('push') from Tajikistan is driven mainly by economic and political factors. Economically, Tajikistan is one of the poorest of the post-Soviet states; during the period studied an estimated one-half of its population lived in poverty and 20 per cent in extreme poverty, with malnutrition among children common (Hemmings 2010: 10). A devastating five-year civil war from 1992–7 damaged economic and social infrastructure and led to many deaths and large-scale displacement. The healthcare system, severely under-resourced in financing, personnel and infrastructure, contributes to some of the worst health outcomes in Central Asia. The large parts of the country that are rural and mountainous constitute a major source of migratory labour for Russia. Rapid population growth has produced a booming youth population with few and poor employment opportunities in Tajikistan. By the late 2000s migrating to Russia had become the default option for many male Tajik school-leavers.

Promoting and facilitating out-migration has been a proactive government strategy, pursued to raise living standards and 'ease the social climate driven by the idleness of the work force' (FIDH 2011: 23). In 1998 and again in 2001 the Tajik government approved 'Concept' papers that outlined incentives to promote migration, most significantly tax exemptions for remittances; a network of government-run and private advising, support and 'recruitment' services; and efforts (largely unsuccessful) to negotiate bilateral agreements on migrants' labour and social rights with Russia and other receiving states. The Tajik government and some international organisations argued that remittances would finance and spur internal development. Migrants were expected to transfer back money and return with knowledge and skills that would contribute to growth of domestic infrastructure and technological modernisation. But this has virtually not happened in Tajikistan, which has the highest recorded remittance rate in the world (see Figures 8.1 and 8.2). Transfer back of knowledge and technology has been modest, and most remittances go to immediate consumption or are saved for emergencies, including medical care. Instead migration has created an ethnically stratified regional labour market in which Tajiks live and work as a marginalised stratum while remittances have driven growth of Tajikistan's GDP in the absence of significant domestic economic development (Buckley and Hofmann 2011; Heleniak 2012; International Labour Organization 2010).

The major 'pull' or demand factors from Russia are economic, demographic and cultural/communal. After a decade of economic decline in the 1990s, Russia's economy grew rapidly from 2000–8, then resumed growth after the 2008–9 recession. Demand for labour grew while Russia's population and labour force were declining because of low birth rates and high premature mortality of working-aged males. Migrant labour was the main source available to fill the gap left by the shrinking domestic labour force (see Figure 8.3). Tajiks were drawn to Russia by employment opportunities and especially high regional wage differentials – average wages even for unskilled work in Russia were four times the Tajik average during the 1990s. By 2000 migrants comprised 8–10 per cent of Russia's total employment. Despite the Putin government's pronatalist and 'compatriot resettlement' campaigns, increasing numbers of migrants from 'other' ethnic communities were needed to compensate for labour deficits.

Labour migrants are concentrated in particular niches of Russia's economy, mainly in the secondary labour markets of a few major 'global cities', of which Moscow is the prime example. Russia's economy, heavily dependent on exports of energy resources, has produced an extraordinarily heavy concentration of wealth in a few large cities that function as banking, business,

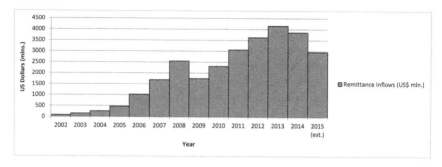

Figure 8.1 Remittance Inflows from Russia to Tajikistan for 2002–15
Source: Figure created by Colin Johnson. World Bank website, www.worldbank.org/
en/topic/migrationremittancesdiasporaissues/brief/migration-remittances-data; accessed
March 10, 2016.

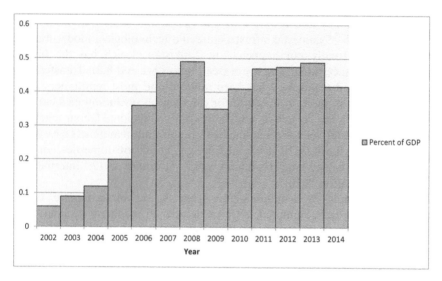

Figure 8.2 Remittances as a Percent of GDP in Tajikistan for 2002–14
Source: Figure created by Colin Johnson. World Bank website, www.worldbank.org/
en/topic/migrationremittancesdiasporaissues/brief/migration-remittances-data; accessed
March 10, 2016.

communications and technical centres. These cities become magnets for upper
SES (socio-economic status) mainly Russian professionals whose demands
produce a secondary labour market with little pay, stability, or opportunities for
advancement. As qualified native workers are not attracted to these jobs,
particularly in a low-unemployment environment such as that of 1990s
Moscow, global cities generate demand for immigrant workers (Massey 1999:
305). Tajiks who migrate to Moscow are concentrated mainly in services and
construction. Most form part of a fungible, disposable labour force without

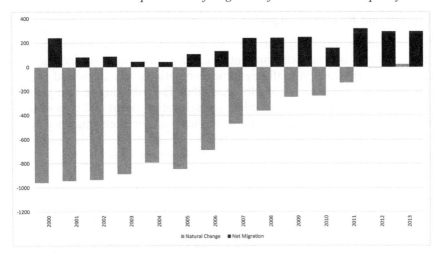

Figure 8.3 Facets of Russia's population change (2000–13)
Source: Figure created by Colin Johnson. *Demographic Yearbook of Russia 2002 and 2015*, www.gks.ru/bgd/regl/B15_16/Main.htm; accessed March 10, 2016.

rights that is vulnerable to both economic and political pressures to go home when their labour is no longer needed.

Cultural and communal ties, i.e. shared history and established networks for migration, constitute the third set of 'pull' factors. As a general rule, 'the immigration stream shows a strong tendency to continue as migrant networks grow, migratory behaviour spreads in the sending community, and network expansion becomes self-perpetuating' (Massey 1999). Tajikistan and Russia form part of a postcolonial (post-Soviet) 'shared space', including language, educational systems, and everyday social practices, that mitigates cultural distance between the mainly Christian Slavs and the mainly Islamic Central Asians. Russia's secularism, in contrast to Islamic religious practice in potential migrant-receiving states of the Middle East (such as Saudi Arabia) also make it attractive to the Tajik government as a destination. The migration flow is facilitated by the visa-free regime that allows Tajik and other Central Asian citizens to travel to Russia and remain temporarily, but not to reside or work legally; legal or 'registered' residence and employment require a work permit. Mainly because Russia's government set the quota for permits far below labour demand during most of the period studied, the majority of Tajik migrants stayed and worked in Russia without registration. While the percentages are uncertain and have varied over time, it is generally considered that a substantial majority – an estimated 70 per cent or more – has remained unregistered. Socially excluded and legally illegible, they populate and rely on Russia's informal (shadow) labour and social economies.

Migrants and Russian social policy

This section considers migrants' *de jure* and *de facto* social rights. The first section reviews international conventions and agreements that bind the Russian government and cover all migrants, then national legislation and policies that apply to those who are legally registered. The following section presents evidence on *de facto* access according to registration status and type of medical needs. The conclusion considers implications for both migrants' social welfare and the informal economy. It also considers alternative providers, including NGOs and formal and informal private markets.

De jure *rights*

International and bilateral agreements make some provision for migrants' social rights. The Russian government is a signatory to the UN International Convention on the Protection of Rights of All Migrant Workers and Members of Their Families, which stipulates a universal right to emergency medical care regardless of legal status. (It should be noted that this is the minimum standard for unregistered or illegal migrants also in many European and other countries.) As a signatory to the UN International Convention on the Rights of the Child, the Russian Federation guarantees education for all school-aged children living on its territory. As a member of the World Health Organization (WHO) and other international health bodies, it is committed to follow international protocols on treatment of tuberculosis (TB) for any diagnosed patient. As later discussion of *de facto* access will show, Russian practice broadly conforms to the UN conventions: public health facilities routinely provide emergency assistance regardless of migrants' registration status, and all school-aged children have the right to attend, though with some caveats in each case. Evidence on treatment of TB is more mixed.

Beyond these agreements most migrants have no access to publicly funded social services or social insurance. Russia's government has not signed the International Labour Organization (ILO) conventions on migrants' social security rights. While migrants who are citizens of one or two Central Asian states have been granted more extensive social rights through bilateral agreements, Tajiks have not. According to interviewees in Dushanbe, the government and Ministry of Health have tried to negotiate with their Russian counterparts on behalf of migrants, but the Russian government is generally uncooperative. Tajik health authorities have attempted to set up a system of health checks and certificates for departing migrants that would be recognised by their Russian counterparts, without success. Rather, the large scale of migration and heavy dependence on remittances undermine the potential bargaining power of the Tajik government, making it vulnerable to Russian political pressure on a range of issues. Far from being able to negotiate on behalf of its citizens, the Tajik government is subject to threats that its nationals will be arrested and deported by Russian authorities when political problems or tensions arise between the two states. Neither the government nor international health organizations, even those that count the Russian Federation as a member, appear to have much influence in advocating for protecting unregistered migrant workers in Russia.

With regard to national legislation, Russia has a system of Compulsory Medical Insurance (CMI) for all citizens and permanent residents, with employers required to pay a Health Insurance tax for those in the labour force (Cook 2007). Until 2011, a minority (perhaps 30 per cent) of Tajiks and other migrants who were legally registered to work were covered by CMI. Their dependent children were regularly accepted at polyclinics for required preschool checks and immunisations and included in medical checks at school. Pregnant women dependents were eligible for routine prenatal care, and newborns were registered for care up to one year. Public policy and practice in Moscow also provided maternity and routine paediatric care regardless of registration before 2011. However, since then most have been excluded from access to publicly funded services.

Social insurance reform in 2011 removed the obligation for employers to issue compulsory medical insurance policies for many migrants working legally in Russia. Now only those with residence permits have mandated coverage. These include a small number of skilled professionals, estimated by a Tajik Health Ministry official at not more than 5 per cent of migrants, who are registered to live and work legally in Russia and have employment contracts. Though some employers provide broader coverage voluntarily, most do not, leaving even registered migrants and their families uninsured, without clear rights even to access the public healthcare system. (Grenfell 2011: 31). Instead the Russian government introduced a new system for registering migrant workers, 'patents' or employment certificates, that require migrants to purchase a health insurance policy through state intermediaries. Initially patents could be sponsored only for migrants employed by individuals, for example working in a household, but the system has been expanded to include a broader group of migrants. The patent system was designed to formalise migrants' employment and bring their jobs and wages out of the 'shadows'. Patents also provide income for the state; they can be purchased only for short periods – months to a year – with a fee paid to the state for initial purchase and each renewal. The health insurance required in order to buy a patent is not expensive but it provides minimal benefits and covers only the migrant worker, not family members. Health insurance policies required for children to attend school are more expensive. Generally the patent system has had limited success because of its high costs in the face of declining wages; in late 2015 the majority of migrants remaining in Moscow were unregistered.

The 2011 social insurance reform was accompanied by broader changes in internal, federal and regional normative documents regulating medical care for members of migrants' families, specifically pregnant women and school-aged children, that led to changes in practice. According to a study by Yulia Florinskaya, a prominent Russian sociologist:

The situation changed drastically in 2011 ... after the change in the order of issuing compulsory medical insurance (CMI) policies to adult migrants legally working in Russia ... regional departments of public healthcare annulled the possibility of receiving free healthcare for migrant children and pregnant women in Russia's institutions of healthcare. Now migrants only have a possibility of paid visits.

(2012)

She reported that health services in public schools and polyclinics that provided basic care (including inoculations) for school-aged children and pregnant women, have been curtailed in the years since the reform.

De facto *access*

Interviews with representatives of NGOs in Moscow and focus groups with returned migrants in Tajikistan confirm that emergency medical care, including hospitalisation for childbirth, is usually provided – here practice follows international obligations.

According to a Moscow NGO representative, whose claim was confirmed by others, for example 'Even without a passport, if there is a real emergency they will take care of you; you have to pay for other treatment'. Particularly in cases of employment-related and other accidents, unregistered migrants are poorly protected. As one Moscow respondent stated the case, typically, 'Doctors provide emergency assistance, then look for a residence permit. When there are accidents, we collect money among ourselves and send the injured person home' (FIDH 2011: 16, citing Sharq survey). Some focus group respondents recounted experiences of employers or public medical facilities providing longer-term care. Some expressed preferences for getting medical care in Moscow, if it was affordable or they had some access to the public system, because the quality was much better than in Tajikistan. However, the cost of non-emergency care was prohibitive for most, and those with injuries that prevented their continuing to work returned home.

The situation with regard to infectious diseases is more complicated. On the basis of its membership in international health organisations and approval of WHO protocols, the Russian government is required to provide treatment to anyone diagnosed with TB until the patient has a negative test result, i.e. is no longer infectious. But according to interviewees in both Moscow and Dushanbe, migrants found to be infected are normally not registered for treatment, nor are they treated unless they can pay. According to one Moscow source:

If a migrant has TB, legally he has to be treated in Russia, but it is expensive, no one wants to deal with it, so it is resolved in an informal manner – he goes home, conditions are created for the migrant to go home, he can be treated in Moscow if he has money, but it is very expensive, so often they are not treated here.

Interviewees from international health organisations in Dushanbe were especially critical about this issue, echoing one another in their claims that the Russian government regularly failed to follow international agreements, protocols and practices on treatment of infectious diseases, particularly TB, with migrants. Several told a consistent story about Russian authorities stonewalling when pressed on these issues: at high-level meetings Russian health officials agreed to cooperate, but there was little or no follow-through, initiatives were smothered in bureaucracy. In sum the IOs had little effective leverage.

These practices are confirmed by reports from the focus group whose participants had returned to Tajikistan infected with TB. A separate report on in-depth interviews with ten TB patients who had returned from Moscow to Tajikistan found that all left because the cost of treatment was prohibitive in Moscow, and much less expensive in Tajikistan, where at least medicine was provided free of cost. Two of the ten infected returnees had spent all of their savings from their work in Moscow on medical care (Gilpin et al. 2011).

Healthcare access for migrant women is also complicated, varying with the type of care needed. Childbirth is considered a medical emergency that qualifies for guaranteed medical care regardless of legal status. Moscow respondents reported that women were normally accepted at hospitals to give birth ('If/a pregnant woman is/ill or in labour, the hospital will provide services whether they have money or not'). However, unregistered migrant women must pay for prenatal care, and women who lack certification of prenatal testing and screening were in some cases refused care at local facilities and taken to a specialised infectious disease hospital. Focus group respondents reported that hospitals sometimes demanded residence permits before admitting women who were in labour, though it is not clear that any were ultimately denied hospital admission. The post-2010 restrictions on access to healthcare have been a particular hardship for women, who generally require more routine health services than men even when they are healthy. Even when care is accessible, language and cultural barriers sometimes raise obstacles to its effectiveness.

The right of migrant children to attend school in Moscow is of course very significant, providing opportunities for them to learn the Russian language, get a strong general education, and integrate into Russian society. Attendance does pose some obstacles. All children need medical certificates and insurance to enter school, and the cost is significant. Admission can also be problematic. In Moscow, as in all cities with large middle classes, admission to schools is competitive in many districts, migrant children are often disfavoured and sometimes must attend schools far from their homes. Nevertheless interviewees report that nearly all migrants' children attend. It is more difficult to find placements for preschool and younger children. Extended families in Tajikistan often take the very young, but it is significant that migrant women reportedly abandon newborns in Moscow hospitals at a significantly higher rate than average.

Alternative providers: NGOs, formal and informal private markets

What alternatives do migrants have if they cannot meet healthcare needs in public facilities? Where in Moscow can they get routine and non-emergency health services, health certificates and other documents required by Russian authorities? The three possible alternatives are NGOs, formal and informal (shadow economy) paid private services. Each will be considered below.

As stated in the introduction to this chapter, one purpose of my research is to assess the role of NGOs in meeting needs or filling 'gaps' left by the state and public sector. There has been a great deal of attention recently to the growth of NGOs, particularly in the area of public health. In 2012 I interviewed representatives of Moscow-based NGOs identified as working with migrants on social issues, including health services and advocacy; follow-up interviews were conducted with several in 2013 or 2015. I found none that directly provided health services. Licensing is difficult, regulations complicated; even an international health organisation that delivered services elsewhere struggled with licensing requirements in Moscow. A few organisations help migrants get access to healthcare by connecting them with health personnel who are willing to treat them, advocating on their behalf with hospitals, giving money for services, or providing legal advocacy for those hurt in work or traffic accidents. In the most extensive effort I found, one organisation coordinated with other NGOs to organise a network of willing providers, ran a hotline to connect migrants with needed specialists and did health education outreach. According to its representative, the organisation ran:

> Small projects to help migrants with access to healthcare, education – Tajiks are the worst of the worst, the most marginalised; our reach is not great, most of the projects are implemented by volunteers, doctors … they created a 'hotline', referring to specialists if there is one in the network; they also hold periodic awareness sessions on health.

A few others engage in advocacy, urging the Russian government to provide insurance or to address potential public health risks resulting from deficient healthcare for migrants. The Moscow and Dushanbe offices of the International Organization for Migration (IOM) have outreach efforts to provide migrants with information about health risks, insurance, etc.

In sum, the resources and capabilities of Moscow NGOs that work with migrants can, despite their best efforts and ingenuity, do little to fill gaps in provision of health services. Few to begin with, they often have limited and temporary funding. During the three years of my research one organisation that had helped a number of migrants, including a young child requiring surgery for a cardiac defect (for whom they successfully cobbled together a California-based medical charity that provided Internet-based diagnostics, a doctor in a distant Russian province to perform the surgery, and some funding) ran out of money and ceased operation. The IO (mentioned previously) that was seeking a medical licence left Moscow. The most stable organisation, that had constructed the provider network, remains active but the network has largely collapsed. These NGOs are created and staffed mainly by more established members of the Central Asian diaspora, their professional volunteers mostly have ties to the region, they rely on contingent funding and volunteers. One organisation provided services for orphaned migrant children and at-risk families, but it has also ceased functioning. More NGOs in Moscow provide legal services and advocate for migrants' and human rights. It should be noted that international health organisations, most prominently the Global Fund and including UNDP (United Nations Development Project), WHO (World Health Organization) and US AID (Agency for International Development) ran a network of public health clinics and services in Tajikistan, in cooperation with the government. These services included clinics intended for returned migrants that offered anonymous testing and treatment for infectious diseases (STDs, TB, HIV). These efforts by the international health community in effect filled some of the gaps left by Russia's exclusion of most migrant workers from most health services.

Migrant workers also rely on formal and informal private health services. Moscow now has a medical facility run by doctors and others from the Kirghiz diaspora, which is somewhat longer and better established in Moscow. *Mayak*, commonly known as the Kirkhiz Clinic, offers a broad range of paid medical services provided by native speakers of the three main Central Asian languages spoken by migrants, culturally sensitive treatment, a welcoming atmosphere (it advertises to migrants, who are shunned in many public places) and an implicit understanding that there will be no questions about registration status. It meets needs for those with sufficient income or urgent medical problems. *Mayak*, however, is formally a clinic rather than a hospital; it does not meet the standards for full hospital accreditation in Moscow.

For other medical services, most commonly certificates of health checks and other documents required by Russian government authorities, migrants often turn to informal and shadow services that provide documents for a fee, often without performing the health checks they are certifying. One can see such document services advertised at bus stop shelters all over Moscow, including its upscale districts, typically offering a range of documents including health for a set fee. Some of these services produce fakes, others are run by people who have connections with officials and are allocated numbers of 'real' documents or stamps that are registered and recognised by government and migration authorities. In fact reliance on these more-or-less 'shadow' document services has a prominent place in migrants' coping and survival strategies, driven by their informal status and the complexities and risks of trying to use formal, official channels. According to Bhavna Dave, an authority on the topic, migrants are forced by their status, 'to resort to a variety of semi-legal or outright illegal ("corrupt") transactions through the intermediaries in order to "get things done"' (Dave 2014: 2). It is impossible to obtain necessary documentation without resorting to quasi-legal or corrupt practices. I will return to discussion of migrants and the shadow economy in the conclusion.

Role of diaspora communities

It is commonly claimed that diaspora communities provide networks of support in migration. Interviewees in both Moscow and Dushanbe reported that when migrants faced health emergencies or crises, they could rely on help from their migrant ethnic communities – that it is the tradition and responsibility of people in diaspora communities, with shared cultural roots, to help and support one another in times of hardship. One respondent, for example, said:

> Migrants are organised by village, they have informal migrant organisations, they provide for emergencies but not for primary care; informal migrant associations have their own leaders; they get no support from government or embassies, so they have to organise themselves; so if someone is sick or dies, people from the village pool funds, but they can do so only for emergencies.

This quotation illustrates both the possibilities and limitations of help from the diaspora community, which is willing to aid ill or injured migrants, but has very limited resources with which to do so. According to another interviewee, migrants rely on groups based on village, people from home whom they know and trust, to help one another cope with difficulties in Russia. The following was the response to a question about whether migrants relied on traditional healers or treatments when they could not get access to care:

> The Tajik community is united in Russia. If an accident happens or a migrant becomes ill, relatives will help, if they are there, to gather money for doctors ... The migrant community in Russia will almost always pitch in and help the worker in need. They will use state clinics, or someone in the community will have connections with a doctor... and the injured migrant can go there. Sometimes the older migrants can help, or the ones who have lived in Russia the longest, and will tell the injured migrant where to seek help.

However, the circumstances of Tajik migrants in Moscow raise questions about the extent of help that is possible. They do not live in an enclave, but are spread among construction sites and apartments, often on the outskirts of the city. Focus group respondents who faced medical problems spoke of help from family members. Other evidence confirms that migrants who are seriously ill usually return home for treatment, because they have access to some free and/or lower-cost care, and have family to help them. The capacity of the diaspora community appears limited to short-term, ad hoc or emergency help, with returning home as the default option for migrants who can no longer work. It may be that the limited number of women among Tajik labour migrants, especially women outside the labour force, limits the resources available for care-taking of ill or injured migrants.

Conclusion: risks, realities, implications for the welfare state

Some research indicates that migrants generally, and Central Asian migrants to Russia in particular, exhibit a 'healthy migrant effect' – that most are in good health when they arrive, but there is no effective system of medical monitoring to provide evidence of Tajiks' pre-departure health. Once in migration, they confront several risk factors. First, accident rates are high in construction, the most common area of male Tajiks' employment in Russia. Russia's Federal Labour Inspectorate reports that the majority of workplace accidents, and nearly 40 per cent of deaths, occur in construction, where few even skilled workers were found to be familiar with safety regulations. Injuries among migrant workers are reportedly common, some return home as invalids, and hundreds reportedly die each year in building and road construction accidents (Olimova 2003). Work in trade, which is relatively common for women, produces injuries related to lifting and loading as well as exposure to cold in outside markets. As long as workers are informal, employers effectively bear no responsibility for health and safety conditions.

Housing conditions also present risks, particularly poor, crowded, unsanitary living quarters. Many Tajik migrant workers – reportedly 70 per cent – live on construction sites, or in non-residential buildings and barracks or other marginal housing provided by employers. Others rent rooms or apartments, often in buildings far from the centre, sometimes with several people sharing a room and sleeping in shifts. According to both survey evidence and interview informants, it is common for migrants to live in cellars and unheated dwellings, and for as many as 20 to share an apartment. Isolation from their families potentially contributes to risky sexual behaviour. Several studies have shown low levels of information about transmission, prevention, diagnosis and treatment of common infectious illnesses (i.e. TB HIV/AIDS) (Gilpin 2012; Weine 2008). In addition, unregistered migrants are often subject to arrest and sometimes deportation; in either case they may be held in Russian prison facilities where levels of TB, including multi-drug-resistant TB, are high; xenophobic violence is also a risk.

Despite these risks, there is no definite evidence that Tajik labour migrants suffer more health problems than their non-migrating counterparts. Of surveyed migrants who have returned to Tajikistan, 11 per cent consistently reported 'worsening of health' as their reason for returning; and that medical care in Moscow, while preferable to that in Tajikistan because it is higher in quality, was too expensive and difficult to get without legal residence or citizenship (Hemmings 2010: 17; International Labour Organization 2010: 18). Dushanbe doctors report illnesses related to hypothermia and a rise in TB and HIV/AIDS among returnees (FIDH 2011: 16). Most of the international health workers I interviewed believed that migration produced negative health effects. However, the Tajik government's health data does not include a separate category for migrants; studies by international organisations based on limited sampling have produced inconsistent results. My study is not premised on a claim that migration worsens health. Rather, it has aimed to understand how health and other social service needs experienced in migration are addressed in Russia.

As for social policy, my research reveals that the Russian welfare state has become fragmented, with different populations, defined by ethnicity and political/citizenship status, having access to dramatically different levels of services and healthcare. Russian citizens and legal residents have employer-paid medical insurance and can access the public sector, though even for citizens a significant level of informality in the public system creates obstacles to access (Cook 2014). Many migrants working legally in Russia have had their rights (and rights of accompanying family members) to medical insurance curtailed since 2011, and related changes in policy and practice have restricted access for migrant women and children. Unregistered migrants have virtually no rights to the public health system beyond emergency care. Nor are NGOs able to compensate much in filling 'gaps' left by the state. As the chapter shows, Moscow-based NGOs' efforts to provide health services or related advocacy for migrants appear to be few and weak. International organisations that administer global public health regimes have little leverage to affect migrants' rights. Other migrants in the diaspora may help, but Tajiks in Moscow constitute a dispersed community; the resources it can provide appear to be ad hoc and short term, often amounting to collection of funds to send an injured or ill migrant home. When migrants do receive more and better care, focus group participants indicate that it comes either through personal connections, or the ethics of individual employers and medical professionals.

There are two sets of implications for the welfare state. The first is strongly negative.

Migration has grown large, socially excluded populations in Moscow and other major Russian cities. These marginalised populations live precariously, eroding levels of human security. Most by necessity work in informal labour markets and rely on informal social service markets, contributing to expansion of a shadow economy that the state cannot regulate, tax or to a large extent see; much of migrants' lives are legally invisible and exempt from the state's surveillance. The shadow economy erodes the tax base that finances the public sector. Private employers and government officials develop vested interests in persistence of informal and corrupt networks and practices. The state's capacities to govern and allocate resources are undermined.

On the other hand, the marginal status of migrants creates beneficiaries, and arguably facilitates the labour market adjustment and welfare retrenchment that are inevitable in the current economic downturn. Migrant labour, characterized by lack of rights, minimum wage or social taxes, is cheap, benefiting employers and upper-income Russians who hire domestic and service workers. The profit migrant labour creates contributes to the social benefits of workers in the formal sector, and to some extent all with social rights. Migrants constitute a disposable labour force that has no claims on the employment system. They are highly vulnerable to economic and political pressures. Facing the economic downturn, many have simply left. The Russian government can and does also put downward pressure on their numbers by selectively tightening enforcement of rules and restrictions, increasing harassment, deportations and long-term bans on individuals' return, and increasing costs of patents. The disposability of migrants facilitates labour force adjustment, opening jobs that may now be attractive to some locals, and allowing the government to push out the poorest and concentrate its resources on those who retain social rights.

Notes

1 Acknowledgments: Support for this research, provided by a Visiting Fellowship from the Center for Russian Studies, Russian Presidential Academy of the National Economy and Public Administration (RANEPA), Moscow, Russia and the US International Research and Exchanges Board (IREX), is gratefully acknowledged. Thanks to Colin Johnson of Brown University and Gavhar Hamroeva in Dushanbe for excellent research assistance.
2 Interviews were conducted by the author with support from RANEPA and IREX.

References

Abdurazakova, D. 2011. 'Social impact of international migration and remittances in Central Asia', *Asia-Pacific Population Journal*, 26(3): 29–54.

Amirkhanian, Yu. A. et al. 2011. 'Male labor migrants in Russia: HIV risk behavior levels, contextual factors, and prevention needs', *Journal of Immigrant Minority Health*, 13: 919–928.

Baldyshtova, I. M. 2004. 'Characteristics of labor migrants' households in Russia', *Sociological Research*, 43(1): 46–61.

Buckley, C., B. Ruble and E. Trouth Hofmann. 2008. *Migration, Homeland and Belonging in Eurasia*. Baltimore, MD: Johns Hopkins University Press.

Buckley, C.-J., E. Trouth Hofmann and Y. Minagawa. 2011. 'Does nativity matter? Correlates of immigrant health by generation in the Russian Federation', *Demographic Research*, 24(32): 801–824.

Cammett, M. and L. M. MacLean. 2011. 'Introduction: The political consequences of non-state social welfare in the Global South', *Studies in Comparative International Development*, 46: 1–21.

Cook, L. J. 2007. *Postcommunist Welfare States: Reform Politics in Russia and Eastern: Europe*. Ithaca, NY: Cornell University Press.

Cook, L. J. 2014. '"Spontaneous privatization" and its political consequences in Russia's postcommunist health sector', in M. Cammett and L. M. McLean (eds.), *The Politics of Non-State Social Welfare*. Ithaca, NY: Cornell University Press, pp. 217–236.

Cook, L. J. and C. Johnson. 2013. 'Maximizing Returns: The Social Politics of Central Asians' Migration to Russia." Presented at the Annual Meeting of the American Political Science Association, Chicago, IL, Aug. 29–Sept. 3.

Dave, Bhavna. 2014. 'Becoming "legal" through "illegal" procedures: the precarious status of migrant workers in Russia', *Russian Analytical Digest*, 159, 20 December.

Dzhatoeva, F. 2010. 'Tuberculosis in labor migrant donor countries to the Russian Federation', *Economics of Public Health*, 8: 14–18.

FIDH (International Federation for Human Rights) 2011. *Tajikistan: Exporting the Workforce – At What Price? Tajik Migrant Workers Need Increased Protection*

Florinskaya, Yu. F., 2012. 'Migration of families with children to Russia: Integration problems (based on materials of sociological queries conducted by the Center for Migration Studies)', *Studies in Russian Economic Development*, 23(4): 408–413.

Ganguli, I. 2009. 'Tajik labor migration to Russia: Is Tajikistan at a crossroads?' Washington, DC: IREX Scholar Research Brief.

Gilpin, C. et al. 2012. 'Exploring TB-related knowledge, attitude, behavior, and practice among migrant workers in Tajikistan', *Tuberculosis Research and Treatment* [published. online 19 January 2012. Article ID 548617].

Glen, R. 2009. *Broshennye zheny Tadzhikskikh trudovykh migrantov.* Dushanbe: MOM.

GoskomstatRossii, *Sotsial'noi polozhenie i uroven zhizni naselenie Rossii: Offitsial'noe Izdanie* (annual, various years).

Goskomstat Rossii, Trud i zaniatost' v Rossii: Offitsial'noe Izdanie (annual, various years)

Grenfell, P. 2011. 'Social security and international migrants: global examples and lessons for Russia' (draft paper).

Grogor'ev, M. and A. Ocinnikov. 2009. *Nelegal'nye Migranty v Moskve.* Moscow: Izdat. 'Evropa'.

Heleniak, T. 2008. 'An overview of migration in the post-Soviet space', in Buckley et al. (eds), *Migration, Homeland and Belonging*, pp. 29–68.

Heleniak, T. 2011. *Harnessing the Diaspora for Development in Europe and Central Asia.* Washington, DC: World Bank.

Heleniak, T. 2012. 'The ECA's diaspora populations: Can aid growth and development', *Knowledge Brief: Europe and Central Asia* 46. Washington, DC: World Bank.

Hemmings, H. 2010. *Remittances, Recession … Returning Home: The Effects of the 2008 Economic Crisis on Tajik Labor in Moscow.* Washington, DC: Woodrow Wilson Center.

Hertzer, L., S. D. Klump and M.E. Malinkin (eds) 2009. *Transnational Migration to New Regional Centers: Policy Challenges, Practice, and Migrant Experience.* Washington, DC: WWICS.

International Labour Organization. 2010. *Migration and Development in Tajikistan: Emigration, Return and Diaspora.* Moscow: ILO.

International Organization for Migration. 2010. *Trudovaya Migratsiia I Voprosy Zdravookhraneniia.* Moscow: IOM.

International Organization for Migration. 2011. *Migration Health: Report of IOM Activities.* Moscow: IOM.

Keshavjee, S. and M.C. Becerra. 2000. 'Disintegrating health services and resurgent tuberculosis in post-Soviet Tajikistan: An example of structural violence', *JAMA: The Journal of the American Medical Association*, 283(9): 1201.

Khodjamurodov, G. and B. Rechel 2010. 'Health Systems in Transition'. *Tajikistan: Health System Review*, 12(2): 1–154.

Kulmala, M. 2011. 'Russian State and Civil Society in Interaction: An Ethnographic Approach', *Laboratorium*, 3(1): 24–56.

Kumo, K. 2012. 'Tajik labor migrants and their remittances: Is Tajik migration pro-poor?', *Post-Communist Economies*, 24(1): 87–109.

Laruelle, M. 2007. 'Central Asian labor migrants in Russia: the "diasporization" of the Central Asian States', *China and Eurasian Forum Quarterly*, 5(3): 101–119.

Massey, D. S. 1999. 'International migration at the dawn of the twenty-first century: The role of the state', *Population and Development Review*, 25(2): 303–322.

Migranty v Rossii: Otchet mezhdunarodnoi issledovatel'skoi missii. 2007. International Federation for Human Rights.

Mughal, A.-G. 2007. *Migration, Remittances, and Living Standards in Tajikistan: A Report Based on Khatlon Remittances and Living Standards Measurement Survey.* Dushanbe: IOM/Tajikistan.

Olimova, S. and I. Bosc 2003. *Labor Migration from Tajikistan.* Dushanbe: IOM.

Olimova, S. 2009. 'Vernyvshiesia migrant: ekonomicheskaia i sotsial'naia rol'. Dushanbe: Sharq Research Center.

Olimova, S. 2005. 'The economic impact of labor migration: The case of Tajikistan' (paper presented at the annual meeting of the International Studies Association, March).

Olimova, S. 2010. 'The impact of labour migration on human capital: The Case of Tajikistan', *Revue Européenne des Migrations Internationales*, 26(3): 181–197.

Remington, T. 2011. *The Politics of Inequality in Russia.* Cambridge: Cambridge University Press.

Rozanova, M. S. 2012. *Migration Processes and Challenges in Contemporary Russia.* Washington, DC: Wilson Center.

Schenk, C. and U. Nazurbaev. 2013. 'Caught between formal and informal: coping strategies of Central Asian migrants in the Russian Federation' (paper presented at Apr. 2013 BASEES conference).

Trudovaia migratsiia i voprosy zdravookhraneniia. 2010. Moscow: Bureau MOM/IOM.

Trudovaia migratsiia iz Tadjhikistanta. 2003. MOM Tajikistan, SHARQ Research Center.

Tsai, L. L. 2011. 'Friends or foes? Nonstate public good providers and local state authorities in nondemocratic and transitional systems', *Studies in Comparative International Development*, 46: 46–69.

UNDP. 2009. *Migration and Human Development: Opportunities and Challenges.* New York: National Hum Dev Report.

Weine, S. et al. 2008. 'Unprotected Tajik male migrant workers in Moscow at risk for HIV/AIDS', *Journal of Immigrant Minority Health*, 10: 461–468.

World Bank. 2005. *Tajikistan Gender Review.* Washington, DC: World Bank.

World Bank. 2007. *Tajikistan Living Standards Measurement Survey.* Washington, DC: World Bank.

World Bank. 2008. *Republic of Tajikistan: Public Welfare Dynamics. State of Health and Educational Sectors.* Washington, DC: World Bank.

World Bank. 2009. *Republic of Tajikistan: Poverty Assessment*, Washington, DC: World Bank.

Yudina, T. N. 2005. 'Labor migration into Russia: The response of state and society', *Current Sociology*, 53(4): 583–606.

9 Conclusions

Societal and political consequences of the shadow economy in Russia

Anna-Liisa Heusala and Kaarina Aitamurto

The shadow economy leads to direct monetary losses for the state and indirect, complex and serious societal consequences through unhealthy market competition, loss of entrepreneurial innovativeness, structural corruption, unsafe working conditions and, often, a poorer quality of products and services. The shadow economy overwhelms the positive economic impact that migration can produce, since the human capital of employees is not used or developed in a sustainable manner. In Russia, recorded immigration is a small part of the total inflow of immigrants, and a substantial proportion of migrants work in the shadow economy. The dependence of a country on the workforce in the shadow economy has profound significance for its political and societal development. As a societal force, the shadow economy is similar to corruption, which can initially be used to enter a specific market, but which becomes more problematic and costly over time as the market position becomes entrenched. The competition in the corrupted market can become increasingly hostile as those who got into the markets earlier using the available unofficial networks 'try to turn against those same networks in order to reinforce their hegemonic positions' (Sajó 2003: 174).

This joint volume was set up to examine the impact which the large-scale use of migrant workers in the shadow economy is having on Russian societal transformation. The case studies have varied from an ethnographic study among the migrant workers themselves in Moscow to an analysis of the dynamics between Russia's foreign policy goals in the Eurasian Economic Union and its labour market developments. We have analysed the concrete effects of societal transformation in three areas: politics, institutions and law, at different hierarchical levels and geographical dimensions of the Russian state and society. Our aim was to see how questions of human security are inextricably linked to domestic and international politics. We understand societal transformation as a complex, non-linear process which consists of incremental learning processes and adaptation, often characterised by unintended consequences. We have also given some consideration to how expected and welcomed (Perri 2010) some of the changes in Russian society have been.

Migration from the former Soviet republics to the Russian Federation has become a part of the globalised scene of inequality, political stagnation and

DOI: 10.4324/9781315657424-9

social instability, similar in many ways to the migration flows in other parts of the world, including Europe. Globalisation forces societies to balance their domestic policy goals and the demands of international economic and political regimes. In the case of Russia, this has produced an institutional tension between the demands of technocratic, narrow economic and institutional modernisation and more inclusive modernisation, which would involve political changes in the current authoritarian market society (Gel'man 2015: 104–14). In Russian politics, we see the internal–external nexus of the shadow economy in which migration policies, regional relations and identity politics come together. Hypotheses of migration, concerning such questions as economic and cultural threats (Buckler 2008) are used in domestic discussions which have for a long time overshadowed the political problematisation of practices in the Russian labour market. Instead, questions of security threats and challenges of cultural diversity come to the fore.

In real terms, however, integration policies in the Eurasian Economic Union have forced the Russian government to engage in the modernisation of its migration policies. This includes enforced control of legality and the dismantling of bureaucratic obstacles to the legal registration of migrant workers. The availability of opportunities for work in Russia affects the economies, security situation and longer term political stability of Russia's Southern neighbours. Domestically, the economic fall caused by the drop in oil prices and the Western sanctions has hit the Russian economy hard since autumn 2014. In the current situation, the number of Russian citizens who find themselves in the shadow economy due to the loss of official employment is growing and creating new unofficial competition for work. Thanks to the fall in the rouble, migrant labourers have begun to regard Russia as a less attractive destination. The Central Asian states have depended on money transfers from Russia as a substitute for state-sponsored welfare, and their younger generation has been able to find opportunities in Russia which are lacking at home.

Understanding and tackling the question of the shadow economy in the current situation presents a major challenge for Russia, since the organisation of societal and economic interests in Russian society is still rather weak. Interest representation in the Russian labour market relates to some core issues of its societal transformation. The current exclusion of the objects of policy – the migrant workers – and the insufficient power and cooperation between trade unions and employee organisation at a national level on key policy questions slow down the strengthening of public interest or 'common good' (Vincent-Jones 2002: 33), which could increase responsiveness to law and regulations. As both an unintended consequence of the financial crises and a consequence of the integration process of the Eurasian Economic Union, there has been some activation of labour market institutions in recent years. As a result, attention has been directed to such questions as workers' qualifications, quality of work and work safety, harmonised standards and the integrity of employees as keys to the development of the Russian labour market and industry. Better policy processes, which routinely take into full account the professional and social concerns of both Russian employers and trade union representatives, could considerably advance the modernisation of Russian labour market conditions, in line with the Programme of Migration policy until 2025.

Interest representation in the Russian labour market is affected by current policies towards civic activism in general. The Russian authorities have shown suspicious attitudes towards various kinds of bottom-up initiatives and NGOs which are working with the migrants. The current state policy underlines a 'securitised' control of civil society and prefers the NGOs to work as part of official state programmes. Negative public attitudes about migrant workers have so far intensified the control dimension in the state's reactive policy measures. In the future, more inclusive third sector participation is required to reach the ambitious and more proactive goals of Russia's recent migration policy.

As several chapters of this book demonstrate, a cycle of negative side effects exists, connected with institutional fragility in the Russian state. One of the key impressions is the dynamic between corruptive institutional practices and ways of thinking, which are fostered by the shadow economy and uphold its grip. As Johnston points out, 'we tend to think of corruption in terms of specific transgressions and individuals, but in fact its main societal impact comes from its collective dimension', which Johnston describes as 'a loss of ability, on the part of an entire system of leadership and order, to command loyalty and pursue a vision of the common good' (2012: 332).

The 'unintentionality' of the 'unintended consequences' of the policy decisions or inaction of the Russian government can also be questioned. In Russian political rhetoric, illegal/irregular migration and the shadow economy appear as a major social problem demanding a solution. However, the pace of action has been slow and its comprehensiveness weak, which raises the question as to whether this has been due to unintended transitional constraints (level of institutional maturation, such as the FMS finding its position inside the Russian administration) or more an intended political choice influenced by Russian market conditions. For years, developments in the Russian Federation have been characterised by new conflicts and unintended obstacles to the observance of legality in the implementation of migration rules. Institutional corruption has even intensified in some cases, through legal changes intended to facilitate control.

Migrant workers have formed a work reserve which is not able to effectively organise through unions or political movements. Therefore, it is not surprising that in spite of the rhetoric on the societal impact of illegal migration, serious attempts to control or limit the number of illegally working migrants have encountered obstacles and proven inefficient. The effects of the use of large scale migrant workforce in shadow economy have resulted in societal transformations which have many similar qualities found in other industrialised societies. Discriminatory attitudes create an environment which makes equitable implementation of new legislation and regulations difficult (van Aerschot and Daentzer 2014: 4). The assimilation of the migrant workers into their surrounding communities has been slow and nationalistic sentiments have been effectively used in Russian politics. The widely shared negative attitudes towards large foreign communities has influenced the lack of political motivation to let migrants legalise their status and bring their families to Russia, a situation which resembles the situation of the *Gastarbeiter* in Europe during the 1960s and 1970s (Massey *et al.* 1998: 5).

The chapters of this volume give reason to argue that illegal/irregular migration and its intimate links to the shadow economy are crucial elements in the difficulties in countering corruption in Russian institutions and strengthening the rule of law in Russian society. The hindrances that the massive use of the illegal migrant force set before the formation of an effective trade union movement further suggest that it also has a negative effect on the development of a civil society and political system which was more firmly anchored to the promotion of collective interests than, for example, the personal charisma of political leaders.

The level of transparency in society influences the real societal outcome of both legislation and governmental programmes. Sajó's work shows how in countries with large-scale structural corruption, vigorous anti-corruption policies might be in place because the governments wish to maintain their monopoly of corruption. Policymaking around anti-corruption measures may be about securing the governmental monopoly on bribery and legislation used to legalise and normalise this situation. Furthermore, public discussion on corruption can continue to emphasise negative labels attached to individual actors (Sajó 2003: 177–8, 180), instead of paying more comprehensive attention to the political, legal and economic structures which sustain the practice. Finally, corruption is connected to a 'broader web of illegalities that become part of the exercise of political power'. In an economy, which is heavily dependent on crime, corruption serves to facilitate other crimes and prevents the institutions and powerful individuals involved in these crimes being called to account (Sajó 2003: 189).

Even as globalisation necessitates the harmonisation of rules and practices, it also reproduces old forms of social integration. Particularly in the shadow economy, migrant workers import and adapt practices to their new surroundings, which are outside regulated communication and decision-making. Definitions of 'legality' and 'illegality' are affected by the legal cultures of their home states and local communities. Difficulties found in obtaining legal status with its related social security benefits and possibilities to integrate into the surrounding society, for instance through training and education, continue to uphold unofficial and underground practices. Personal relations dominate over the observance of rules and regulations, which has long-term negative consequences for both the migrants and their Russian communities.

The short-term profitability of the shadow economy and the inconsistent and conflicting government responses to the matter ensure the continuation of societal fragmentation and the atomisation of rights. Finally, structural corruption, like the large-scale shadow economy, essentially betrays public trust in the political system itself (Sajó 2003: 176). As public trust erodes, interest representation is further atomised, even to the level of individual survival techniques, as is the case for illegally working migrants. The shadow economy can be seen as a major factor in Russian society's persistent culture of 'personal ties', resistance to strict forms of legality (Brisbin 2010: 26) and fragmented institutional trust. Thus, societal transformation in Russia depends to a significant degree on the issues raised here.

References

Brisbin, R. A., Jr. 2010. 'Resistance to legality', *Annual Review of Law and Social Science.* 6: 25–44.

Buckler, K. 2008. 'Public opinion on illegal immigration: A test of seven core hypotheses'. *Journal of Crime and Justice*, 31(1): 113–47.

Butler, M. J. R. and P. M. Allen. 2008. 'Understanding policy implementation processes as self-organizing systems', *Public Management Review* 10(3): 421–440.

Gel'man, V. 2015. *Authoritarian Russia. Analyzing Post-Soviet Regime Changes.* Pittsburgh, PA: University of Pittsburgh Press.

Johnston, M. 2012. 'Corruption control in the United States: Law, values, and the political foundations of reform', *International Review of Administrative Sciences* 78: 329–345.

Mahoney, J. and K. Thelen (eds). 2010. *Explaining Institutional Change. Ambiguity, Agency and Power.* Cambridge: Cambridge University Press.

Massey, D. S., J. Arango, G. Hugo, A. Kouaouci, A. Pellegrino and E. J. Taylor. (eds). 1998. *Worlds in Motion. Understanding International Migration at the End of the Millennium.* New York: Oxford University Press.

Perri 6. 2010. 'When forethought and outturn part: Types of unanticipated and unintended consequences', in H. Margets, 6 Perri and C. Hood (eds.), *Paradoxes of Modernization. Unintended Consequences of Public Policy Reform.* Oxford: Oxford University Press, pp. 44–57.

Sajó, A. 2003. 'From corruption to extortion: Conceptualizing of post-Communist corruption', *Crime, Law & Social Change* 40: 171–94.

Van Aerschot, P. and P. Daentzer. (eds). 2014. *The Integration and Protection of Immigrants. Canadian and Scandinavian critiques.* Ashgate: Farnham.

Vincent-Jones, P. 2002. 'Values and purpose in government: Central–local relations in regulatory perspective', *Journal of Law and Society* 29(1): 27–55.

Index

For Product Safety Concerns and Information please contact our EU representative GPSR@taylorandfrancis.com Taylor & Francis Verlag GmbH, Kaufingerstraße 24, 80331 München, Germany

Printed and bound by CPI Group (UK) Ltd, Croydon, CR0 4YY

08/05/2025

01864353-0001